The
Hummingbirds
of
North America

Paul A. Johnsgard

Smithsonian Institution Press

Washington, D.C. 1983

©1983 by Smithsonian Institution. All rights reserved.
Color plates © by James McClelland
Printed in the United States of America
First edition

Second printing, 1984

Library of Congress Cataloging in Publication Data
Johnsgard, Paul A.
Hummingbirds of North America
Bibliography
Includes 6 appendixes, glossary, and index.
1. Hummingbirds. 2 Birds–North America. I. Title.

Cover:
Green violet-ear (*C. t. thalassinus*) male and lucifer
hummingbird pair visiting *Salvia henryi*.

ISBN 0–87474–562–4

Contents

APPENDIXES

To the memory of Charles Darwin,
Without whom hummingbirds might have seemed
as unlikely as unicorns.

COLOR PLATES

PLATE 8A.
Green violet-ear (*C. t. thalassinus*) male and lucifer hummingbird pair visiting *Salvia henryi*.

PLATE 8B.
Bahama woodstar pair and Cuban emerald (*C. r. bracei*) male visiting *Tillandsia fasiculata*.

PLATE 8C.
White-eared hummingbird (*C. l. leucotis*) pair (right) and broad-billed hummingbird (*C. l. magicus*) pair (left) visiting *Bouvardia ternifolia*.

PLATE 8D.
Violet-crowned hummingbird (*A. v. ellioti*) female (above) and males visiting *Castilleja miniata*.

PLATE 8E.
Buff-bellied (*A. y. chalconota*) (above), berylline (*A. b. viola*) (middle), and rufous-tailed (*A. t. tzacatl*) (bottom) males visiting *Erythrina flabelliformes*.

PLATE 8F.
Blue-throated hummingbird (*L. c. bessophilus*) pair visiting *Zauschernia californica*.

PLATE 8G.
Rivoli hummingbird (*H. f. fulgens*) male and two females visiting *Mimulus cardinalis*.

PLATE 8H.
Plain-capped starthroat (*H. c. leocadiae*) male and bumblebee hummingbird males and female visiting *Agave lechuguilla*.

J. McClelland

J. McClelland

PLATE 8C

J. McClelland

J. McClelland

J. McClelland

J. McClelland

J. McClelland

J. McClelland

Preface

*I*t is frequently difficult to remember just when the germ of an idea for a book emerges, but the one for this book certainly arose when an impudent female calliope hummingbird constructed her nest near my cabin in Grand Teton National Park while I was doing fieldwork there in the summer of 1975. Watching the progression of her incubation and brooding, often from only a meter or two away, was a fascinating exercise in ecology and behavior. Thus, I resolved to investigate the whole group of hummingbirds more carefully someday.

That day came in the spring of 1980, when I found the time to write a fairly short and not-too-technical book on an appealing subject. After only a little thought, I settled on hummingbirds. My first idea was simply to produce a series of essays on the breeding biologies and natural histories of the North American hummingbirds. Almost immediately, however, I realized that limiting my coverage to the strictly North American forms would eliminate the vast majority of hummingbirds and their biology. Thus, I decided to incorporate a series of introductory chapters on comparative hummingbird biology, not restricted to North America. This approach, in turn, supported the inclusion of a complete synopsis of the hummingbirds of the world, together with a limited amount of information on their ranges and identification.

From the outset I believed that the book should contain suitable illustrations, inasmuch as hummingbirds are among the most spectacularly plumaged of all birds. Since my own photographic files were almost totally lacking in hummingbird subjects, I asked James McClelland, a highly gifted watercolor artist of Lincoln, Nebraska, if he would consider doing a series of plates for me. This he immediately agreed to do, and his fine efforts have greatly assisted me in illustrating this book. The University of Nebraska Herbarium loaned specimens to me as needed, and whenever possible Glen Drohman kindly provided fresh plant material for me. C. F. Zeillemaker, Gary Stiles, and Richard Zusi undertook critical readings of the entire manuscript.

I have received valuable assistance from many other persons, including David Willard of the Field Museum of Natural History, Chicago, and Robert Mengel of the University of Kansas Museum of Natural History, for loan of specimens. Specimen information was also provided me by Lloyd Kiff, Western Foundation of Vertebrate Zoology, Los Angeles; David Niles, Delaware Museum of Natural History, Greenville; Fernando I. Ortiz-Crespo, Museum of Vertebrate Zoology, Berkeley; Dwain Warner, James Ford Bell Museum of Natural History, Minneapolis; and George Watson, National Museum of Natural History, Washington, D. C. Other information or assistance was provided by James Bond, John A. Crawford, Crawford Greenewalt, Lester Short, Jr., and Charles G. Sibley. A grant from the Frank Chapman Fund of the American Museum of Natural History allowed me to visit that museum and obtain necessary specimen and library information available there. I am also indebted to the School of

Life Sciences, University of Nebraska–Lincoln, for providing me with the facilities necessary for undertaking this project and for secretarial assistance in manuscript preparation.

Introduction

"*Of* all the numerous groups into which the birds are divided there is none other so numerous in species, so varied in form, so brilliant in plumage, and so different from all others in their mode of life." Thus did the American ornithologist Robert Ridgway introduce the hummingbirds in a monograph almost a century ago, and no writer before or since has been able to refer to this incredible group of birds without resorting to superlatives. John James Audubon described a hummingbird as a "glittering garment of the rainbow," and John Gould called them "wonderful works of creation."

The all-too-human tendency initially to admire such beauty and then to demand to possess it has been responsible for an impassioned interest in hummingbirds, which has lasted for several hundred years. At its heyday in the mid-1800s, the market for hummingbirds was so great that hundreds of thousands were killed in South America to supply the upper-class Europeans with specimens for collections and for ornamental uses. A Brazilian port once shipped 3000 skins of a single hummingbird species on one consignment, and public sales in London for one month in 1888 included more than 12,000 hummingbird skins. London auctions sold some 400,000 bird skins that year, a good percentage of which were doubtless hummingbirds. During that period ornithologists discovered numerous new hummingbird species from among the vast number of specimens flowing into England and the Continent. Many of these came from unspecified parts of northern South America, and a few of them have never been found again.

The period of maximum importation of hummingbirds, occurring at the peak time for animal monographs with magnificent hand-colored plates, spawned many sumptuous volumes on the subject. One of the first of significance was that by the Frenchman R.P. Lesson, who published the first portion in 1829, added a "supplement" in 1830–1831, and completed the third and last section in 1832. Although the three volumes were discrete works with separate titles, they formed a comprehensive treatment of the roughly 110 species known to him and contained many colored plates. But Lesson contributed early to the confusion of hummingbird nomenclature by indiscriminately renaming many previously described species.

Between 1849 and 1861 John Gould produced a five-volume monograph on hummingbirds. This magnificent folio production, one of the most beautiful of all bird monographs, contained 360 hand-colored lithographic plates and collectively catalogued some 416 "species," many described for the first time. But the chaotic state of hummingbird taxonomy at that time is evident from the frequent divergence between the names on the plates and those in the accompanying letterpress. Nevertheless, the monograph set a level in book production and in bird art that has rarely been surpassed (if ever).

During the later decades of the nineteenth century a host of new hummingbird species were described, and many new names were applied to species already known. Nevertheless, in 1878 D.G. Elliot produced a landmark monograph of the whole group. This work made a serious effort at redefining all genera, describing all the known species, and providing an identification key as well as detailed illustrations of representatives of all the genera accepted by Elliot.

About a decade later—in 1890—Robert Ridgway provided his equally outstanding contribution on the subject, including an extended survey of the characteristics of the hummingbird family as a whole, as well as individual treatments of the 17 species that had been found within the boundaries of the United States. In 1911 he published a larger work, which included all of the nearly 150 species that Ridgway accepted as occurring north of the Isthmus of Panama and in the West Indies. This is still the most valuable and definitive single volume on the hummingbirds of North and Central America, particularly for its keys and plumage descriptions.

Surprisingly few monographic approaches to the entire family have appeared during the 1900s, despite the tremendous interest of the preceding century. One of the few—an *Histoire naturelle* of the hummingbirds, published by E. Simon in 1921—was little more than a revised taxonomy of the group. It had none of the strengths of Elliot's earlier approach and burdened the hummingbird literature with what has proven to be the ultimate in generic and specific names. But Simon's classification clearly affected the subsequent taxonomies of the group, especially James Peters' classification, which has been the standard authority since its appearance in 1945.

Although the London Zoo acquired its first living hummingbird as early as 1905, the bird died within two weeks. It was not until the development of rapid transatlantic air travel and suitable diets that hummingbirds began to appear regularly in European zoos. The English aviculturalist Alfred Ezra established the importance of adding proteins, fats, minerals, and vitamins to the basic honey diet of hummingbirds, and later Walter Scheithauer in Germany experimented extensively to establish specific optimum requirements for these food components. Scheithauer's popular book *Hummingbirds*, published initially in German in 1966 and in English translation the following year, not only provided this information, but also included superb color photographs of 31 species as well as a detailed discussion of the flying abilities of these birds. A few years earlier in North America, Crawford Greenewalt produced a similar volume, also titled *Hummingbirds*, which contained 69 outstanding color photographs of 59 species, a relatively technical discussion of flight characteristics, and detailed analyses of the physics of flight and iridescent coloration.

Comprehensive summaries of the biology of hummingbirds are almost as scarce as works dealing with other aspects of these birds. A.C. Bent described the life histories of 18 North American species in 1940, and J. Berlioz (1944) and A. Martin and A. Musy (1959) provided more general approaches. One of the most attractive introductions to hummingbird biology is the 1973 volume by Alexander F. Skutch, *The Life of the Hummingbird*, with splendid color illustrations by Arthur Singer.

Over the last decades there has been a major resurgence of interest in the hummingbirds, particularly in their physiology, foraging ecology, and coevolutionary relationships with bird-pollinated flowers. The last of these areas of research was marked by the appearance in 1968 of *Hummingbirds and Their Flowers*, by Karen and Vernon Grant, but the other topics have yet to be summarized in book form.

Because Bent's materials on the natural history and breeding biology of North American hummingbirds are now more than 40 years old, and because of the great advances in most areas of knowledge of hummingbirds, I thought a new approach to the hummingbirds of North America would be appropriate. Initially I envisioned the major emphasis as a group of up-to-date species accounts of the North American species. However, I soon recognized the need for summarizing certain comparative information, and realized that a few preliminary chapters on comparative ecology, behavior, physiology, and the like might best serve this end. Moreover, these sections could contain information for the non–North American species, which would not be included in the species accounts. Lastly, it seemed desirable to provide a new synopsis of the entire family of hummingbirds, including both common and scientific names and a limited amount of information on the species not given separate descriptive accounts. Thus, I have included an index to available color plates for identification purposes and a simplified descriptive key of distinctive characteristics to facilitate identification of unknown species.

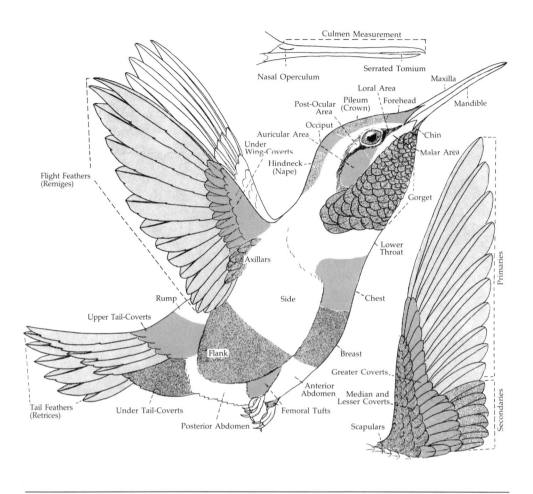

Culmen Measurement

Serrated Tomium

Nasal Operculum

Maxilla

Loral Area

Mandible

Post-Ocular Area
Pileum (Crown)
Forehead

Occiput

Chin

Auricular Area

Malar Area

Under Wing-Coverts

Hindneck (Nape)

Gorget

Flight Feathers (Remiges)

Lower Throat

Axillars

Chest

Rump

Side

Upper Tail-Coverts

Primaries

Flank

Breast

Greater Coverts

Anterior Abdomen

Median and Lesser Coverts

Tail Feathers (Retrices)

Under Tail-Coverts

Femoral Tufts

Secondaries

Posterior Abdomen

Scapulars

Body and feather areas of hummingbirds, showing features mentioned in the keys or text.

PART ONE

COMPARATIVE BIOLOGY OF HUMMINGBIRDS

COLOR PLATES

PLATE 16A.
Costa hummingbird pair visiting *Fouquierria splendens*.

PLATE 16B.
Anna hummingbird pair visiting *Ribes speciosus*.

PLATE 16C.
Ruby-throated hummingbird pair visiting *Lobelia cardinalis*.

PLATE 16D.
Black-chinned hummingbird pair visiting *Castilleja chromosa*.

PLATE 16E.
Calliope hummingbird pair visiting *Ipomopsis aggregata*.

PLATE 16F.
Rufous hummingbird pair visiting *Ribes sanguineum*.

PLATE 16G.
Allen hummingbird (*S. s. sasin*) pair visiting *Aquilegia formosa*.

PLATE 16H.
Broad-tailed hummingbird pair visiting *Penstemon barbatus*.

J. McClelland

J. McClelland

J. McClelland

J. McClelland

J. McClelland

J. McClelland

J. McClelland

J. McClelland

CHAPTER ONE

Classification, Distribution, and General Attributes

Although most bird lovers readily recognize hummingbirds on sight because of their unusually small size, distinctive "humming" flight, and attraction to nectar-producing flowers or feeders, an introduction to the family Trochilidae should begin with a fairly formal definition. In brief, hummingbirds are small (2–20 grams) nectarivorous and insectivorous members of the avian order Apodiformes, but differing from others of that group (the swifts) in having long, slender bills and extensile bitubular tongues. They always have 10 primary feathers, 6 or 7 secondaries, 10 rectrices (rarely fewer), and an extremely large sternum. Their feet are small and rather unsuited for walking, but the toes are well-developed for perching, with three directed forward and one posteriorly. Their wings are moderately long and pointed, with unusually short arm and forearm bones, but relatively long hand bones. They fly by a unique method of rotating the entire wing with little or no wrist and elbow flexing, which makes them capable of forward, backward, and prolonged hovering flight. Adults virtually lack down feathers, and their body feathers are often scale-like and highly iridescent. Sexual dimorphism in adult plumages is common, and non-monogamous mating systems are typical. The entire family is confined to the New World, and is mostly tropical in distribution.

This relatively detailed and technical description totally fails to portray the beauty and attractiveness of hummingbirds. Nevertheless, their common names, such as woodstar, starfrontlet, sapphire, emerald, topaz, ruby, sylph, mountain-gem, sunbeam, firecrown, fairy, and sunangel, portray some of the romance which has traditionally endowed the group. In France they are often referred to as *colibri* or by the less attractive name *oiseau-mouche* (fly-birds); in Spanish-speaking countries they are usually called *picaflores* (flower-peckers); and the Portuguese sometimes use the delightful term *beija flor* (flower-kissers). In the Antilles and Guiana they are sometimes called *murmures* (murmurers), *bourdons,* and *frou-frous* by the Creoles; likewise, their native names in parts of Central and South America include a variety of terms of descriptive or metaphorical nature, such as "rays of the sun," "tresses of the day-star," "murmuring birds," and the like (Ridgway, 1890).

Even if hummingbirds were not so beautiful, they would be able to draw our attention simply because probably no other group of birds can lay claim to so many unique or extraordinary characteristics, such as the following:

• They include perhaps the smallest of warm-blooded vertebrates, and have the greatest relative energy output of any warm-blooded animal.

• They are the largest nonpasserine family of birds, and the second largest family of Western Hemisphere birds in number of living species.

• The smaller species have the most rapid wingbeat of all birds (reportedly to 200 per second during courtship, and reliably to 80 per second in forward flight), and are among the fastest fliers of small birds (50–65 kilometers per hour in forward flight to 95 kh in dives).

• The ratio of their heart size to their body size is the largest of all warm-blooded animals, and their heartbeat rate reaches 1260 beats per minute (second only to some shrews).

• They have the relatively largest breast muscles of all birds (up to 30 percent of total weight), and are the only birds whose upstroke provides as much power as the downstroke.

• Their plumage is among the most densely distributed of all birds, and the feather structure is among the most specialized; but they have the fewest total feathers of all birds (often less than 1000).

• Their brain size is among the relatively largest of all birds (up to at least 4.2 percent of body weight).

• They have a unique flight mechanism, capable of prolonged hovering and rapid backward flight.

• They are the only birds that regularly become torpid at night, with a drop in body temperature of as much as 19° C; however, their normal body temperature is among the highest (40° C) of all birds.

• Individual hummingbirds often consume more than half their total weight in food and may drink eight times their weight in water per day.

Although various regions of the Old World possess nectar-sucking birds, such as the similar sunbirds, these groups do not approach the hummingbirds in their degree of specialization for nectar feeding, nor do they exhibit the great array of color and species diversity for which the hummingbirds are well-known. Thus, hummingbirds are perhaps the most notable of all New World bird groups, and, like the birds of paradise of Australia and New Guinea, they were the source of great interest and folklore by the early explorers of the New World. French colonists of Brazil mentioned them as early as 1558, and in 1671 the nest and eggs of a ruby-throated hummingbird were first described in the *Philosophical Transactions* of Great Britain as a "curiously contrived Nest of a Humming Bird, so called from the humming noise it maketh whilst it flies." The same journal published a description of the bird itself in 1693, in which the author noted that "they feed by thrusting their Bill and Tongue into the blossom of Trees, and so suck the sweet juice of Honey from them; and when he sucks he sits not, but bears up his Body with a hovering Motion of his Wings. . ." (Ridgway, 1890).

By the time of Linnaeus, several species of hummingbirds were known; the 10th edition of his *Systema Naturae* (1758) included descriptions of 18 species known to him, which have since been reallocated to 11 currently recognized species. Thereafter relatively few species were described, until a veritable plethora were discovered in the middle of the 19th century (Table 1). By 1945, when James Peters provided what is still the most widely accepted classification of hummingbirds, the golden age of hummingbird discoveries was essentially over. Nevertheless, in the 35 years since Peters' classification appeared, an additional 13 species of hummingbirds have been described (4 more than were described in the previous 35 years). Six of these species were discovered in the 1970s alone, which suggests that there may still be more in the American tropics.

Partly because of the great taxonomic problems associated with their classification,

Table 1   *Historical Sequence of Discovery of Hummingbird Species (Based on Taxonomy of Peters, 1945)*

Time of Discovery	Number of Species Described	Cumulative % of Total
1758	11*	3
1761–1770	5	5
1771–1780	1	5
1781–1790	17	10
1791–1800	1	10
1801–1810	3	12
1811–1820	15	16
1821–1830	29	25
1831–1840	54	42
1841–1850	79	66
1851–1860	43	79
1861–1870	18	84
1871–1880	14	89
1881–1890	9	91
1891–1900	12	95
1901–1910	7	97
1911–1945	9	100

*The 18 species of Linnaeus represent 11 recognized by Peters.

Table 2   *Summary of Genera and Species Accepted by Various Authorities*

Authority	Genera	Species
Linnaeus, 1758	1	18
Brisson, 1760	2	36
Gould, 1861	123	416
Gray, 1861–71	163*	469
Elliot, 1878	127(37)†	327
Simon, 1921	188(84)†	489
Peters, 1945	123(73)†	327
Morony et al., 1975	116(64)†	338
This work, 1983	102(58)†	342

*Including subgenera.
†Monotypic genera in parentheses.

it is virtually impossible to state with certainty how many hummingbird species actually exist. Table 2 provides a summary of the total numbers of genera and species of hummingbirds recognized by various authorities since Linnaeus. The most recent authorities (Morony et al., 1975) list 338 species; I list 342 in appendix 3 of this book. Yet 23 of these are of distinctly uncertain taxonomic status, and at least some are certainly hybrids or aberrant specimens probably representing other known species. Thus, a minimum of 319 distinct species of hummingbirds certainly exist, and the actual number probably exceeds 330.

Although hummingbirds are usually associated with tropical rainforests, their actual distribution is somewhat at variance with this conception. Certainly the largest number of hummingbird species reside near the equator, but it is the Andes rather than the Amazon basin that supports the greatest hummingbird diversity. As may be determined from Table 3, the country that supports the largest number of hummingbird species is Ecuador, followed closely by Colombia. By comparison,

Table 3   *Hummingbird Diversity in Various Regions*

Country or Region	Hummingbird Species		Area (1000 km²)	Land Area per Species*	Reference
	Total	No. Endemic			
Argentina	24	0	2,808	117.0	Olrog, 1963
Belize (British Honduras)	19	0	23	1.3	Russell, 1964
Bolivia	63	2	1,079	16.9	de Schauensee, 1966
Brazil	90	22	8,549	93.6	Ruschi, 1979
Canada	5	0	10,108	2,022.8	This work
Chile	7	2	744	106.6	Johnson, 1967
Colombia	135	12	1,144	8.3	de Schauensee, 1964
Costa Rica	52	3	42	0.8	Slud, 1964
Ecuador	163	5	276	1.6	Greenewalt, 1960b
El Salvador	21	0	34	1.6	Dickey and van Rossem, 1938
Guatemala	37	0	117	3.1	Land, 1970
Guyana	36	0	216	5.9	Snyder, 1966
Honduras	40	1	153	3.6	Monroe, 1968
Mexico	50	8	1,976	39.0	Peterson and Chalif, 1973
Panama	54	3	73	1.3	Wetmore, 1968
Paraguay	12	0	408	33.8	Olrog, 1968
Peru	100	15	1,253	12.5	Zimmer, 1950–53
Surinam	27	0	140	5.2	Haverschmidt, 1968
United States†	19	0	5,972	312.0	This work
Uruguay	4	0	187	46.8	Olrog, 1968
Venezuela	97	5	915	9.4	de Schauensee and Phelps, 1978
West Indies	17	13	212	12.5	Bond, 1971

*1000 km²/species.
†Excluding Alaska and Hawaii.

Brazil supports only about half as many as either one, in spite of its far greater surface area. If adjustments are made for differences in land areas, then such small Central American countries as Belize, El Salvador, Costa Rica, and Panama all exhibit a diversity of hummingbirds as great or greater than that of most South American areas. Yet, from the vicinity of Panama northward there is a progressive decline in actual species of hummingbirds along a general latitudinal gradient, with the diversity remaining greatest in areas supporting montane forests and other diverse vegetational habitats (see Figure 1).

A summary of the types shown in Table 3 fails to distinguish the kinds of hummingbirds in various regions, as is especially illustrated by the seemingly more "primitive" hermit hummingbirds. This group of generally plain-colored birds with relatively long and often decurved bills are largely associated with equatorial regions and are most abundant in the lowland forests of the Amazon basin. They seem to be more insectivorous than the hummingbird types that have colonized North America, and their bill shapes appear to be highly adapted for extracting insects and nectar from the flowers of such tropical forest plants as *Heliconia*, *Centropogon*, and the like.

Although the hermits comprise a distinctive and reasonably isolated group, which Gould designated as a separate subfamily as long ago as 1861, the remainder of the family is much less readily characterized. Ridgway (1911) listed three subfamilies—the hermits (Phaethornithinae), the coquettes and thorntails (Lophornithinae), and all the remaining species (Trochilinae)—which he distinguished primarily on the basis of the location and relative development of the nasal operculum. Most recent classifications, such as that of Peters, do not contain subfamilies, although Zusi (1980) supported Gould's original recognition of two subfamilies, Phaethornithinae and Trochilinae, with the former more specialized for gleaning arthropods and the latter for nectar-feeding. He listed five genera (*Glaucis*, *Threnetes*, *Ramphodon*, *Phaethornis* and *Eutoxeres*) in the subfamily Phaethornithinae, excluding *Doryfera* and *Androdon*, although the latter is convergent with *Ramphodon*. However, Ruschi (1965) noted that, although *Doryfera* fits with the Trochilinae in having a typical ventrally supported cup-like nest, *Androdon* (like *Ramphodon* and the other hermit-like forms) builds a nest attached laterally to the underside of a palm leaf, with hanging streamers below. Thus, the form of the nest seems to be a very good trait for separating the two subfamilies—if one believes that *Androdon* actually belongs with the hermits and *Doryfera* with the typical hummingbirds.

Although the hermits seem to be more specialized for insect-feeding than are the typical hummingbirds, all the species consume a certain proportion of animal food. Indeed, ancestral hummingbirds were probably exclusively insectivorous, probing vegetation and especially flower blossoms for tiny insects. During evolution, their bill and tongue structure likely became progressively more suitable for obtaining nectar as well as solid foods. Thus, reciprocal evolution began to occur between plants and birds, as the plants evolved pollination adaptations through developing nectar production and floral structures that both attracted the birds and tended to restrict the range of potential pollinators. Eventually, a special class of bird-pollinated (ornithophilous) plants emerged in the Western Hemisphere, and the hummingbirds were the principal beneficiaries. (The floral adaptations associ-

1. Species-density map of hummingbirds, showing total numbers of breeding or resident species within the enclosed areas. In part after Cook
(1969); South American map based on incomplete information and subject
to modification. Areas enclosed by lines represent the numbers of species
and hummingbirds breeding within each area. Increasing species density
toward the tropics is indicated by four levels of overlay patterning.

ated with such pollinating adaptations as distinctive coloration, high nectar production, tubular blossoms, and lack of insect-attracting devices are described in a later chapter.) This process has clearly played an important role in the shaping of blossom types in many families of Western Hemisphere plants, as well as in affecting the structure of the bill and tongue in nearly all hummingbirds.

The major evolutionary forces that produced the astonishing array and beauty of hummingbird plumages are quite different. Scarcely a single species of hummingbird is not iridescent in at least some feather areas, most generally on the dorsal surface and, in the more highly specialized forms, in the neck region, where an often highly differentiated "gorget" occurs. In some relatively dull-colored forms, such as the hermits, males and females are frequently almost identical in appearance; in the more sexually dimorphic groups, the male invariably exhibits the elaborate crests, trains, and highly colorful plumages.

Apart from the unpigmented white areas, hummingbird feathers possess only two fairly simple melanin pigments, producing blackish or rufous coloration. Light refraction by specialized feathers generates the metallic colors, which range through the entire visible spectrum from ruby red to intense violet. Further, the precise angle at which the light strikes the feathers alters the color, so that a feather may shift in apparent coloration with only slight changes in angle relative to the light source. In hummingbirds, the barbules of the iridescent feathers are highly flattened and twisted, so that the microscopic feather surface faces the observer. The melanin granules within the barbules are themselves responsible for the light refraction; in some other bird groups the interference is caused by the outer keratin layer, and the melanin simply prevents the reflection of other colors. The melanin granules of hummingbirds are distinctively shaped into rows of oval platelets, with each platelet containing numerous small air bubbles. The specific colors reflected depend on the thickness of the platelets and the sizes of the enclosed bubbles (Greenewalt, 1960).

One of the most highly developed attributes of hummingbirds is their tongue (see Figure 5, p. 34). Besides being extremely long, it is capable of considerable extension because of the elongated hyoid apparatus that curls backward and upward around the eye sockets in species so far studied. Although long known to be split, forming a double tubular structure at the tip, the tongue was once believed to be hollow as well. Recent research (Weymouth et al., 1964) has effectively disproved that contention, although the terminal portions of the tongue are probably able to take up liquids rapidly, perhaps by capillary action. A foraging hummingbird does not keep its tongue continuously in the fluid, as a moth does, but rather rapidly inserts and removes it. Insects do not appear to be sucked up directly, although they may well be caught up in the sticky material adhering to the fringed edges of the tongue. Further, although a few hummingbirds have distinctly serrated edges on the bill, which may facilitate the holding of insects, generally hummingbirds seem incapable of manipulating insects with the bill or even holding them in it for more than a few seconds (Thompson, 1974).

For almost two centuries we have known that hummingbirds feed at least in part on insects, although the actual proportion of animal foods in their diet has remained controversial. For one thing, nectar is very rapidly assimilated and thus is usually absent from the stomach contents of dead individuals. On the other hand, often their stomachs are almost entirely filled with minute insects and spiders, especially among the insect-adapted hermits and their allies. Furthermore, nestling hummingbirds no more than two days old are frequently fed almost exclusively on these items (Ridgway, 1890). The unusually well-developed crop of young hummingbird nestlings nonetheless seems to be equally adapted for holding large volumes of arthropods and fluid foods. The crop is retained into adulthood and, at least in some species, can be expanded to fill the area above the neck vertebrae. Moreover, the entrance and exit openings of the stomach are very close together, so that the gizzard, when filled with arthropods, will not interfere with the passage of nectar.

If the hummingbirds have any deficiencies, one may be their general lack of vocalizations. The voice-producing organ (the syrinx) is located very far forward in the windpipe or trachea, and thus the bronchi are unusually long. Further, the major muscles that originate on the sternum and insert on the trachea of most birds are completely lacking, although two pairs of special intrinsic muscles are present. Thus, hummingbird vocalizations are generally simple and of a twittering and high-pitched nature. One of the few species that has anything like a true song is the tiny vervain hummingbird of the West Indies, which warbles in a weak but sweetly melodious manner for as long as 10 minutes (Ridgway, 1890). The fairly closely related wine-throated hummingbird of Central America also utters a "sweetly varied outpouring" of sounds lasting for almost a minute (Skutch, 1973). Further, the male Anna hummingbird has a fairly elaborate courtship vocalization, as compared with that of most other North American species.

Although hummingbirds may have vocal limitations, their abilities to generate instrumental sounds through feather vibrations are certainly substantial, as indeed the name "hummingbird" implies. For example, the attenuated outer primaries of such genera as *Selasphorus*, *Lafresnaya*, and *Aglaectis* probably are adapted chiefly for sound production, and the unusually narrowed outer rectrices of some species of *Archilochus* and the typical "woodstars" of the genus *Acestrura* may serve similar functions.

In their mating systems the hummingbirds are surprisingly uniform, yet it is exactly this uniformity that may be responsible for the incredible diversity of male plumage patterns and elaborate displays for which the group is noted. In general, the sexes live apart from one another, with little or no association until the breeding season; then the males begin their advertisement displays. They often are dispersed in widely separated breeding territories, but may at times gather in loose courtship groups. "Singing assemblies" composed of a few to about 20 or more birds may develop, with each male defending a small but discrete territory within a larger "lek" area. These assemblies seem most prevalent among the hermits and other essentially forest-dwelling species, where poor illumination requires vocalizations rather than visual displays for the greatest attraction powers. On the other hand, most of the more temperate-climate species tend to display solitarily in well-illuminated areas, which enable the males to exhibit their magnificent gorgets and other iridescent colorations effectively; thus, their weak vocalizations contribute little or nothing to the total display valence.

The male plays virtually no role in the reproductive process beyond fertilization; male participation in incubation or rearing of young has been reported for very few species. The female builds the nest alone, which is normally cuplike and incorporates spider webbing or similar silken materials to bind it to the substrate. She almost invariably lays two eggs, which are white and unusually long and elliptical, and, with rare exceptions, she alone incubates them for 14 to 21 days. The young hatch virtually naked (psilopaedic), helpless, and blind (altricial); they must stay in the nest (nidicolous) until they fledge 18 to 40 days later, depending on food supplies and weather conditions.

CHAPTER TWO

Evolution and Speciation

*T*he evolutionary history of hummingbirds is essentially conjectural because there are no fossil remains to use as guidelines. A few fragments of probable swift fossils from the earliest Oligocene strata in France provide us with a rough approximation of the temporal origin of the order Apodiformes. Most scientists believe that hummingbirds and swifts evolved from a common ancestral nucleus, principally because (a) their wing bones have similar proportions; (b) they both lay long, white elliptical eggs, usually in small clutches; and (c) their young are altricial, psilopaedic, and nidicolous.

In contrast to the hummingbirds, swifts feed only on insects, which they capture while in flight. Moreover, swifts have extremely weak legs and feet suitable for perching or clinging, but not for walking. Some swift species build nests on the undersides of palm leaves, making tubular nests of feathers and plant fibers in a manner similar to that of hermit hummingbirds, but swifts secure the nest with sticky saliva rather than with spider webbing. Further, among swifts both sexes typically assist in nest building, incubating the eggs, and brooding. Finally, some swifts and hummingbirds are capable of entering a state of torpidity.

In spite of these considerable similarities, some recent investigators are uncertain whether the swifts and hummingbirds are truly closely related or whether they have simply undergone convergent evolution toward a similar flight mechanism. After close examination of this question, Cohn (1968) determined that the major skeletal similarities (enlarged sternum, strong wing bones, a short humerus and forearm but greatly elongated hand bones) are somewhat superficial and that actually no linear measurements exist that have the same relationship to body weight in both groups. Thus, the ulna and carpometacarpus of hummingbirds are relatively shorter than the corresponding bones in swifts, but the digits are relatively longer. The trunk and humerus of hummingbirds are also relatively longer than those of swifts, but the hummingbird wings are relatively shorter. In most aspects of the wing and associated skeletal girdle, hummingbirds resemble the perching birds (Passeriformes) and related orders, whereas the swifts resemble the goatsuckers (Caprimulgiformes).

Hummingbirds are unique in that they are able to reverse their primaries during hovering flight through rotary movements at the shoulder and the wrist and in the bones supporting the outer primaries. The swifts, however, which are larger, fly in the same wing-flexing manner as more typical birds, and their wrists are reinforced against rotation (Cohn, 1968). The forearm musculature of both groups achieves a strong fanning action during flight, but in swifts this fanning is apparently associated with speed and maneuverability rather than with development of hovering capabilities. Because of these differences, Cohn suggested that the phyletic relationships of the hummingbirds might be best reflected by erecting a special order, Trochiliformes, for them.

Whether or not hummingbirds are closely related to swifts, their ancestral home must have been South America. Not only is the largest number of species still found there, but also the more insectivorous types (the hermit group) are still essentially confined to that region. A bill type of the form currently found in various hermit species, which combines a moderate degree of elongation for probing into the corollas of flowers with a limited ability for grasping and extracting insects from them, would seem to be the generalized hummingbird bill type. From this beginning, progressively more specialized types have emerged, as coevolution between plants and particular species of hummingbirds has gradually refined the relationship of bill and tongue structure to specific food sources in nectar-producing plants. In many species of hummingbirds the tip of the tongue is essentially bitubular and probably highly effective in nectar-gathering; in others it is more brush-tipped and evidently effective both in obtaining nectar and in entrapping small insects.

The evolution of a very small clutch-size may have provided the first steps in the shift to a non-monogamous mating system. Selection favoring small body size probably imposed this system and thus improved hovering abilities and survival on limited food resources as the birds became progressively more nectarivorous. Quite possibly the earliest hummingbirds, like the swifts, were monogamous, with both sexes participating in incubation and brooding. Although some swifts lay clutches of up to six eggs, the reduction of the clutch size in hummingbirds to two eggs (or only one, in rare cases) has reduced both the energy drain on the female during egg-laying and the amount of foraging required to feed the developing young during their fledging period. The gradual emancipation of the male from nesting duties may thus have fostered tendencies for successive matings with additional females during the long tropical nesting periods, eventually almost eliminating all pair-bonding tendencies in both sexes.

The origins of flower groups specifically adapted to foraging and pollination by hummingbirds also remain speculative, but they may at least in part have emerged from flower groups previously pollinated largely by bees and butterflies. Plants adapted for pollination by these insects probably already had some of the important attributes, such as daylight blossoming, large showy flower parts, considerable quantities of nectar, and (perhaps) sufficient odor to attract not only bees or butterflies but also tiny insects that exploit the nectar without achieving pollination. To the extent that hummingbirds attracted to these flowers for their insect fauna may have inadvertently achieved pollination, it became progressively more advantageous for the flowers gradually to shift from insect- to hummingbird-pollination mechanisms (by reducing odor production, shifting away from the blue and violet end of the color spectrum for blossom parts, etc.). Thus, the flowers adapted in ways that reduced nectar loss to "illegitimate" insect foragers and (perhaps) increased the total diversity of available pollinators, thereby reducing interspecific pollination possibilities.

The earliest hummingbird forms may well have been largely confined to relatively wooded environments rich in insect life that would thrive among the dense forest vegetation. However, as the birds became progressively more nectarivorous, the hummingbirds probably began to move into edge environments. There flowering shrubs, vines, and herbs grew abundantly in sunny areas, and individual flowers became more noticeable through large blossom sizes and colors that effectively contrasted against the background substrate. At about this time, the males might have become more prone to promiscuous mating systems, and selective pressures began to favor increased male conspicuousness. Thus, greater nectarivory may well have fostered sexual selection for male advertisement devices such as brilliant plumages and conspicuous behavior, especially visual displays like aerial posturing in a well-lighted environment.

In Trinidad, the flowers of trees that are visited by hummingbirds have only a low incidence (4 of 19 species) of red blossoms, but those of herbaceous plants and vines have a high incidence of red coloration (9 of 14 species) (Snow and Snow, 1972). Further, the smaller species of hummingbirds in that area tend to forage on plants with fairly small corollas and pale colors; the larger species more often forage on the larger and more colorful blossom types. As Snow and Snow (1972) suggested, the larger species of nectar-adapted hummingbirds may have evolved in parallel with certain flowers, as the latter evolved mechanisms of size or structure that effectively excluded most insects. Even the more insectivorous hermits studied by the Snows apparently preferred to forage at red flowers, so the association between red coloration and hummingbird attraction is probably a very ancient one, which apparently is not specifically associated with advanced groups or well-lighted environments. Rather, as has been suggested by various other investigators, it may simply be due to the fact that red is one of the most effectively contrasting colors against a green background for daylight-foraging vertebrates. It also is essentially the "leftover" portion of the visible spectrum that has previously been unutilized by plants adapted to pollination by bees, butterflies, and other diurnal insects, whose visual spectrums scarcely reach the red region. Red thus became an ideal device for ornithophilous flowers to achieve maximum visibility to hummingbirds, while at the same time making the flowers relatively inconspicuous to rival nectar-feeders such as bees and butterflies.

Trying to discern trends in the plumage patterns of hummingbirds can be dangerous, but some knowledge has been learned. In comparison with the hermit group, the "typical" hummingbirds of the subfamily Trochilinae exhibit not only a greater tendency toward sexual dimorphism, but also a greater probability of having reddish iridescence in their plumage. Indeed, males of nearly all of the species that have colonized in North America can be considered "flame-throated" to varying degrees, with a well-differentiated iridescent gorget that varies from red to violet or purple in its predominant coloration. Given the obvious visual impact of red on the sensory system of hummingbirds, it is curious indeed that the distribution of this "high-valence" color is so restricted in the group. Thus, many hummingbirds are mostly emerald or sapphire-green in coloration, but almost none has an area of red greater than that of the gorget itself. One of the few species that seems to fall in this category is the crimson-topaz hummingbird, in which the gorget itself is red only in the female. Similarly, hummingbirds lack the bright red carotinoid pigments commonly found in sunbirds and various other passerine groups. Perhaps red is such a powerfully attractive color in hummingbirds that it must be restricted only to a few specific areas, such the gorget. There the bird can effectively expose or hide it at will, thus avoiding constant aggression among the males and also providing directed, periodic exposure to others at appropriate times.

The evolutionary diversity of the hummingbirds is so great, and the species that have been closely studied anatomically or behaviorally are so few, that detailed presentations of probable evolutionary relationships below the subfamily level are impossible at present. There are approximately 300 species within the subfamily Trochilinae alone, with a still uncertain number of genera that should be recognized. This book covers but 23 species and about a dozen of these genera, thus providing only the slightest taste of evolutionary diversity within the entire hummingbird group. However, I here present (Figures 2 and 3) a highly tentative and greatly oversimplified diagrammatic representation of the possible relationships among them, in my judgment, to point out some of the obvious ways in which the groups seem to differ from one another and may be partially characterized at the generic levels. Much more detailed descriptions of each genus are provided in Part Two of this book, and the diagrams here are for general information only.

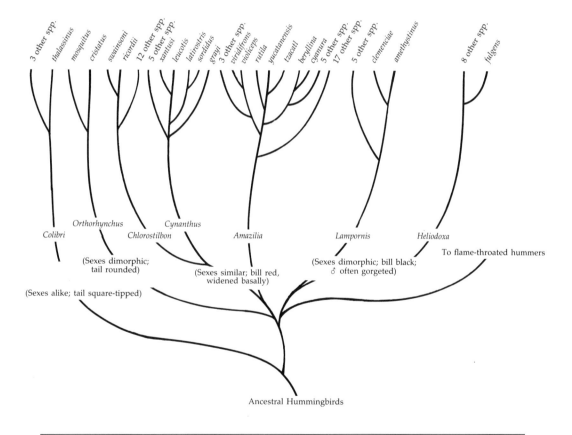

2. Dendrogram of presumptive relationships among North American hummingbirds, exclusive of the flame-throated species.

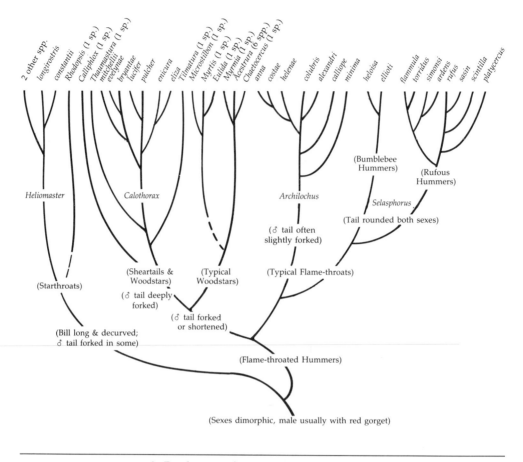

3. Dendrogram of presumptive relationships among North American flame-throated hummingbirds.

In Figure 2 are the presumed affinities of 7 genera and 11 species of predominantly Central and South American trochiline hummingbirds having populations that usually barely reach the North American borders or are only accidental visitors to the United States. Excluded are more than 60 genera and well over 100 species, which occur in linear taxonomic sequence between *Colibri* and *Heliodoxa* but have not been reported within the United States boundaries. Thus, it is a very simplified dendrogram indicating highly speculative relationships.

In Figure 3 are the seemingly more advanced groups that have the center of their breeding distributions in Central America, with a few species reaching South America and many breeding regularly within the United States. This dendrogram includes all of the genera and species occurring in linear taxonomic sequence between *Heliomaster* and *Selasphorus*, even if they do not reach the United States boundaries. Nevertheless, this too is a quite hypothetical and tentative diagram, which should not be interpreted too literally.

Although discussions of the probable evolutionary affinities of each of the species having separate accounts are provided in Part Two, coverage of some general questions of evolution and speciation patterns in North American hummingbirds is appropriate here. If the suggested phylogeny in Figure 3 is acceptable, then North America has been colonized by a group of hummingbirds having their distributional center primarily in the highlands of Central America. They are generally smaller than the more southern-adapted forms, and they have fairly short beaks that are relatively straight and allow for foraging from a wide diversity of nectar-producing plants. There is a rather surprising uniformity in bill length of the North American species of both *Selasphorus* and *Archilochus,* and a correspondingly great apparent potential for different species to forage on the same food plants as well as for a single species to forage from a wide diversity of food plants. Thus, Austin (1975) noted that the ruby-throated hummingbird has been observed foraging on at least 31 plant species that represent 18 different families, and that at least 19 species of eastern North American plants have undergone evolutionary changes favoring pollination by hummingbirds. This is a remarkable statistic, since in the course of hummingbird-flower evolution a fairly specific plant-bird relationship was probably favored to minimize interspecific pollination probabilities. Part of the answer to this anomaly may lie in the fact that over much of eastern North America the only available bird pollinator is the ruby-throated hummingbird, and thus numerous plants have adapted to this single species. In turn, it has retained a rather generalized bill shape that allows exploitation of all of these flower types, thus maximizing the potential geographic breeding range of the species.

The western states contain a much larger total number of ornithophilous plant species as well as a much greater diversity of hummingbirds, as documented by Grant and Grant (1968). Here, speciation in the hummingbirds has resulted in the evolution of seven endemic species of breeding hummingbirds of the "flame-throated" group (broad-tailed, rufous, calliope, black-chinned, Costa, Allen, Anna). These species exhibit limited but varying amounts of geographic overlap during the breeding season and exploit the same or similar food plants in at least some parts of their ranges. Correspondingly, their bill lengths differ only by a matter of a few millimeters in average length, and all possess essentially identical bill shapes. Interspecific territoriality is fairly common in situations where more than one species coexist (Pitelka, 1951a); likewise hybridization among the species is relatively common. At least 9 interspecific hybrid combinations occur among these 7 species, which represents almost half of the total 21 mathematically possible combinations. Further, at least 6 of the undescribed combinations are impossible or unlikely on the basis of breeding range configurations; 6 other possible hybrids may exist on the basis of known breeding ranges, but have yet to be described (Figure 4). The single reported hybrid specimen involving the calliope and Costa hummingbirds is an unexplained anomaly. Although it was reportedly taken in California (Banks and Johnson, 1961), there are no areas of probable breeding overlap either in that state or elsewhere, except possibly in Nevada. This surprisingly high incidence of hybridization implies that the differences in male plumage do not always serve as absolute isolating mechanisms; the close similarities in the plumages of the females are likely to be a much better index to their actual relationships. Furthermore, given this potential for hybridization and interspecific competition for limited resources,

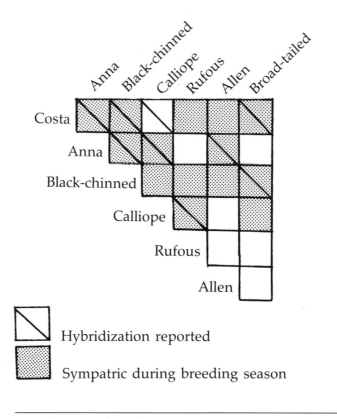

4. Summary of hybridization records of North American flame-throated hummingbirds.

each of the western hummingbirds should show a tendency for ecological isolation from its relatives. This indeed seems to be the case (see chapter 4),although local contacts between two species are certainly prevalent in some areas, and rarely as many as three hummingbirds may breed in fairly restricted areas (Pitelka, 1951b).

CHAPTER THREE

Comparative Anatomy and Physiology

From their iridescent feathers to their tiny skeletons, the hummingbirds offer an amazing number of specializations that can be matched by few if any other bird groups. On the basis of their wings alone, the hummingbirds are preeminent among birds. The remarkable elongation of the hand bones and the associated length of the ten primary feathers are examples. The secondaries, however, are greatly reduced in both length and number. There are typically only six, but sometimes a rudimentary seventh feather is present. The rectrices are also almost invariably ten, although one species—the marvelous spatuletail—has only four, two of which are highly specialized.

The skeletal characteristics (Figure 5) of hummingbirds exhibit many obvious specializations for their unique mode of flight. The sternum, which is greatly enlarged in comparison with more typical flying birds (Figure 6), is also deeply keeled, and the eight pairs of ribs (versus six in most land birds) protect it during the great stresses of hummingbird flight. Further, the unusually strong coracoid is attached to the sternum by a shallow ball-and-cup socket, in a manner that is unique to hummingbirds and swifts (Ridgway, 1890).

The tongue of a hummingbird is essentially as long as the species' bill, yet, by virtue of the elongated hyoid bones, it can be greatly extended from the tip of the bill, thus increasing its effective length for foraging in deeply tubular flowers. For about the anterior half of its total length, the tongue is divided into two separate units, which are fringed along the membranous outer edges, probably in conjunction with the amount of insect foods usually consumed (Figure 5e). The bill itself varies in length from less than a centimeter in *Ramphomicron* to sometimes more than 10 centimeters in *Ensifera*; it is often slightly decurved and is very rarely recurved. In a few genera, such as *Heliothryx* and *Schistes*, the bill is greatly compressed laterally, forming a fine tip when viewed from above. In nearly all hummingbirds the nostril is to some extent covered from above by a distinct shelf-like scale, or operculum. Whether this is related to protection of the nasal cavity from inhaling pollen and the like or has some other unrelated function is unknown.

In nearly all species, the primary feathers are progressively longer from the inside outwardly, and in all but a very few the outermost primary is the longest. The exceptions have an outermost primary that has obviously been modified in structure to generate sound, yet in the streamertail it is shorter than the second primary but not specialized in shape. In some genera, particularly *Campylopterus* and *Aphanto-chroa*, the shafts of one-to-three of the outermost primaries are greatly thickened in males, possibly related to a general strengthening of the outer primaries or perhaps for some unknown display purposes.

Although there is a remarkable consistency in the number of tail feathers, the

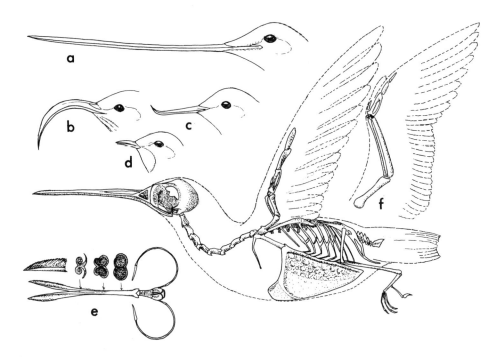

5. Skeleton, bill, and tongue characteristics of hummingbirds, including bills of (a) Andean swordbill, (b) white-tipped sicklebill, (c) avocet-bill, and (d) thornbill. The (e) tongue of the green-throated carib is also diagramed. The wing of a typical flying bird (duck)—drawn to the same scale—is included for comparison (f). (Partly after Ridgway, 1890)

shape of the tail varies substantially among hummingbirds, with differential lengthening of the feathers resulting in forked, scissor-like, wedge-shaped, rounded, graduated or pointed tails, or other variations (Figure 7). In several species the outer tail feathers are appreciably narrower than the more centrally located ones, and these probably are set into vibration during aerial display; the Costa and Anna are examples among North American species. On the other hand, in the rufous male the pair of rectrices adjacent to the middle pair are curiously notched near the tip. They possibly also generate special sounds, although Baptista and Matsui (1979) suggested that, in the case of the Anna, the dive-noise is largely or entirely vocal in origin.

Generally, neither the remiges nor rectrices of hummingbirds are extensively iridescent, perhaps because the structural specializations in the barbules responsible for this coloration seem to inhibit the ability of the separate feather barbs to "knit" together and maintain an unbroken airfoil when subjected to stresses. However, with the exception of these feathers, nearly all of the other feather regions of hummingbirds are relatively iridescent. Their body feathers are also extremely small

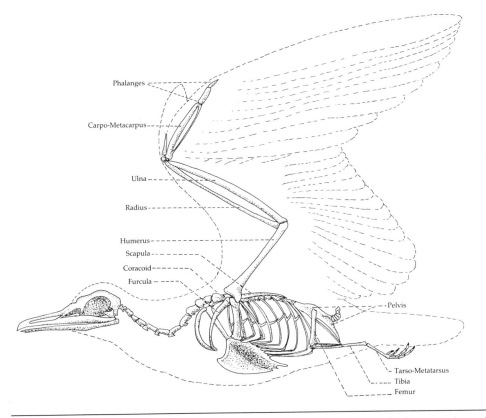

Phalanges
Carpo-Metacarpus
Ulna
Radius
Humerus
Scapula
Coracoid
Furcula
Pelvis
Tarso-Metatarsus
Tibia
Femur

6. Skeletal characteristics of a typical flying bird (gull), for comparison with Figure 5.

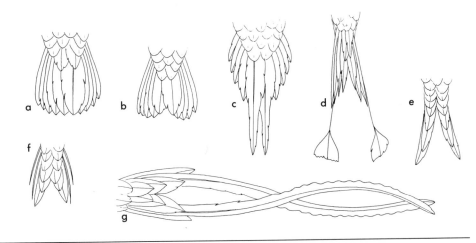

7. Variations in tail shapes of hummingbirds, including (a) rounded, (b) double-rounded, (c) pointed (long-tailed hermit), (d) racket-like (racket-tailed coquette), (e) scissor-like (amethyst woodstar), (f) forked (white-bellied woodstar), and (g) streamer-like (streamertail). (After Ridgway, 1890, 1911)

and closely packed. Aldrich (1956) reported that a male Allen hummingird had 1459 feathers and a female 1659. By comparison, a brown thrasher (*Toxostoma rufum*) had 1920, but this species has a skin surface area about ten times larger than a ruby-throat; thus, the density of feathers in the hummingbird is approximately five times greater (Greenewalt, 1960a).

The highly iridescent feathers of the hummingbird gorgets are among the most specialized of all bird feathers. But even in the male's gorget of a species such as the Allen hummingbird, only about the distal third of each feather is modified for iridescence; the close overlapping of adjacent feathers thus generates the unbroken color effect. The iridescence is produced by the proximal parts of the barbules, which are smooth, flattened, and lack hook-like barbicels or hamuli. Beyond the color-producing portion, the barbule is strongly narrowed and curved toward the distal tip of the feather (Figure 8). The barbicels in this area help to hold together the barbules on one side of the barb, but do not unite the barbules of adjacent barbs (Aldrich, 1956).

Greenewalt (1960a) reviewed at length the aspects of optical theory required for

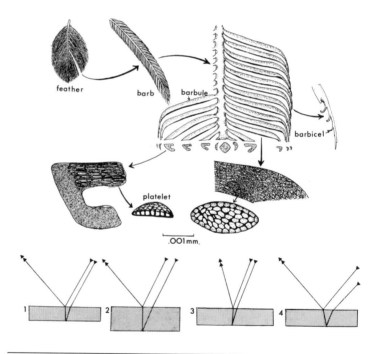

8. Iridescent feather structure of a hummingbird feather, based on photographs in Greenewalt (1960). Below, diagrams of light pathways of optical films having a higher refractive index than that of air, showing effects of variations in film thickness (1 and 2) and in angle of viewing (3 and 4) on reinforcement of particular wavelengths. (In part after Greenewalt, 1960a)

an adequate understanding of iridescence in hummingbird feathers; the following is a brief overview: First, the colors do not directly depend on selective pigment absorption and reflection, as do browns and blacks produced by the melanin pigments of non-iridescent feathers. Rather, they depend on "interference coloration," such as that resulting from the colors seen in an oil film or a soap bubble. Basically, the colors depend on light being passed through a substance with a different refractive index than that of air (1.0), and being partially reflected back again at a second interface. The percentage of the light that is reflected back increases with the difference in the refractive indices of the two media; in addition, the thickness of the film through which the light is passing strongly influences the wavelengths of the light that are reflected back. Put simply, red wavelengths are longer than those at the violet end of the spectrum and generally require films that are thicker or have higher refractive indices than those able to refract bluish or violet light. Thus, the optimum refractive index for red feathers is about 1.85; for blue feathers it is about 1.5.

Hummingbird feathers may attain any refractive index within this range because the iridescent portions of the barbules are densely packed with tiny, tightly packed layers of platelets. These platelets are only about 2.5 microns in length and average about 0.18 microns in thickness, but they vary in thickness and are differentially filled with air bubbles. The platelet's matrix, probably of melanin, evidently has a refractive index of about 2.2, whereas the air bubbles inside have a refractive index of 1.0. Varying the amount of air in the platelets provides a composite refractive index that ranges from the red end of the spectrum (1.85) to the blue (1.5). An analysis by Greenewalt (1960a) indicated that the theoretical structure of the plates should have an "optical thickness" equal to one-half of the particular color's peak wavelength, or an actual thickness equal to the optical thickness divided by the average refractive index. If, then, half the wavelength of red light (0.6-0.7 micron) should be divided by the average refractive index, "red" plates should be about 0.18 micron in average thickness, or the same as the actual thickness indicated by electron microscope examination.

Thus, the actual thickness of the platelets not only significantly determines the quality of the perceived light, but it also affects the amount of air held within the pigment granules and the consequent variations in interference effects. Further, a single pigment granule can produce different color effects according to the angle at which it is viewed. When an optical film is viewed from above, it reflects longer wavelengths than when viewed from angles progressively farther away from the perpendicular (Figure 8). Thus, a gorget may appear ruby red when seen with a beam of light coming from directly behind the eye, but as the angle is changed the gorget color will shift from red to blue and finally to black, as the angle of incidence increases (Greenewalt, 1960a).

In hummingbirds, the color-producing pigment platelets are closely packed into a mosaic surface, and 8 to 10 such layers are then tightly stacked on top of one another in typical iridescent feathers. Far from confusing the visual effects, such stacking actually tends to intensify and purify the resulting spectral color, which is probably why hummingbirds have possibly the most intensively iridescent feathers known in birds (Greenewalt, 1960a).

Iridescence is only one of the many respects in which hummingbirds outdo other birds. When flying, all birds expend a relatively high amount of energy. In most strongly flying birds the two pairs of muscles originating on the sternum's keel occupy from about 15 to 25 percent of the total body weight, but in hummingbirds these muscles comprise from 25 to 30 percent. Further, the muscle that elevates each wing is approximately half the weight of that responsible for the downstroke; it is usually only 5 to 10 percent in more typical birds (Greenewalt, 1960a, 1962).

The unusually large size of the muscles that elevate the wings is related to the fact that hummingbirds generate power during the upstroke as well as the downstroke, with the wings operating like a variable-pitch rotor. The pitch during the upstroke can modify the thrust generated on the downstroke, so that hummingbirds are readily capable of forward, hovering, and backward flight. These remarkable abilities are achieved by a combination of rotary movements of the outer portion of the wing as well as changes in the plane of the wing movement. Thus, during forward flight the tips of the wings describe a vertical oval in the air, not very different from that of other flying birds. However, during hovering the wings are moved in a manner approaching a horizontal figure eight, with the plane of the movement essentially parallel to the horizon (Figure 9). By a slight backward tilting of the plane the bird can easily move upward and backward, and likewise by tilting the plane downward the bird can begin to proceed slowly forward, much in the manner of a helicopter (Greenewalt, 1960a).

The wings of hummingbirds therefore act like aerial "oars," lacking the flexing at the wrist and forearm joints typical of other birds and operating like mechanical oscillators that have constant-speed motors. Thus, they have a close relationship between wing length and the rate of wing beats, as do other flying birds as well as insects. In fact, hummingbirds appear between insects and other groups of birds when their wing length is plotted against their rate of wing beats, or when their wing length is plotted against average body weight (Greenewalt, 1960a). Their wing length is relatively long relative to body size, and on the average body weight is proportional to the 1.5 power of the wing length (Greenewalt, 1962). Average adult hummingbirds weigh from about 2.1 grams in the vervain species (Lack, 1976) to a maximum of about 22 grams in the giant hummingbird (Lasiewski et al., 1967). The wingbeat rate of the former (as well that of the slightly smaller bee hummingbird) is still undetermined, but in the very slightly larger amethyst woodstar it averages 80 per second (Greenewalt, 1960a). However, that of the giant hummingbird ranges from about 10 to 15 per second. In spite of this species' remarkably large size, it is perfectly capable of controlled hovering and backward flight (Lasiewski et al., 1967).

Plots of frequency distributions of average body weights and average adult wing lengths of hummingbirds reveal some interesting relationships. Table 4 presents the range of adult weights of 166 species as determined by Carpenter (1976), as well as the average adult wing lengths of nearly 300 hummingbirds, as obtained from museum specimens and extracted from literature. The latter total represents about 85 percent of the known species of hummingbirds (data on the remaining species were not readily available to me). According to the table, hummingbirds exhibit an apparent "adaptive aerodynamic peak" in weights at about 4 grams.

9. Stages in wing action during hovering flight in a hummingbird, in side and dorsal views. Numbered points on the central diagram indicate location of wingtip at successive stages. (Modified from Greenewalt, 1960a)

Table 4   *Average Wing Lengths and Body Weights in the Family Trochilidae*

Wing Length (millimeters)	# of Species*	% of Species	Body Weight (grams)	# of Species†	% of Species
29–34	10	3.4	1.5–2.5	13	7.8
35–39	22	7.4	2.5–3.5	31	18.6
40–44	26	8.8	3.5–4.5	34	20.5
45–49	29	9.8	4.5–5.5	24	14.5
50–54	36	12.2	5.5–6.5	27	16.2
55–59	48	16.3	6.5–7.5	14	8.4
60–64	39	13.2	7.5–8.5	16	9.6
65–69	33	11.2	8.5–9.5	5	3.0
70–74	27	9.2	>9.5	2	1.2
75–79	15	5.1			
80–84	4	1.3			
85–90	2	0.7			
>90	3	1.0			

*Based on a survey of 294 species sampled from the literature and museum specimens.
†Based on a survey of 166 species sampled by Carpenter (1976), numbers estimated from graph.

Likewise there is a distinct peak for wing length between 55 and 60 millimeters, although ecologic factors may dictate other size constraints. Near the lower end of the scale, the average weights of female hummingbirds are somewhat greater than those of males, but among the larger species of hummingbirds the reverse is true. This may be because the effects of sexual selection in the larger species favor male dominance, whereas in the relatively small species the energy drain of egg-laying has fostered selection favoring larger female weights as compared to males. Thus, the female vervain hummingbird lays a clutch of two eggs of about 0.37 grams each, and their combined weight equals 34 percent of the average adult weight (Lack, 1976). In the larger species the relative egg weight is considerably less, and the females spend less energy in caring for the relatively smaller young (Brown et al., 1978).

Thus, the hummingbirds seem to have evolved along a very narrow evolutionary corridor, which has kept their body weights low enough to provide for the energy-demanding requirements of their unique flight and associated hovering abilities and has prevented them from becoming larger than their limited food supplies would support. They have also been limited by constraints at the lower end of their potential body size by problems associated with regulating body heat, limits on miniaturization of body parts such as structural strength of bones and minimum brain size, and increasing vulnerability to all sorts of predators, including large insects.

Hummingbirds consume large amounts of oxygen, especially during flight, which often places their circulatory systems under special strains. They have the largest known relative heart size of all birds—up to 2.4 percent of their body weight (in the rufous-tailed)—and likewise the most rapid heartbeat in birds—1260 beats per minute (in the blue-throated hummingbird). Similarly, the density of their erythrocytes is the highest known among birds (6.59 million per cubic milliliter), perhaps as a result of the cells' unusually small size, which is associated with efficient gas-transport capabilities. Body temperatures of active hummingbirds are generally close to 40° C, occasionally reaching as high as 43° C when struggling but restrained (Lasiewski, 1964; Morrison, 1962). The breathing rate in hummingbirds is also very high, approximately 250 per minute for a 3-gram hummingbird at rest.

The rate of metabolism of even a resting hummingbird, as measured by its oxygen consumption, is about 12 times greater than that of a pigeon (*Columba livia*)and 25 times greater than that of domestic fowl (Welty, 1975). A human, metabolizing energy at the rate of a hummingbird, would have to consume roughly double his weight in food such as meat every 24 hours, or about 45 kilograms of pure glucose, and his body temperature would rise to more than 400° C (Scheithauer, 1967). Hummingbirds and the comparably sized shrews among mammals have evidently reached the smallest sizes that are physiologically possible for warm-blooded animals; smaller animals simply could not eat enough food to avoid starvation.

Small birds endure a greater rate of heat loss from the body than do large birds; likewise, small birds are relatively more subject to overheating when placed in an environment that is warmer than their body temperature. Even temperate-zone hummingbirds lack down feathers, and thus are relatively unable to increase their insulation effectiveness by feather fluffing during exposure to cold. Thus, they can maintain body temperature only by increasing their heat production. Working on marginal energy balances, hummingbirds cannot accomplish such maintenance over a prolonged period; so, rather than make the attempt, many enter a state of torpor. The metabolic rate may then drop to about one-fiftieth of the basal rate at normal body temperature, and the rate of water loss by evaporation decreases from one-third to one-tenth that of the normal body temperature; thus torpidity may be important as a water-conservation device. The rates of entry into and emergence from torpor are inversely related to the bird's body size: The smaller the hummingbird, the more rapidly it may enter or emerge from a torpid state.

During torpidity, the rate of heartbeats varies with body temperature, from 50 to 180 per minute, and breathing becomes irregular, with long periods of non-breathing at lower temperatures (Lasiewski, 1964). In many torpid birds the body temperature tends to approximate that of the environment, and in species such as the poorwill (*Phalaenoptilus nuttallii*) lowering the external temperature does not stimulate regulatory processes that prevent the body temperature from either falling further or from arousing. However, a few hummingbird species maintain a minimum body temperature of 18 to 20° C below that of the normal resting temperature in spite of even lower air temperatures. Apparently the regulated level of body temperature during torpidity is related to the minimum environmental conditions that are encountered under normal conditions in the wild (Wolf and Hainsworth, 1971). A study of several species of South American hummingbirds found that average body temperatures during daytime activities were about 39° C, with increases of 2.2° C during maximum activity and a decrease of only 4° to 5° C during deep sleep or torpor conditions. Tropical species of hummingbirds thus seem more sensitive to a lowering of the body temperature than are more temperate-adapted species (Morrison, 1962).

We have long wondered how species such as the ruby-throated hummingbird store enough energy to allow them to migrate across the Gulf of Mexico, a minimum overseas distance of about 800 kilometers, given their limited capacities for fat storage and the high rate of energy utilization during flight. Although earlier calculations suggested that the maximum flight range of this species might be about 616 kilometers, or far below the necessary minimum to make the flight, more recent estimates by Lasiewski (1962) have prompted new conclusions. He estimated that the average adult ruby-throat can store and use 2 grams of fat, which would be enough for about 26 hours flight in males and 24.3 hours in the larger females. Given an average air speed of 40 kilometers per hour, the maximum flight range of a male would thus be 1040 kilometers, and that of a female 975 kilometers— more than enough to make a nonstop flight across the gulf. This was based on the estimate that the birds would burn their energy reserves at the rate of 0.69 and 0.74 calories per hour for the male and female sexes, respectively, and the fact that a gram of fat has an energy content of 9.0 calories.

To keep from "burning out," a hummingbird must spend a good proportion of its waking hours gathering food simply to stay alive. One wild male Anna hummingbird requires a minimum of 7.55 calories (assuming torpidity at night) to 10.32 calories (assuming sleep at night) during a 24-hour period. An average daily period of 12 hours and 52 minutes of activity would require an energy expenditure of 3.81

calories in perching, 2.46 calories in nectar flights, 0.09 calories in insect-catching, and 0.30 calories in defense of territory. The nectar production of about 1022 fuschia flowers could supply this daily need (Pearson, 1954). If the hummingbird will spend the night without becoming torpid, it must consume a substantial surplus of energy during the hours of activity; one study on the rufous-tailed hummingbird estimated that an excess daily intake of 4.07 calories would enable the bird to survive the night without going into torpor (Schuchmann et al., 1979). Studies on a few species of hummingbirds indicated daily energy budgets of 7.78 to 12.4 calories per 24 hours. These energy budgets are 3.1 to 3.6 times the standard ("basal") metabolic rates of the individual species or considerably greater than figures obtained for comparable nectar-feeders among passerine birds (MacMillen and Carpenter, 1977).

CHAPTER FOUR

Comparative Ecology

*T*here are an enormous number of ecological factors associated with several hundred species of hummingbirds and their foraging adaptations, as well as the related adaptations of the hundreds of species of plants which have coevolved with hummingbirds with respect to mechanisms favoring efficient pollination. The relationship between plants and hummingbirds is an old and close one; in western North America alone about 130 species of plants exhibit features apparently modified through evolution for foraging and pollination by hummingbirds (Grant and Grant, 1968). Another 20 or more species of eastern North American plants have been similarly affected (Austin, 1975), so that at least 150 species of North American flowering plants exhibit an "ornithophilous syndrome" (van der Pilj and Dodson, 1966).

Plants exhibiting these adaptations normally bear large flowers that are solitary or loosely clustered in a horizontal or pendant position, usually at the tip of flexible pedicels. The flowers are often red or red and yellow, hold large quantities of nectar at the base of a long, stout floral tube, and the corolla is often thickened or otherwise modified to protect it from accidental piercing by the bird's beak or from nectar thievery by nonpollinators. The plants typically bloom during daylight hours, have little or no scent, and have projecting stamens and pistils that are likely to intercept the crown of the visiting pollinator. They also lack "landing platforms" suitable for nectar-drinking competitors such as bees, and may have other devices that tend to exclude visits by these and other nonpollinating nectar-drinkers, such as butterflies and moths (Grant and Grant 1968).

Van der Pilj and Dodson (1966) have listed some of the typical features of ornithophilous flowers as compared with those adapted for butterfly and bee pollination. As shown in Table 5, there are greater similarities between blossoms pollinated by hummingbirds and butterflies than between those adapted to birds and bees.

According to Grant and Grant (1968), most of the hummingbird-adapted plants of western North America are either perennial herbs or softwood subshrubs, with a few trees and very few annual herbs as well. Many of the plants are dicotyledons with fused corollas, and the vast majority are red or at least partially red. The Grants concluded that the most common ancestral condition for the hummingbird flowers of North America is a bee-pollinated system, with only a few genera from ancestral groups where lepidopteran (butterfly or moth) pollination typically occurs. Further, a few ornithophilous genera are centered in subtropical or tropical America and probably have been associated with birds for long periods. These presumably have followed the hummingbirds northward to occupy their current ranges in western North America.

Table 5   *Typical Characteristics of Flowers Pollinated by Birds, Butterflies, or Bees (after various sources)*

Characteristic	Bird-Pollinated	Butterfly-Pollinated	Bee-Pollinated
Flowering time	diurnal	diurnal	diurnal
Flower shape	weakly zygomorphic or radial	radial or zygomorphic	zygomorphic, usually with landing platform
Blossom color	vivid, often red	vivid, sometimes red	variable but not red
Odor	none	sweet and fresh	sweet and fresh
Nectar	very abundant in broad tubes	abundant, in narrow tubes	sparse, usually hidden
Flower position	horizontal or hanging	erect	horizontal
Petal position	often recurved	usually not recurved	not recurved, thus allowing for landing

The listing of plants provided in Appendix 6 is based largely on that of Grant and Grant, plus all the eastern species listed by Austin (1975) and a few more that recent studies determined to be hummingbird-adapted. The genera and species are alphabetically organized by families, and the families themselves are listed alphabetically within the major monocotyledonous and dicotyledonous groups.

In a review of the effect of the evolution of ornithophily on flowers, Stiles (1978) noted that, because this syndrome is energetically expensive for plants, it should occur only when birds provide the optimum vehicle for pollen flow. Pollinating adaptations exhibited by plants all revolve around nectar secretion and the specific manner of presenting it to birds or other pollinators. In dark habitats, plants may produce enough nectar to make bird pollination profitable; similarly, annual plants would benefit less from long-lived pollinators such as birds than would perennials. Likewise, trees benefit relatively little from hummingbirds, since such a rich nectar source would be divided up into small foraging territories, thus reducing pollen flow from tree to tree. On the other hand, many epiphytes are hummingbird-pollinated; the small plant sizes associated with the epiphytic habit tend to assure outcrossing even in territorial species of hummingbirds. Generally, hummingbird-pollinated flowers tend to bloom over a greater proportion of the year than do insect-pollinated flowers, a tendency which may help to stabilize the presence of the pollinator in the community. Many plant species have flowers that are specialized for hummingbird pollination, but usually not by specific bird species. This general rather than precise structural correspondence and codependence may help to buffer the ecosystem against sudden population fluctuations of any single bird or flower species (Stiles, 1978).

In a study area in the White Mountains of Arizona, nine species of hummingbird flowers coexist, all strongly convergent in flower color, size, and shape. Competition among them for pollination is evidently reduced by differences in orientation of anther and stigma location, so that different parts of the bird transport the pollen. Many of the flower species secrete nectar at similar rates, but the local population of cardinal flower produces no nectar at all, and instead attracts hummingbirds by mimicking the more abundant nectar-producing species (Brown and Kodric-Brown, 1979).

As Grant and Grant (1968) noted, the usual relationship between corolla length and bill length of the typical hummingbird visitor is only a general one; nevertheless, there is often a close relationship in both corolla length and corolla shape in these structures (Figures 10–12). Brown and Kodric-Brown (1979) noted that seven of the nine species of hummingbird-pollinated flowers that they studied had very similar corolla length (20–25 mm), and the average culmen lengths of the three most common hummingbird visitors ranged from 15.7 to 20.2 mm.

A striking case of coevolution between bill length and corolla length in hummingbirds is that of the swordbill, an Andean species of hummingbird that has a culmen length substantially longer than any other known species. The culmen length in adults averages 83 mm, ranging to 105 mm in some individuals. In their study in Colombia, Snow and Snow (1980) observed that this measurement is apparently specifically dependent upon the blossoms of *Passiflora mixta*, a species of passion flower with a remarkably long corolla tube (about 114 mm). The long

10. Andean swordbill and *Passiflora mixta*.

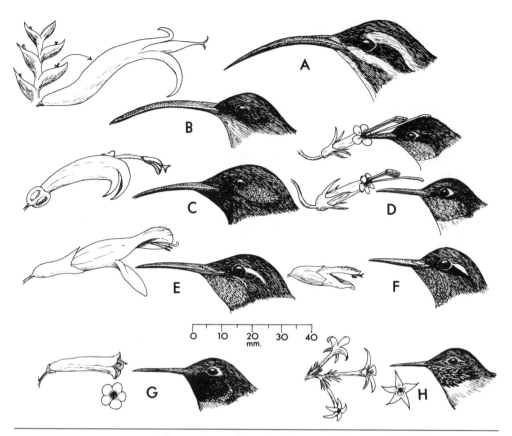

11. Comparisons of corolla shapes and hummingbird bills, showing co-evolved characteristics. *Heliconia bihai*, associated with hairy hermit (A) and green hermit (B); *Centropogon valerii*, with green violet-ear (C); *Macranthera flammea*, with ruby-throated hummingbird (D); *Salvia cardinalis*, with blue-throated hummingbird (E); *Salvia mexicana*, with white-eared hummingbird (F); *Penstemon eatoni*, with black-chinned hummingbird (G); and *Ipomopsis aggregata*, with calliope hummingbird. (After various sources)

bill and extensile tongue of the swordbill species enable it to obtain the nectar from the long corolla tube, which is probably inaccessible to all other hummingbirds (Figure 10). The swordbill is evidently nonterritorial, and forages as a "trapliner" by visiting a large number of plants over a fairly wide area. Likewise, the giant hummingbird in Ecuador is heavily dependent upon the flowers of *Agave americana*, and its distribution seems to have spread with that of the plant (Ortiz-Crespo, 1974).

Many other species of plants, though perhaps not so specifically adjusted to bill length as *Passiflora* may be, nonetheless have remarkable adaptations that ensure cross-pollination. Pickens (1927) described the situation in *Macranthera flammea*, which has the typical hummingbird corolla shape (Figure 11) and color (bright orange), but bears an erect flower. As the corolla begins to open, the pistil quickly emerges and reaches its full length. A day or two later the pistil begins to wither, but by then the stamens have grown to the length of the drooping pistil, with the pollen-bearing anther surfaces tilted toward the center of the flower. By this device, a visiting hummingbird is bound to have its crown intercept either the anthers or the stigma, thus assuring cross-pollination when it visits another blossom at a slightly different stage of floral development, while at the same time avoiding self-pollination.

Wagner (1946a) described a similar situation in the Mexican plant *Centropogon cordifolius*. In the early stages of floral development, the stamens mature first and tilt downward. After the stamens have withered, the stigmas occupy essentially the same position in the blossom, where they are likely to strike the top of the head of a foraging hummingbird (Figure 12). In a similar case, the stigma of *Lamourouxia exserta* develops earlier than the anthers, so only cross-pollination is possible. Even more remarkable is the highly specialized structure of *Marcgravia*, which has a group of nectaries directly below a series of developing flowers located horizontally above on long, thick stalks around the upper part of the main flower axis. The blossoms face downward toward the nectary below and exhibit "protan-

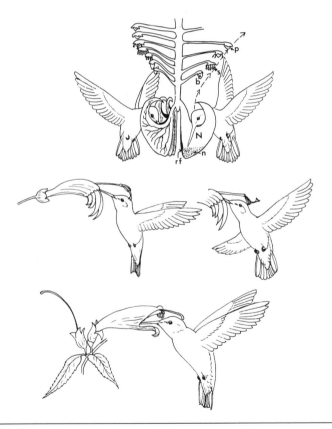

12. Pollination adaptations of *Marcgravia picta* (top), *Centropogon* (middle), and *Lamourouxia exserta* (bottom), after drawings by H. Wagner. See text for explanation. In top drawing, b = bud, N = nectary, n = nectar, p = pistil, rf = rudimentary flower, and s = stamens.

dry," with the pollen-bearing anthers developing first and the stigmas later. As the hummingbird finishes drinking at the nectary and rises backward and upward, its head comes into contact first with the clustered stamens and later with the pistil (Figure 12), again assuring cross-pollination (Wagner, 1946a). Similarly, in the southern Andes, the Andean hillstar pollinates a species of oranged-blossomed composite (*Chuquiraga spinosa*) that exhibits protandrous development of the stamens. As the growing style passes through the corolla tube, it pulls the mature pollen upward with it, coating the inside of the corolla tube and the style itself with pollen. The lobes of the stigma remain closed until the style's elongation has lifted the stigma well above the level of the corolla tube, thus avoiding self-pollination (Carpenter, 1976).

A number of investigators have reviewed the usual association of bird-pollinated flowers and red coloration. Grant and Grant (1968) suggested that a single coloration used by a group of hummingbird-adapted species serves as a common advertisement for food sources, and thus each plant species benefits from becoming a part of a pool of similar nectar-producing species. Moreover, many hummingbird-pollinated forms probably evolved from bee-pollinated ancestors that were usually blue. The shift from blue to red, which is not attractive to bees, may have augmented the development of a bird-adapted flower form. Thus, in the genus *Penstemon*, which is commonly bee-pollinated, the species *P. centranthifolius* is red, with flowers that are trumpet-shaped and attractive to hummingbirds. The closely related form *P. grinnelli*, which has pale blue, widely bilabiate flowers, is bee-pollinated, and a third species, *P. spectabilis*, has smaller blue, somewhat bilabiate flowers and is wasp-pollinated (Straw, 1956). Grant (1952) described a similar case of floral isolation by flower color, shape, and position in two closely related species of *Aquilegia* found in the Sierra Nevada mountains; these differences reproductively isolate a hummingbird-adapted species from a hawk-moth-adapted species.

Hummingbirds do not exhibit any innate preference for red coloration, but they certainly can learn to associate particular colors with nectar sources. Thus the development of red coloration in bird-adapted flowers provides a convenient, uniformly recognized "flag" for the birds, which is conspicuous against a green background. It is also unlikely to attract bees, which have color vision ranges that barely reach the red portion of the spectrum.

Studies by Stiles (1976) indicated that hummingbirds respond more strongly to energetic aspects of fluid solutions (concentration of sugar, rate of nectar flow) than they do to taste considerations (composition of sugar), and to taste in turn more strongly than to the color of feeder or flower. Among sugars, they select sucrose over glucose, and glucose over fructose. The preferred colors tend to be near the long-wavelength or red end of the spectrum for both tropical and temperate-zone flowers; thus the presence or absence of hummingbird migratory behavior is probably not significant in fixing the colors of plants.

Besides individualized specialization between birds and plants, specialist foragers such as hummingbirds tend to exhibit a considerable degree of ecological segregation into habitats where interspecific competition from related species are minimal. Of the few quantitative investigations in this area on North American species, studies such as those of Des Granges (1979) have indicated a high degree of interspecific organization of hummingbird guilds in tropical environments. Table

Table 6   *Climatic and Vegetational Affinities of Breeding Hummingbirds in Western North America**

Species	Preferred Climate	Preferred Habitat	
		Region	Dominant Plants
Allen	moist	coastal woodlands	deciduous trees
Anna	mesic	chaparral woodlands	deciduous trees
Black-chinned	xeric	scrub lowlands	deciduous trees
Broad-tailed	xeric	open woodlands	conifers
Calliope	mesic	montane coniferous	conifers
Costa	xeric	desert scrub	shrubs
Rufous	moist	moist coniferous	conifers

*Excluding species centered primarily in Mexico.

Table 7   *Altitudinal and Ecological Affinities of Hummingbirds That Breed in Mexico and Are Occasionally Found in the United States**

Species	Altitude (meters)	Ecological Preference	
		General Area	Particular Habitat
Berylline	900–3000	interior highland	arid pine, pine-oak or fir forest edge
Blue-throated	1800–3900	interior highland	montane meadow, woodland edge
Buff-bellied	0–1200	Atlantic lowland	coastal scrub, forest edge
Bumblebee	1500–3000	interior highland	open pine-oak woodland, cloud forest edge
Green violet-ear	1800–3000	interior highland	humid pine-oak woodland, fir forest
Lucifer	1200–2400	interior highland	arid brush
Plain-capped starthroat	0–1500	Pacific lowland	thorn forest, scrub desert
Rivoli	1500–3300	interior highland	humid pine-oak woodland, cloud forest edge
Rufous-tailed	0–1700	Atlantic lowland	high deciduous forest, rainforest
Violet-crowned	90–2100	interior highland	dry forest, riparian scrub
White-eared	1200–3300	interior highland	scrub oak, pine-oak woodland, arid brush

*Excluding Mexican species not recorded from USA; altitudes and habitats mainly after Edwards, 1972.

6 presents an approximation of the tendencies for ecological segregation in the species of hummingbirds that breed predominantly in western North America, and Table 7 comprises a similar ecological and geographical tabulation of the primarily Mexican species discussed individually in this text. Neither table allows for a precise estimate of ecological overlaps or interspecific competition between any two species, but both tables at least provide some indication of the most probable cases of ecological contact between species while on their breeding grounds. Further seg-

regation of habitat between the sexes exists for at least six of the seven species of North American hummingbirds presented in Table 6 (Pitelka, 1951b; Stiles, 1972b) as well as in such Mexican species as the white-eared hummingbird (Des Granges, 1979) and the blue-throated hummingbird (Wagner, 1952). At least one species of hermit (the saw-billed) is sexually dimorphic in bill shape (Selander, 1966).

In a study area in Mexico on the border of Colima and Jalisco, Des Granges (1979) found a foraging guild of some 21 species of hummingbirds, comprising three different groups; (a) the resident group of tropical species inhabiting particular habitats throughout the year; (b) wandering species that visit several habitats during the year and follow seasonal blooms of flowering plants; and (c) migrants present only during the winter. Most of the resident species are territorial, feeding preferentially on tubular flowers. The wanderers are typically "trapliners"—nonterritorial birds that move about, foraging on a variety of blossom types. The migrant species are territorial, defending flowers that provide nectar in excess of the resident and wanderer's requirements, and supplementing their diets with insects. There were several types of ecological segregation, including special segregation of species (dominant and territorial birds defending the tops of trees and shrubs, or areas of tightly packed flowers, and subordinate or nonterritorial birds defending lower areas and often more scattered flowers), seasonal segregation of some species, and a limited degree of sexual segregation in two species; there was no definite indication of diurnal segregation.

At least in the more tropical areas, the species in hummingbird communities tend to fall into one of four foraging modes. "High-reward trapliners" have relatively specialized bills, which have coevolved with particular blossom types. Such species effectively exploit the nectar sources by repeated visits, but do not defend specific foraging territories. "Low-reward trapliners" are similar, but usually have smaller, straighter bills and are more generalized foragers, visiting more dispersed and less specialized flower types. Typical "territorialists" defend foraging territories, visiting all the suitable flower types within them. Finally, the "territory parasites" are either large species that can feed with impunity in the territories of smaller and less dominant species, or relatively small and fugitive forms that can effectively infiltrate the territories of other species (Feinsinger and Colwell, 1978). Territorial species often have greater flight acceleration and maneuverability than do traplining species, but they hover less effectively and usually have a higher wing-disc loading (the ratio of body weight to the area covered by the outstretched wings) than do trapliners.

In a recent review, Pyke (1980) noted that honeyeaters of Australia show convergences with hummingbirds in that both groups feed on a combination of nectar and insects; both have long, curved bills and tongues adapted to nectar foraging; and both feed at long red flowers. He summarized studies that indicate that 7 nonhermit species of hummingbirds spent about 84 percent of their time gathering nectar and the remainder of their time catching insects. Studies of 15 species indicated that 86 percent of the observations of foraging were associated with nectar-gathering; 14 percent with insect-catching. Hummingbirds catch insects in many ways, including hawking in flight, gleaning from recesses, variants of gleaning, and sometimes even running or walking (Mobbs, 1979).

CHAPTER FIVE

Comparative Behavior

The behavior of complex animals such as hummingbirds can generally be organized into three very broad categories: (a) those concerned with the survival and maintenance of the individual (egocentric activities), (b) those essentially self-directed but tending to bring about aggregations of individuals in common habitats or areas of common activity (quasi-social actions), and (c) those directed toward and dependent upon the presence of other organisms for their expression (social behaviors).

Egocentric behaviors of hummingbirds include such fundamental features of individual survival as respiration, ingestion, defecation, and the like, as well as more complex activities such as preening, oiling, shaking, and stretching, all of which might fall under a collective heading of "comfort activities." Unlike most birds, hummingbirds sleep with the neck retracted, head directed forward, the bill pointed upward at a distinct angle, and the body feathers variably fluffed. Essentially the same posture is typical of fully torpid individuals (Figure 14F). Upon awakening, the bird arches its neck and raises its partly closed wings. It then opens one or both wings fully and stretches them down alongside the body, but not to the rear as in most birds (Figure 14A and C). The tail may be fanned simultaneously. Although hummingbird feet are very small, perching on a single foot has been observed in several genera (Mobbs, 1971).

Apparently hummingbirds never engage in mutual preening, but instead spend a good deal of time in self-preening. For most of this, in common with other birds, they use the bill (Figure 13B), but hummingbirds are remarkably adept at preening themselves with their claws (scratch-preening) in areas of the head and neck that cannot be reached by the bill. Sometimes the claws are used to preen the wing-coverts, but not the primaries themselves. Most hummingbirds scratch by raising the foot up and over the wing, as do typical perching birds (Figure 13C), but some long-billed species scratch by bringing the foot forward under the wing (Mobbs, 1973).

Hummingbirds seem to enjoy bathing very much, and will often bathe in the water film that has accumulated on a large, flattened leaf. At other times they may fly into the flowing water of a small waterfall or other spray and bathe while hovering in the air. When flying around in the jet of a water spray coming from below, the birds will allow themselves to be drenched from beneath and will sometimes catch individual drops of water in the bill with great skill. When bathing on a leafy surface, they will rub their abdomens against the leaves and move backwards and forwards over the wet leaf surface (Figure 13A), occasionally sliding off into the air only to fly back and begin the activity again (Scheithauer, 1967).

Quasi-social behaviors include investigative, shelter-seeking, and similar activities that bring individuals into social contact, even though this is not the chief purpose

13. Hummingbird behavior patterns, including (A) leaf-bathing by rufous-tailed hummingbird, (B) preening by blue-tailed sylph, (C), over-the-wing preening by horned sungem, (D) threat display by green thorntail, (E) singing with aggressive tail-wagging by long-tailed hermit, and (F) copulation by long-tailed hermit. (After various sources)

of the activity. Thus, aggregations may develop around limited foraging areas, in localized bathing or roosting sites, and even in favorable nesting sites (albeit rarely). Examples of nesting aggregations include a clustering of five Andean hillstar nests in a small cave in Ecuador (Smith, 1949) and the presence of six Costa hummingbird nests within a 30-meter radius in a cocklebur thicket (Bent, 1940).

The remarkable tendency of hummingbirds to investigate unusual features of their environment probably is related to their constant need to find new and rich sources of food. Thus, they are likely to examine almost anything that is brightly colored, from a red tin can on a camp table to a bright-colored cap. I have seen rufous hummingbirds closely investigate the red stripes of canvas that support the poles of my tent, and of course they will visit red hummingbird feeders almost immediately after one installs them in areas the birds frequent. Such curiosity occasionally can be disastrous, as, for example, when a bird gets caught in the sticky head of a purple thistle and is unable to escape, or is otherwise trapped in an unfamiliar situation.

Closely related to a hummingbird's curiosity is its apparently excellent memory, which enables it to locate food sources perhaps remembered from previous years. Hummingbirds have a remarkable capability of associating food sources with location and color (Miller and Miller, 1971; Scheithauer, 1967), which fosters foraging success. Fitzpatrick (1966) recounted an amazing example of a hummingbird's memory and capabilities for detailed human recognition: He placed a hummingbird feeder outside his bedroom window while he was recuperating from tuberculosis in a California sanitarium. Soon a rufous hummingbird took possession of the feeder, and thereafter Fitzpatrick watched it closely for several months. When he was finally able to go outside in a wheelchair, Fitzpatrick was immediately "greeted" by the hummingbird, which careened around his head and hovered in front of his eyes. After almost a year, when Fitzpatrick returned to his home some 13 kilometers away, the rufous somehow managed to follow him and took up residence near his house. Later, the bird usually accompanied him on his daily walks. It sometimes called his attention to the presence of other animals that he might have otherwise overlooked—once noting a half-hidden rattlesnake—and eventually rode on the rawhide lace that served as a rifle sling. When he had fully recovered from his illness, Fitzpatrick left his house for a month. Yet, only moments after he returned and got out of his car, the hummingbird was there, zooming about his head and hovering in front of his eyes!

This remarkable story introduces the area of social behavior, comprising all aspects concerned with individual interactions within and between species. Social behavior includes such altruistic responses as care-giving and care-soliciting behavior, which in hummingbirds is essentially limited to relationships between parents and offspring, although there are a few cases of adult hummingbirds feeding youngsters other than their own. Thus, parental nurturing (Figure 14D) is probably the only type of altruistic behavior among hummingbirds; there is no evidence of succoring behavior between adults, although Weydemeyer (1971) reported seeing a possible example of this. Adults rarely even touch each other, although Poley (1976) photographed contact behavior between two adult female hummingbirds and also photographed what seemed to be typical courtship feeding behavior (Fig-

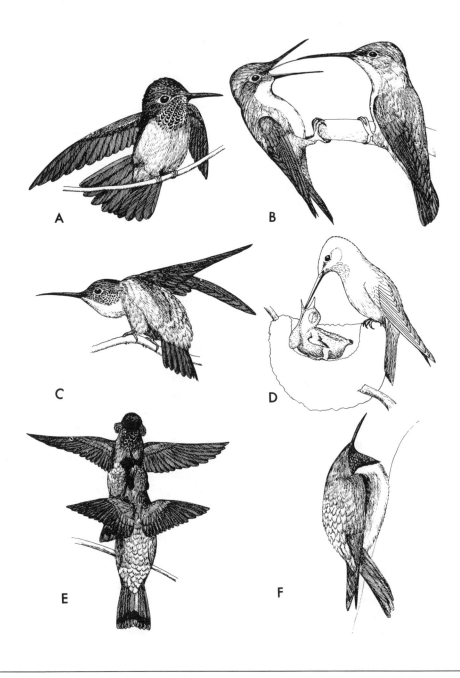

14. Hummingbird behavior patterns, including (A) unilateral wing-stretch-ing, (B) "courtship feeding" in Andean emerald, (C) bilateral wing-stretching, (D) feeding of young by female, (E) fighting by sparkling violet-ear, and (F) nocturnal torpor of Andean hillstar. (After various sources)

ure 14B). However, the existence of true courtship feeding in hummingbirds is still unproven.

The other major aspects of social behavior are agonistic interactions (attack-escape behavior) and sexual activities. In hummingbirds the two components are extremely difficult to separate, for a good deal of what passes for sexual behavior is probably little different from agonistic responses (Figures 13D and 14E). For example, male territoriality in most hummingbirds centers on a supply of food for itself, rather than encompassing a nesting site or available food resources for the female and any offspring. Thus, except in lek-forming species, only secondarily does the territory serve as a mating station, and the display flights of male hummingbirds are probably essentially an intimidation device (Pitelka, 1942). Thus, the bright coloration exhibited by males during territorial advertisement and defense may be essentially agonistic rather than sexual in function. Yet, to the degree that females can discriminate among individual males, and possibly tend to mate with those that are relatively more dominant or conspicuous, the role of sexual selection in the evolution of male plumages and displays cannot be overlooked.

Perhaps the most complete attempt to understand the diversity and significance of hummingbird sexual behavior is that by Wagner (1954), based on his long experience with numerous species of Mexican hummingbirds; a brief summary of his observations can serve as a basis for further discussion. According to Wagner, the female hummingbird searches for a mate only after nest completion. She is likely to mate with the first conspecific male that she meets, and their period of union lasts for only a few hours.

The courtship of the male has two phases: "luring" the attention of females that are ready to mate by species-specific plumage display and associated behavior, followed by the nuptial flight, performed by both sexes immediately before copulation. The luring phase is generally associated with not only posturing but also sound production effected either mechanically or by feather vibration during display flights, and vocalizations. Vocalizations in turn include short-note "songs" of a single bird, group singing in "song-assemblies," and sounds produced during display flights.

For the courtship phase, or nuptial flight, the male must take the initiative, although the female's actions determine the locality of the activity. In different species there are widely varying degrees of sexual dimorphism and coloration associated with precopulatory behavior. In Wagner's experience the degree of sexual dimorphism in plumage is closely correlated with the degree of differentiation of the nuptial flight; the more complicated the latter, the greater the degree of sexual dimorphism. In some species this phase of courtship consists only of a high intensity of activities typical of the luring phase; in others it is comprised entirely of different instinctive movements.

However, Pitelka's (1942) study regarded male display flights, as well as singing assemblies, essentially as devices for territorial proclamation and intimidation of conspecifics, including females, and courtship or invitation roles were not apparent in their performance. In his opinion, displays in which both the male and female participated did not indicate the height of courtship, but the contrary, with the female's displays perhaps only an effort to resist the male. He believed that most descriptions of hummingbird copulation were actually simply examples of the usual aggressive clashes between sexes, and that very few credible descriptions of copulation actually exist.

Observations by Scheithauer (1967) tend to confirm the idea that males probably attain copulation primarily by intimidation rather than courtship. For example, a male blue-tailed emerald displayed for weeks in front of a female, hovering in front of her only 12 millimeters from the tip of her bill as she perched on a branch, following his rapid movements with her head, so that their bills pointed at one another like needles. Invariably, before he was able to take the decisive step toward mating she would dart away and elude him, so that the two birds never paired. Yet, in another case when a female brown inca completed a nest but had not yet secured a mate, she courted a male fawn-breasted brilliant by "dancing" up and down in front of him with a piece of cottonwool in her bill.

Similarly, Stiles (1982) reported that the dive displays of North American hummingbirds are essentially aggressive displays associated, in most cases, with the defense of the breeding territory. However, they may also play some role in the initial phases of courtship. The most important displays in courtship per se are close-range, back-and-forth flights by the male, above or in front of the perched female. These "shuttle-flights" are accompanied by species-specific sounds (song in *Calypte* species, wing strokes in other genera), and they are highly species-specific in terms of rate, direction, and amplitude of the "shuttles." The displays immediately precede copulation in nearly all cases, but have never been explicitly described, probably because they usually occur in dense vegetation (as does copulation itself).

Among the most interesting of the social behaviors of hummingbirds are the song assemblages of territorial males, especially the hermits. Such singing assemblies are present in Trinidad little hermits from about November until the post-breeding molt in July. During this eight-month period each male is at its singing perch for a high proportion of the daylight hours—in one case, 70 percent of the entire time. While on its perch, the male sings about once every two seconds (or 12,000 times a day). The songs of individual males vary considerably, but males with neighboring perches tend to have similar song-types. The singing assemblies apparently function as leks, which the females visit for the sole purpose of mating. However, actual copulation in the species has not yet been observed, according to Snow (1968). A study of song-types in the little hermit has tended to confirm Snow's finding that there are similarities among the song patterns of different singing assemblages, perhaps around a founding individual that performed an imperfect imitation of a previously existing song pattern. The surprisingly elaborate songs of the species may have resulted from the fact that the birds display in relatively dark locations, unsuited for visual displays, and also to facilitate the differentiation of song dialects (Wiley, 1971).

Stiles and Wolf (1979) recently completed a more thorough study of lek behavior for the long-tailed hermit. Of the approximately 30 species of hermits, at least 3 form leks throughout their ranges (long-tailed, green, and little), and a fourth (reddish) forms leks in part of its range. Others, such as the planalto hermit, evidently do not form leks at all. Lek behavior has been observed in the genera

Threnetes and *Eutoxeres*, but seems to be especially typical of the genus *Phaethornis*. In the long-tailed hermit, leks have been active on the same site for as long as 12 years, with as many as 25 males occurring in a single lek. Territories in the leks evidently serve as mating stations only, and are never sufficiently rich in flowers to affect the energy budgets of the resident males.

Song display (Figure 13E) was the major type of territorial advertisement noted by Stiles and Wolf, and visual displays were observed only between birds close to each other. The sexes are identical in this species, and the same displays were given to females as to male intruders. Females apparently signal their sex simply by sitting still long enough for the male to mount, so there have been both heterosexual and homosexual mating copulations (Figure 13F). Mating sequences apparently always begin within the male's territory, although actual copulation may take place elsewhere.

In the leks of this species, at least, the most dominant males occupy central territories, and subordinate individuals are restricted to more peripheral areas. These central territories were the most stable over time, and the most strongly contested. Resident males returned to the same territories in subsequent years or moved into vacant territories closer to the center of the lek. Most movements toward the lek center occurred after the deaths of central residents, but the dominance status of individual males seemed to change little with age, even over several years. The rate of turnover of lek residents was about 50 percent annually, a high mortality rate, which surpasses that of the green hermit in Trinidad, where nearly all resident males survived more than one year (Snow, 1974). In this species mating takes place on the male's territorial perch. Moreover, "false matings" by males with leaves or other objects occur frequently in this and other hermit hummingbirds. Male green hermits have visited active nests as well, but nest defense by males has not been recorded.

As is the case with leks of grouse and other lek-forming species such as the ruff (*Philomachus pugnax*), females may cue on activity centers in lek-forming hummingbirds; unlike these species, however, there is no sexual dimorphism in plumage and very little weight dimorphism. In the hermits, the peripheral males apparently have at least some chance of mating, and as a result there is seemingly a less steep dominance/fitness gradient in these birds than in grouse or other species with highly structured leks and extremely localized mating opportunities. This is perhaps partly a result of the rapid turnover rate in resident males, the dense vegetation of the lek that restricts effective widespread dominance by a single male, and the fact that even dominant males must frequently leave the lek to forage, thus increasing mating opportunities for all the remaining individuals. Since nearly all hummingbirds possess the essential prerequisites for lek behavior—male emancipation for breeding participation and extensive available nonmaintenance time and energy for territorial advertisement and defense as well as courtship—it is perhaps surprising that so few species have adopted this breeding strategy. Lek behavior seems to have evolved more frequently in the hermit group than in the more widespread trochiline hummingbirds, because the former have concurrently evolved a high degree of morphological specialization for exploiting but not defending flowers that have coevolved with these species. However, feeding-resource–centered, territorial, defensive behavior seems to be the most efficient use of male activities for most of the trochiline species, including the North American forms (Stiles and Wolf, 1979).

CHAPTER SIX

Comparative Reproductive Biology

Among hummingbirds virtually all of the activities associated with nesting and the rearing of the young are the sole responsibility of the female. No other major avian family seems to have adopted so overwhelmingly this trend toward male emancipation from nesting responsibilities and consequent promiscuous mating tendencies. J.J. Audubon ironically believed that the beauty of hummingbirds must cause one to "turn his mind with reverence toward the Almighty Creator." Yet, were it not for their remarkable mating system and a high degree of associated territorial advertisement behavior, these birds might well have been no more esthetically attractive than their drab relatives the swifts, which have consistently held to a monogamous mating system. In adopting an adventurous and specialized life-style, involving a high degree of nectar-dependency, a prodigal expenditure of energy during flight, and a seemingly devil-may-care mating system, the hummingbirds epitomize a unique kind of high-risk but potentially high-reward strategy for survival.

Female hummingbirds are among the most tenacious and persistent of mothers. They often build or rebuild their nests in the most vulnerable locations, and audaciously attack any man or animal that ventures too near, including large hawks that might easily consume the bird in a single swallow. For their part, the males are no less admirable in their stalwart defense of foraging or mating territories, and on a few rare occasions have been observed incubating eggs or helping to feed the young. The most notable examples of male incubation were reported by two independent observers of wild individuals of the sparkling violet-ear (Moore, 1947; Schäfer, 1952). More recent investigators have also studied the species, however, and have been unable to confirm if participation in incubation or parental feeding is a regular pattern of male behavior either in the wild or in captivity.

There have been reports of males of a few other tropical species of hummingbirds helping in incubation or feeding the young, including members of the genera *Glaucis* and *Phaethornis*. A few scattered observations of male incubation have been reported in North America, as for example in the ruby-throated (Welter, 1935) and the rufous hummingbirds (Bailey, 1927). Both of these species are most northerly of all hummingbirds in breeding distribution; in such a climate, with relatively cold environmental temperatures and limited food resources, a monogamous mating system with male participation in incubation and brooding would be most advantageous. There is also a single reported observation of an adult male Anna hummingbird feeding young (Clyde, 1972).

Although the male fiery-throated hummingbird does not defend or feed the young fathered by him, he allows females with which he has mated to forage within his territory, probably because of the considerable sexual segregation in foraging behavior exhibited by this species (Wolf and Stiles, 1970). This species does not exhibit a definite pair bond, but does show this remarkable cooperation of the sexes in their reproductive biology. Perhaps the pair-bonding system in this species should be considered polygynous rather than promiscuous.

The first step in hummingbird nesting is construction, which normally occurs well before fertilization, and produces some of the most remarkable of all avian structures. Almost invariably the nest contains extensive wrappings of spider webbing or similar silken materials, which are used to bind it together and to lash it to a solid substrate. In addition, nests of all species contain a very soft inner lining, usually made of a cottony seed material, the wooly surface material of some leaves, or soft bird feathers as may be locally available. Finally, in most species the nests are "decorated" (camouflaged) on the outside with fragments of lichens, bark, moss, or other similar materials, which blend them almost perfectly with the immediate environment.

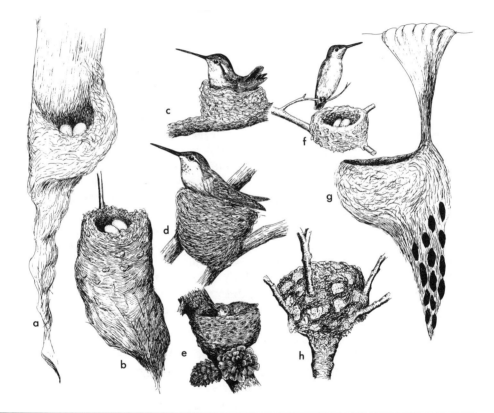

15. Nesting sites and nests of hummingbirds, including (a) palm-leaf nest of long-tailed hermit, (b) hanging nest of blue-throated hummingbird, (c) saddled nest of black-chinned hummingbird, (d) doubly supported nest of Costa hummingbird, (e) pine-cone clump nest of calliope hummingbird, (f) fork nest of vervain hummingbird, (g) counterbalanced nest of sooty-capped hermit, and (h) crotch-supported nest of white-eared hummingbird. (After various sources)

Although the hummingbird nests are relatively similar in composition, they are placed in a wide variety of locations and substrates. They may be saddled on horizontal branches, partially suspended in a fork or in crotches of trees, adhered to the walls of rock faces, or suspended from above by pendant strands (Figure 15). In the subfamily Phaethornithinae, the typical substrate consists of a hanging leaf, such as that of a palm, with the nest supported on its underside along the leaf and with a long "trailer" of leafy matter hanging downward from the nest. Such seemingly precarious locations are probably quite secure, and protect the nest from rain and from most terrestrial predators.

A few hummingbirds, including the sooty-capped hermit, enhance the equilibrium of the nest by incorporating small bits of clay or pebbles into its bottom and sides to counterbalance the weight of the sitting female (Figure 15). Similarly, the Andean hillstar increases the nest materials unequally on one side, achieving the same result (Ridgway, 1890). The nests of the latter species are otherwise unusual in being remarkably large and thick-walled, which increases the insulating value of the nest for these high Andean birds (Carpenter, 1976; Dorst, 1962). They nest in extremely well-protected and inaccessible locations, sometimes in shallow caves of deep ravines, and as many as five active nests have been found within a radius of only 2 meters in such favored locations (Smith, 1949)—an amazing concentration for any hummingbird, given the bleak environment. An equally remarkable breeding concentration of crimson topaz hummingbirds was reported by Ruschi (1979), who found 10 occupied nests of this species in an area of 100 square meters.

The length of time required to construct the nest probably varies greatly, but in a few observed cases the work has been virtually completed in a day or two (Bailey, 1974; Welter, 1935). More often it takes about a week, and sometimes the work may be spread out over two weeks (Legg and Pitelka, 1956). Frequently the female continues to add materials to the nest after she lays the eggs, and sometimes she continues this behavior well into incubation.

The eggs are pure white and almost invariably two in number. The tiny bee hummingbird of the West Indies probably lays the smallest egg of any species, but measurements are not available. However, the eggs of the slightly larger vervain hummingbird of the same area are about 7.0 × 5.0 millimeters (Ridgway, 1890) and weigh only about 0.37 grams each. A normal clutch of two such eggs would thus be equal to about 34 percent of the weight of the adult female (Lack, 1976). The largest hummingbird eggs are those of the giant hummingbird, which average 20 × 12 millimeters (Figure 16) and which probably weigh very close to 1.5 grams each; a clutch of two would thus represent about 15 percent of the weight of the adult bird. So, in common with other birds, the energy drain of laying eggs is probably less severe on females of larger species than of smaller ones.

In many species (or individuals) of hummingbirds the female begins to incubate immediately after laying the first egg, and the eggs thus hatch in the same approximate time sequence with which they were laid. The eggs are typically laid in the morning and are usually deposited about 48 hours apart. However, they are frequently laid on subsequent days and sometimes three days apart. When the eggs hatch synchronously or nearly so, incubation probably did not begin until the laying of the second egg.

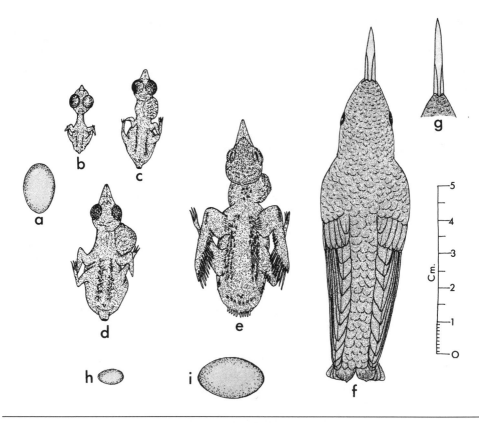

16. Eggs and nestlings of hummingbirds, including egg (a) and nestlings of blue-throated hummingbird at 1 day (b), 3 days (c), 6 days (d), 12 days (e), 24 days (f), and final bill length (g). Also shown are eggs of vervain hummingbird (h) and giant hummingbird (i). (Mostly after Wagner, 1952)

Incubation periods of hummingbirds have commonly been seriously underestimated, perhaps because of their very small size, and some published estimates of periods of as little as 9 to 12 days have appeared. In spite of the eggs' small size, incubation periods are actually long, perhaps because females usually have to leave the nest for extended periods of time to forage every day. This factor may cause a general prolongation of the minimum incubation period to 15 to 17 days (with a few reliable observations of 14-day periods). The longest known incubation periods are those of the Andean hillstar, which average about 20 days, and sometimes require 22–23 days (Carpenter, 1976; Dorst, 1962).

Young hummingbirds are hatched in a nearly naked, blind, and totally helpless state. At the time of hatching they seem to be nearly all "head," but their eyes are tightly closed and the beak is barely indicated. Yet even newly hatched hummingbirds have a well-developed crop, and shortly after they hatch the female begins to "inject" extraordinary amounts of food into her young. She inserts her needle-like bill into the nestling's mouth and regurgitates food from her own crop to that of the young. Even nestlings but a few days old are fed large quantities of tiny insects and probably also nectar, which soon causes their crops to protrude from the sides of their necks like gigantic goiters (Figure 16c, d, e).

Hummingbird youngsters lack a distinct downy feather stage; instead, the definitive contour feathers emerge directly from the pinfeathers. Yet, in spite of the lack of downy insulation, the young birds are remarkably tolerant of short-term temperature fluctuations. Moreover, by the time they are about 12 days old, before they are well-feathered, they have often acquired a considerable degree of temperature control (Calder, 1971). Depending on the species, the female may continue to brood them until they are from 12 to about 18 days old. Species that rear their young under relatively cold conditions may have a prolonged fledging period; the Andean hillstar, for example, usually requires about 38 days, but favorable conditions may lessen it to as little as 22 days (Carpenter, 1976). Even after fledging the tail feathers and the bill of young hummingbirds continue to grow for some time before they reach their adult length (Figure 16), and maternal care and feeding of the young often continues for awhile after the young leave the nest. Skutch (1973) has summarized information on the duration of parental care in various hummingbirds, and for five species the observed range of the last observed feeding was from 40 to 65 days after hatching.

Sometimes adult hummingbirds attempt to feed young that are not their own. Thus Wagner (1959) observed wild adult white-eared hummingbirds feeding both nestling and fledgling birds that were not their own offspring. Under aviary conditions there have also been instances of adult birds "adopting" young not their own.

Even in tropical areas, most hummingbirds do not breed the year round, but rather exhibit seasonality in breeding that is probably associated with the relative intensity of blooming of preferred flower sources during wet or dry seasons. However, some equatorial species do breed throughout the year, as does the Andean hillstar in Ecuador (Smith, 1949) but not in southern Peru or northern Chile (Carpenter, 1976). Year-round breeding has also been reported for the Anna and Allen hummingbirds in southern California (Wells et al., 1978).

Although the incidence of multiple brooding still remains to be studied thoroughly, it is probably of relatively widespread occurrence in tropical hummingbirds. It has also been reported for several North American species, including the blue-throated hummingbird, where it seems to be fairly common. In other species such as the Anna, Allen, and black-chinned, it is less frequent, but probably all species attempt to nest a second time if their initial clutch or brood is lost prior to fledging.

In the species that sometimes exhibit multiple brooding, the female typically begins building a second nest while still feeding young from the first brood. Several instances of such concurrent care of two nests have been described for various North American species, including the white-eared (Skutch, 1973), ruby-throated (Nickell, 1948), and black-chinned hummingbirds (Cogswell, 1949).

In spite of the great perseverance and courage shown by female hummingbirds while defending their nests, the reproductive success of these birds in general is relatively poor. Such low rates for hatching and fledging young (Tables 8 and 9) are probably the result of high vulnerability of hummingbird nests to loss of eggs or young from accidents, weather-associated catastrophes, and predation. Indeed,

Table 8   *Various Nesting Success Rates Reported for Hummingbirds*

Species	Authority	Total Nests	Total Nests in Which			Percent Nesting Success	
			Eggs Laid	Young Hatched	Young Fledged	All Nests	Nests with Eggs
Allen	Legg & Pitelka, 1956	18	16	—	4	22.2	25.0
Andean hillstar	Carpenter, 1976	19	18	—	16	—	88.9
Anna	Stiles, 1972b	85	68	42	23	31.3	44.2
Black-chinned	Stiles, 1972b	55	47	27	15	27.3	31.9
Costa	Woods, 1927	—	29	—	12	—	41.4
Rufous-tailed	Skutch, 1931	22	17	10	6	45.4	58.8
White-eared	Wagner, 1959	39	—	—	12	30.7	—

Table 9   *Various Hatching and Fledging Success Rates Reported for Hummingbirds*

Species	Authority	Total Nests	Eggs Laid	Eggs Hatched	Hatching Success (% of Eggs Laid)	Total Young Fledged	Fledging Success (% of Eggs Laid)
Andean hillstar	Carpenter, 1976	19	37	—	—	22	59.4
Broad-tailed	Waser & Inouye, 1977	52	102	—	—	60	58.9
Costa	Woods, 1927	—	58	35	60.3	19	32.7
Green hermit	Snow, 1974	19	37	12	32.4	10	27.0
Rufous-tailed	Skutch, 1931	22	32	18	56.2	11	34.4
White-eared	Skutch, in Bent, 1940	9	18	9	50.0	3	16.7

one of the most successful species of nesting hummingbirds is the Andean hillstar, which avoids high predation losses in its cold and unfavorable nesting environment. In other tropical species, as well as North American ones such as the Anna hummingbird (Stiles, 1972b), predation accounts for much of the nest mortality (Carpenter, 1976).

In addition to their persistent efforts at nesting, hummingbirds have long potential breeding spans. Very few have been banded in any number, but at least one male ruby-throated that was banded as a juvenile was recaptured 5 years later in the same locality (*Bird-banding* 42:51). Some less convincing accounts assert 10–

12 years for blue-throated hummingbirds (see species account in this book); others have survived as long as 10 years in captivity.

Although reliable data on mortality rates in hummingbirds are not yet available, Baumgartner (1981) obtained some recent recapture data on ruby-throated hummingbirds. Of the 384 hummingbirds she captured between 1977 and 1979, she recaptured 88 birds (23 percent) the following year, 31 of 268 birds (11.5 percent) the second year after banding, and 10 of 110 birds (9.9 percent) banded in the third year. These figures indicate a minimum annual survival rate of 23–46 percent, and, because undoubtedly some survive but are not recaptured, the actual rate must be considerably higher.

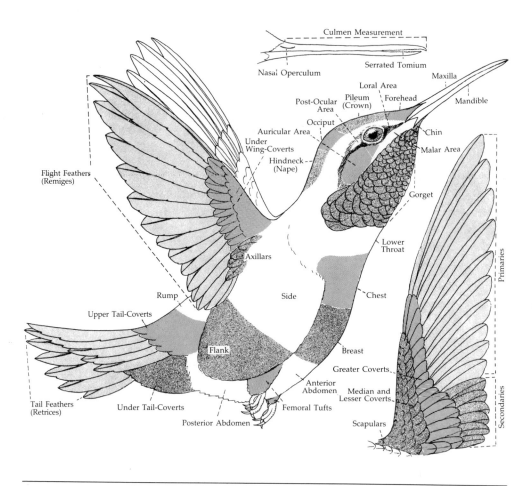

Culmen Measurement

Nasal Operculum

Serrated Tomium

Maxilla

Mandible

Loral Area

Pileum (Crown)

Forehead

Post-Ocular Area

Occiput

Auricular Area

Chin

Under Wing-Coverts

Malar Area

Hindneck (Nape)

Flight Feathers (Remiges)

Gorget

Lower Throat

Axillars

Rump

Side

Chest

Upper Tail-Coverts

Flank

Breast

Greater Coverts

Median and Lesser Coverts

Anterior Abdomen

Tail Feathers (Retrices)

Under Tail-Coverts

Femoral Tufts

Scapulars

Posterior Abdomen

Primaries

Secondaries

Body and feather areas of hummingbirds, showing features mentioned in the keys or text.

PART TWO

NATURAL HISTORIES OF NORTH AMERICAN HUMMINGBIRDS

This section includes all species of hummingbirds that have been reliably reported from anywhere north of the Mexican border, although several of them are not truly North American in the sense of having been proven to breed in the United States or Canada. West Indian species are also included, but only if they have been reported from the mainland of North America.

All descriptions are in typical field-guide terminology, which I have included in the Glossary and on the hummingbird figure facing this page. In addition, identifying characteristics of some species vary depending on the position of the bird and the angle at which the viewer sees it. Therefore, some descriptions are worded according to one or more of the following positions:

- Position *a*: Viewer's eye between bird and light, bird's bill toward eye, bird nearly horizontal.
- Position *b*: Viewer's eye directly above bird, bird's bill toward light, bird nearly horizontal.
- Position *c*: Same as position *a*, but bird reversed (tail, instead of bill, toward eye).

Genus *Colibri* Spix 1824

*T*his genus includes four species of Middle and South American hummingbirds, which are medium to large in size (wing 55–75 mm) and which all have a post-auricular tuft of violet, violet-blue, or violet-red feathers and a long, broad tail of blue, green, or olive color, with a darker subterminal band. The bill is blackish and varies from shorter than the head to somewhat longer, straight to slightly decurved, and nearly round but slightly depressed basally; the culmen is contracted at the base into a narrow ridge. The edge of the maxilla is smooth or has minute serrations near the tip. The nasal operculum is mostly concealed by overhanging feathers, which extend forward beyond the end of the nostrils. The wing is from three to four times as long as the exposed culmen, and the outermost primary is the longest. The tail is up to two-thirds as long as the wing, and is rather square-tipped. The rectrices are broad, with rounded tips. The sexes are alike, and are rather uniformly dark green or brownish except for the tail and ear-tufts.

1. Residential distributions of green violet-ear (cross-hatched) (races t = *thalassinus*, m = *minor*, c = *cabanidis*) and Cuban emerald (stippled) (races b = *bracei*, r = *ricordii*).

GREEN VIOLET-EAR

Colibri thalassinus (Swainson)

Other Names　None in general English use; Verdemar, Colibre orejiviolaceo verde, Chupaflor pavito (Spanish).

Range　Breeds in the upper tropical and temperate zones of Mexico from Jalisco, San Luis Potosi, and Veracruz south through Middle America to Peru and Bolivia. Accidental in North America (Texas). (See map 1.)

North American Subspecies　(After Friedmann et al., 1950.)

C. t. thalassinus (Swainson). Breeds commonly in the temperate zone (up to 2850 meters in Michoacan) from Jalisco and San Luis Potosi south to Guatemala. Probably winters at lower elevations.

Measurements　Wing, males 63–70 mm (ave. of 6, 66.9 mm), females 60–63 mm (ave. of 16, 61 mm). Culmen, males 18–22 mm (ave. of 6, 20.2 mm), females 19–22 mm (ave. of 16, 20.3 mm) (Ridgway, 1911). Eggs, ave. 13.6 × 8.8 mm (extremes 13.1–13.9 × 8.7–9.1 mm).

Weights　The average of 24 individuals of both sexes was 5.24 grams (Feinsinger and Colwell, 1978); averages of 15 males and 12 females were 5.7 and 5.0 g, respectively (Wolf et al., 1976).

Description　(After Ridgway, 1911.)

Adult male. Above metallic green or bronze-green, darker or duller on pileum; tail metallic bluish green or greenish blue (middle rectrices sometimes green or even bronze-green) crossed by a broad subterminal band of blue-black; remiges dark brownish slate or dusky, very faintly glossed with bronzy purplish or violet, the secondaries more or less glossed at tip and on edges with metallic green or bronze-green; loral, suborbital, and auricular regions rich metallic dark violet-blue, sometimes invading (somewhat) sides of neck; malar region, chin, and throat bright metallic green—varying from slightly bluish to yellowish emerald green—each feather with a darker mesial streak or spot; center of chest dark metallic blue or violet-blue, passing laterally into metallic-green; breast, sides, flanks, and abdomen metallic green or bronze-green, duller posteriorly, where sometimes slightly broken by faint pale grayish brown or pale grayish buff tips or margins to the feathers; under tail-coverts metallic green or bronze-green, margined or edged with pale buffy brownish or grayish buffy; bill dull black; iris dark brown; feet dusky grayish brown.

Adult female. Similar to adult male, but smaller and slightly duller in coloration.

Young. Similar to adult female, but much duller in coloration, the upper tail-coverts and feathers of rump (sometimes pileum also) narrowly and indistinctly margined with pale grayish buffy; green of underparts much duller and suffused with grayish, the feathers indistinctly margined terminally with pale grayish; blue of chest absent or only slightly indicated.

Identification   (See Plate 8A.)

In the hand. The only member of the violet-ear group likely to be found in North America; the nearest other species is *C. delphinae* (of Guatemala southward), which is generally brownish rather than metallic green. The presence of a subterminal band of bluish black on the tail, the ear-patch, and the large size (wing 60–70 mm) all serve to identify the species.

In the field. Occurs in oak woods and clearings, and appears almost uniformly green; utters a loud double note, *chip-tsirr*, often while high in trees, repeated endlessly during the breeding season; also utters snapping little rips (Slud, 1964).

Habitats   In Mexico, this species breeds in high mountain forests. In the Valley of Mexico these include not only the original forests of mixed oak, cypress, and pines, but also cutover areas with overgrown gullies, shrubbery, and remaining high trees at the edges of fields. Between breeding seasons the males sometimes occur in forests of firs (*Abies religiosa*) at 2640–3450 meters of elevation in the Valley of Mexico, whereas in Chiapas they have been found at corresponding periods in open areas or clearings of forests between 990 and 1980 meters of elevation (Wagner, 1945).

Farther south, the species is also associated with the highlands; in Guatemala it breeds from 1500 to 3300 meters, in Costa Rica from 1500 to 3000 meters, and in Venezuela occurs from 900 to 3000 meters of elevation. Probably in all these areas the higher altitudes are associated with the breeding season, and lower altitudes are used outside the breeding season. On the Sierra de Tecpam, Guatemala, the birds breed mainly in forests of cypress (*Cupressus bethamii*) above 2700 meters, where forest openings or edges provide abundant flowering plants, particularly certain species of *Salvia* (Skutch, 1967). Generally in Costa Rica the species seems to thrive in parklike pastures and "elfin woodland" that succeed the partial removal of mountain forests. Its total vegetational range extends from the middle of the subtropical belt upward to timberline on the high volcanoes (Slud, 1964).

In El Salvador, the birds have been recorded from 1900 meters in the pine zone to 2400 meters in the cloud forests, and are mainly found in sunny areas such as along trails or clearings (Dickey and van Rossem, 1938). In Honduras the species is common in cloud forests, and less frequently occurs in pine-oak forests, from 990 to at least 2370 meters elevation (Monroe, 1968).

In Panama, the birds occupy open mountain slopes, where shrub and tree growth is scattered or open. Their altitudinal range there is from 1335 to 2070 meters, or (rarely) to 2625 meters (Wetmore, 1968).

In South America the species is found in the subtropical and temperate zones, extending in Venezuela through cloud forest and open woodland to the edge of the páramo, between 890 and 2970 meters elevation (de Schauensee and Phelps, 1978).

Movements   This is a distinctly mobile species, which may perform some real migrations in Mexico. Wagner (1945) believed that at the northern end of its range in the Valley of Mexico all the females, the young, and a variable percentage of the adult males fly south in October or early November and return to their breeding grounds in July, possibly migrating as far as Chiapas, Guatemala, or even farther south. Males, however, remain in the area in varying numbers, moving to fir forests where flowering plants are available in all but the driest winters, when they too may have to migrate.

Skutch (1967) found no evidence of violet-eared hummingbirds crossing the Isthmus of Tehuantepec. Instead, he believed that probably the birds of central Mexico simply move to lower altitudes during the nonbreeding season, as is the case elsewhere in Central America. He noted that, although the birds breed in Costa Rica at altitudes above 1650 meters, during the dry season they can be found on the plains at the base of the mountains at about 630 meters. There are differences in the timing of these seasonal migrations, which are associated with regional differences in the length and intensity of the dry season. Thus, in the western highlands of Guatemala the dry season lasts from mid-October to mid-May, whereas in the higher parts of the Costa Rican mountains it extends only from about January to early April. Likewise, in El Salvador, there are apparently seasonal shifts of one or both sexes. Dickey and van Rossem (1938) found only females and young of the year in the vicinity of Los Esemiles, the males apparently having moved to higher or lower altitudes.

Probably the few occurrences of this species in the United States can be attributed to their mobile tendencies. As summarized by Oberholser (1974), there were three or four sightings of the birds in Texas during the 1960s and early 1970s. The first was seen in Hidalgo County, in heavy brush of the Santa Ana National Wildlife Refuge, during July 1961. Another was seen in Cameron County in April 1964, feeding on shrubs with ruby-throated hummingbirds. A third was seen and photographed at various times between August 25 and September 18, 1969, in Travis County, between Austin and Oak Hill; during the same period there was a possible sighting in Austin at a *Leucophyllum* bush. A definite fourth record occurred in 1976, when a bird was seen at a feeder in the Wimberly area of Hays County between July 3 and August 13 (*American Birds* 30:96). A year later the species was seen at the same site between May 21 and July 6 (*American Birds* 31:199).

Foraging Behavior and Floral Ecology

In Mexico, the distribution of montane flowers, especially several species of *Salvia*, seems to determine the local distribution of this species (Wagner, 1945). Likewise, in Guatemala several mint species, including both red-flowered types such as *S. cinnabarina* and the blue-flowered *S. cacaliaefolia*, are favorite foraging plants. There the birds also feed on the scarlet blossoms of a bean (*Phaseolus*) that climbs over old stumps in cornfields, the purple-white flowers of an alpine thistle (*Cirsium consociatum*), and the red-flowered cupheas (*Cuphea infundibulum*) found in pastureland groves. They have also been seen, along with several other hummingbird species, feeding on a planted shrub (*Stachytarpheta*) sometimes used in hedgerows through the pastures (Skutch, 1967).

Limited studies involving colored sugar solutions (Lyerly et al., 1950) with a single female of this species indicated that, among the four colors used—red, green, blue, yellow—she preferred yellow-colored solutions significantly less than the others. There were no significant differences among the other colors.

Observations by Lyon (1976) in the montane pine habitat of Oaxaca indicated that males of this species controlled relatively small feeding territories (average of four, about 230 square meters). They dominated the smaller white-eared and bumblebee hummingbirds, but were in turn dominated by the larger blue-throated and Rivoli hummingbirds. Some violet-ears established and maintained their territories for short periods, but eventually these birds were displaced by blue-throats or Rivoli hummingbirds.

A study by Wolf, Stiles, and Hainsworth (1976) in Costa Rica indicated that this species concentrated most of its foraging and all of its territorial behavior on only two species of flowers (*Centropogon valerii* and *C. brumalis*). The birds also often obtain insects by hawking them in the air (Skutch, 1967).

Breeding Biology

In some parts of Mexico males are evidently sexually active almost the entire year, being silent only during the molt in April and during days of unfavorable weather. They typically choose exposed perches, usually high in a tree, and continuously utter their repeated calls. Often several males gather in a small area, but this is probably because of the distribution of food plants rather than any social tendencies (Wagner, 1945).

The "song" of the male is a metallic *k'chink chink k'chinky chink*, endlessly repeated from morning to evening, often uttered from an exposed dead twig between 4.5 and 12 meters above ground, rarely much higher or lower. Singing is not restricted to a single perch, but rather the bird may use several twigs separated by 6 to 9 meters, frequently moving from one to another. The birds begin to sing at dawn, as soon as the light is strong enough to see form and color, and they pause during the day only to forage, court females, and chase intruders from their territories. During an 83-minute period of observations, one male foraged on *Salvia* blossoms for about 7 minutes and spent more than 70 minutes singing from his perches. The periods of singing ranged from less than 1 to 11 minutes of nearly continuous vocalizations (Skutch, 1967).

Males usually sing in sight and hearing range of several other males, but they leave one another alone as long as their territorial limits are respected. Depending on the type of terrain and the locations of good perching sites, these territories may be from 45 to 90 meters apart. In both Costa Rica and Mexico a particular male having a distinctively recognizable voice may defend the same territory in subsequent seasons; in Mexico one such bird occupied the same tree for four consecutive years (Wagner, 1945).

Wagner (1945) described three different forms of calls, based on three rising degrees of sexual excitement. The usual one, apparently comparable to that described by Skutch as repeated metallic notes, was described by Wagner as variants of *huit ti titatia, huit tita*. During the peak of sexual excitement the male continuously repeats a *huitta huitta* phrase, or a softer variant during flight. Often at this time he will fly from tree to tree in an undulating flight, keeping his wings spread and quivering for several seconds on alighting. This level of display occurs when the females have completed their nests and are looking for mates. Evidently the far-reaching call and display flights of the males help the females to locate them.

As soon as a female comes into view, the male follows her through the length of his territory. The two birds fly side by side in a fluctuating wavy path through a stretch that probably includes the nesting area of the female. In the later stages of the flight they may clap their wings in a pigeon-like manner. The female may then descend from the crown of a tree in a wavering flight with wing-clapping, skirt the ground, and then fly up and perch on a small twig. She repeats this movement until the male leads her on a final wild flight preceding copulation. Actual copulation has not been described, but it evidently does not occur in the vicinity of the nest (Wagner, 1945). However, in the related species *C. coruscans* copulation occurs immediately after a hovering display flight by the male directly in front of the female (R. J. Elgar, *Avic. Mag.* 88:26–33, 1982).

In central Mexico, females arrive at the breeding grounds at the end of July, and immediately begin to build a nest. There they produce only one brood per season, and replace lost clutches only if the nest is destroyed during the first half of the breeding cycle (Wagner, 1945). In Costa Rica nests have been found from October to March, and male singing extends over a somewhat longer period (September to March). The season in Costa Rica is long enough to allow for two or perhaps three broods (Skutch, 1967). In El Salvador, young birds are common during February and March, suggesting a similar breeding period there (Dickey and van Rossem, 1938).

Nests in Mexico have been found mostly in fairly open areas; five of eight found by Wagner were in densely overgrown barrancas with steep sides covered by small oaks. The nests themselves were on oak branches less than 2 meters above the ground. Another nest was in the branches of a small oak that had grown up from an old root, and the two remaining nests were placed on the forks of a stem of *Salvia polystachya* in dense brush growth. Skutch found four nests in Guatemala among the horizontal lower branches of cypress saplings, from 1 to 2 meters above ground level. He found four more in Costa Rica, all of which were attached to downward-drooping stems or dangling roots or vines. The latter nests were made by the race *C. cabanidis,* and Skutch suggested that there may be some racial differences in nest construction and nest-site preferences. Although both races apparently prefer to build their nests close to the ground, *C. thalassinus* seems more regularly to construct its nest of mosses and to attach many shriveled leaves and grass blades to the outside. The many long, hanging grass leaves typical of at least the northern race easily distinguish the nests from those of other Mexican hummingbirds. The inner lining may be either of moss, or less frequently of plant down or feathers. The nests are from 50 to 75 mm in diameter, and are often slightly less deep, but grass strands may hang down from the sides as much as nearly 250 mm.

In Wagner's (1945) studies, he found that each female had a nesting territory of some 600 to 1000 square meters, which was surrounded by a neutral zone separating it from adjacent territories. Nests of the species were from 52 to 95 meters apart, but sometimes females of broad-tailed or white-eared hummingbirds would nest within 15 meters of an occupied violet-ear nest.

The exact length of time for nest construction has not been reported, although Wagner (1945) stated that from 55 to 65 days are needed to complete a nesting cycle—from the start of the building until the complete independence of the young. This includes a 16–17-day incubation period, a normal fledging period of 23–25 days, and a postfledging dependency period of 5–7 days; thus, building probably requires 10–20 days. Incubation must begin with the laying of the first egg, since the interval between the hatching of the two young may be as much as 24 hours. Moore (1947) reported a male of a related violet-ear species (*C. coruscans*) assisting in incubation, and Schäfer (1952) also observed one incubating and feeding young at a nest; Schmidt-Marloh and Schuchmann (1980), however, did not find positive evidence of this for the green violet-ear.

The fledging period varies considerably in this species, with extremes of 19 to 28 days depending on weather, food availability, and the number of young in the nest. In one case, by the 8th day after hatching the pinfeathers were beginning to break and the eyes were starting to open. By the 11th day the eyes were open, the back feathers were breaking free of their sheaths, and the pinfeathers of the tail were emerging. By the 15th day the body feathering was nearly complete, the primaries were 14–15 mm long, and the tail feathers were emerging from their sheaths. Feathering was completed by the 18th day, and by the 22nd day, at fledging, all the feathers were completely unsheathed. The bill was more than half the adult length and had become entirely black, having gradually changed from yellowish at hatching (Wagner, 1945).

Skutch (1967) has contributed some observations on the care of the young in this species. In a nest that contained two young that were 5 and 7 days of age, the female brooded them eight times over a 4-hour period, for intervals of from a few seconds to 24 minutes, but collectively for only 48 minutes (20 percent of the total period). During the afternoon hours the total brooding time was likewise only 22 percent of the total observation period. The young birds thus endured several hours of very cold, nearly freezing air, and also some periods of intense radiation during the middle part of the day. During an 8-hour period they were fed 21 times, apparently mostly of *Salvia* nectar as well as minute insects caught by the mother in the air above the nest.

Evolutionary and Ecological Relationships

The green violet-ear is clearly part of the closely related *Colibri* group, and on the basis of plumage would seem to be the nearest relative to *C. coruscans*, which coexists with it in South America from Venezuela southward.

Not much is yet known of bird-plant relationships for this species, but Colwell et al. (1974) reported that the Costa Rican shrub *Centropogon valerii* is primarily pollinated by the green violet-ear. In the southern Costa Rican highlands the birds' territories often center on clumps of this plant, which they defend from their own and other species. Observations by both Skutch and Wagner suggest that various species of *Salvia* are also locally important plants for the green violet-ear.

Genus *Orthorhyncus* Lacapede 1799

Synonyms: *Chrysolampis* Boie 1831

*T*his genus of West Indian and South American hummingbirds consists of two medium-sized species (wing 45–58 mm) having a blackish bill that is round, straight, and slender and about as long as the head, but is from a third- to half-covered with frontal feathers, which hide the nasal operculum and extend variably far anterior to it. The culmen is rounded except basally, where it is contracted into a ridge, and the edges of the maxilla are smooth or very minutely serrate. The wing is at least four times as long as the exposed culmen, and the outermost primary is the longest. The tail is more than half as long as the wing and is somewhat rounded. Adult males have a metallic-colored crest, which is broad and rounded or flat and pointed, whereas females and young males are crestless, colored bronzy-metallic above and grayish below, and have gray or white tips on the outer rectrices.

ANTILLEAN CRESTED HUMMINGBIRD

Orthorhyncus cristatus (Linnaeus)

Other Names	Doctor bird, Frou-frou, Little doctor bird; Zumbardorcito (Spanish); Oiseau mouche huppé (French).
Range	Resident in extreme eastern Puerto Rico and adjoining islands eastward and southward through the Virgin Islands and Lesser Antilles to Barbados and Grenada. Hypothetical (one record) in Texas.
North American Subspecies	(Presumed; no specimens available.) *O. c. exilis* (Gmelin). Resident from eastern Puerto Rico eastward and southward to St. Lucia.
Measurements	Of *O. c. exilis*: Wing, males 46–51.5 mm (ave. of 72, 49.6 mm), females 44–49 mm (ave. of 35, 46.3 mm). Exposed culmen, males 7.5–10 mm (ave. of 72, 8.8 mm), females 9–12 mm (ave. of 35, 10.6 mm). Eggs, ave. 11.6 × 8.1 mm. (*Auk* 58:369).
Weights	The average of 18 males was 2.75 g (range 2.2–3.2 g); that of 11 females was 2.42 g (range 2.0–3.0 g) (David Willard, personal communication).
Description	*O. c. exilis* (after Ridgway, 1911).

Adult male. Forehead and whole crown, including much the greater part of occipital crest, very bright metallic green, golden green, or golden, the longer feathers of the crest usually more bluish green, but never distinctly nor abruptly blue (as in other subspecies); hindneck and sides of head behind eye and beneath crest dark metallic green or bronze-green, appearing nearly black when viewed from in front; back, scapulars, wing-coverts, rump, and upper tail-coverts metallic bronze-green or bronze; tail black, glossed with purplish bronze; remiges dusky, faintly glossed with purplish; loral, suborbital, and auricular regions and underparts of body (including under tail-coverts) very dark sooty grayish, becoming paler sooty gray on chin and throat; sides glossed with bronze or bronze-green or mostly of this color; femoral tufts mixed sooty gray and whitish; bill dusky; iris dark brown; feet grayish brown or dusky.

Adult female. Above metallic bronze-green or greenish bronze, including middle rectrices; other rectrices purplish black, the two or three outer pairs broadly tipped with light brownish gray and with basal portion dull metallic greenish or bronzy, the one next to middle pair with greenish or bronzy basal area more extended; remiges dusky, faintly glossed with violaceous; underparts sooty

81

gray, slightly deeper laterally and posteriorly, paler on chin and throat; bill, etc., as in adult male.

Immature male. Similar to adult male, but without any crest, the pileum dull metallic green, and feathers dusky basally.

Identification *In the hand.* Although the bill of this species is not extremely short, it is distinctively feathered for at least half of its length (more in males), reaching to the anterior end of the nostrils, leaving an unfeathered culmen of no more than 12 mm, or less than one-fourth the total length of the wing.

In the field. This very small hummingbird is the only West Indian species that is generally blackish on the underparts and has a distinct crest, which is glittering green in the northern forms. The female lacks a crest, but is green above and whitish below, with a relatively short, straight beak. The birds often perch on telephone wires along roadsides.

Habitats This species is common within its limited range in the Lesser Antilles, being perhaps the most abundant hummingbird of the region, occurring on every island from the sea to the highlands (Lack, 1973). It is apparently partial to drier areas having open vegetation, and is especially common where cactus and agaves occur (Robertson, 1962). It is probably rare or absent only from the highest levels of some of the larger islands, and is locally absent from the densest rainforest habitats, although it does occur in wet cloud forest in the mountains of Dominica.

Movements These birds are sedentary, and subspeciation has occurred on several of the island groups. My only basis for the inclusion of the species on the list of North American birds is the fact that a specimen was obtained on Galveston Island, Texas, on February 1, 1967. The bird was reportedly netted by two boys, and its remains were subsequently retrieved from a trash can. It was impossible to obtain details on the bird's origin from those who captured it, and the possibility remains that someone actually transported it into the Houston-Galveston area, where it escaped or was released. The bird would have had to fly more than 1600 kilometers over water, which seems to exclude natural dispersal factors. Thus the species should probably be considered hypothetical for North America (Oberholser, 1974).

Foraging Behavior and Floral Ecology Most observers have commented on the wide diversity of plant species utilized and foraging heights frequented by these birds, from ground level to the canopy of the tallest trees and from small nonwoody plants to bushes and large trees. Lodge (1896) reported that the birds feed on almost any kind of flowering plant, but seem especially fond of lime trees, lantana, allamanda, and a few other unidentified flowering plants. Ingels (1976) noted that they often feed at the tops of flowering leguminous trees, including poincianas (*Poinciana pulcherrima* and *P. regia*) and shower trees (*Cassia* sp.); they also use *Hibiscus*, *Ixora* (*I. macrothyrsa*), and several other tropical flowering species. Leck (1973) observed the birds feeding at various succulents such as *Euphorbia* species, where they tended to be dominated by the larger bananaquits and green-throated carib hummingbirds. Diamond (1973) noted that crested hummingbirds on St. Lucia fed close to the ground, usually by probing flowers, especially those of *Lantana camara* and *Stachytarpheta jamaiensis.* Similarly, Schuchmann (1979) reported that, in montane habitats where this species overlaps with green-throated and purple-throated caribs, it usually feeds quite close to the ground, below the levels occupied by the other two species.

Breeding Biology   In this species only the males establish feeding territories, whereas the females trapline along regular routes. The males hold display territories from January to August and advertise them by singing. Displays and copulation occur within the male's territory, and mating occurs after the female has built her nest. After initially chasing her from his territory, the male then allows the female to perch in the center of the area and begins his pre-mating display.

There are three phases to the male's mating display, including a preliminary hovering about half a meter from the female while in a vertical position with the crest erected. The male then flies in "slow motion" toward the perched female, abruptly clapping his wings against the fanned rectrices. Then, immediately in front of the female, he begins to fly at high speed in a semicircle around her, while beating his wings against the spread tail at the end of each arc. This flight is repeated four to six times, and the color of the male's crest changes as he alters its angle with respect to the female. The female's only obvious response to the final phase is a slight opening of the bill. Copulation follows this third phase (Schuchmann, 1979).

Nests of this species are built in bushes or vines from less than 1 to more than 2 meters above the ground. They are lined with soft white plant down, and have very thin tissue-like pieces of bark on the external surface. In one observed case, nest-building was done entirely by the female in 5 days. The eggs were laid almost exactly 2 days apart, and incubation began on the afternoon of the day that the second egg was laid. Incubation required 14 days for both eggs, and the young left the nest 21 days later (English, 1934). Earlier English (1928) reported on four nesting pairs of this species. One pair nested successfully in April, and fledged their young on May 14, after respective incubation and fledging periods of 15 and 20 days. A second nest was found on July 11, containing well-grown young. Another pair nested in late April, but the young were not successfully reared. An abortive second nesting by this pair was begun in late June, and a third nesting effort was made in July. A fledging period of 23–24 days was determined for the fourth pair.

Evolutionary and Ecological Relationships   The evolutionary relationships of this species are clearly with *"Chrysolampis" mosquitus,* according to Ridgway (1911), and it seems reasonable to consider them as congeneric. No hybrids involving the crested hummingbird are known.

Very little is known of the ecological relationships of this species. It is evidently a generalist feeder, with a remarkably broad ecological distribution.

Genus *Chlorostilbon* Gould 1833

*T*his genus includes about 14 species of West Indian, Central American, and South American hummingbirds of medium size (wing 40–50 mm), which have bills that are straight, narrow, and about as long as the head. The culmen is broadly rounded and contracted into a narrow ridge basally. The nasal operculum is broad and feathered on the upper posterior portion, with the frontal feathering reaching the middle or anterior end of the operculum. The wing is three to four times as long as the culmen, and the outer primary is the longest. The tail varies in shape from notched to deeply forked in adult males, and is notched or slightly double-rounded in females. The sexes are dimorphic and rather uniformly metallic green dorsally, which color extends in males to the throat, sides, and abdomen. Adult males have green to blackish tails. Females are brownish gray to grayish white ventrally, and their tails range from green to dusky violet, sometimes with whitish tips.

1. Residential distributions of green violet-ear (cross-hatched) (races t = *thalassinus*, m = *minor*, c = *cabanidis*) and Cuban emerald (stippled) (races b = *bracei*, r = *ricordii*).

CUBAN EMERALD

Chlorostilbon ricordii (Gervais)

Other Names	God bird; Zunzún, Zumbador, Zumbete, etc. (Spanish).
Range	Resident on Cuba, the Isle of Pines, and the northern Bahama Islands (Grand Bahama, Abaco and Andros, rare and local on New Providence). Straggles occasionally to southern Florida. (See map 1.)
North American Subspecies	? (actual subspecies unknown.)
	C. r. bracei (Lawrence). Resident on the Bahama Islands.
	C. r. ricordii (Gervais). Resident on Cuba and the Isle of Pines.
Measurements	Of *C. r. ricordii*: wing, males 50–55 mm (ave. of 13, 52.3 mm), females 48–52.5 mm (ave. of 12, 50.7 mm). Culmen, males 14.5–18.5 mm (ave. of 13, 17.1 mm), females 17.5–19 mm (ave. of 12, 18.1 mm) (Ridgway, 1911). Eggs, ave. 12.62 × 8.2 mm (extremes of 5, 12.5–13.0 mm × 8.0–8.3 mm (U.S. National Museum specimens).
Weights	The average weight of 4 males from Cuba was 3.35 g (range 3.25–3.75 g); that of 3 females was 3.54 g (range 3.25–3.87 g) (George Watson, personal communication).
Description	(After Ridgway, 1911.)

Adult male. Above dark metallic bronze-green, darker and decidedly duller on pileum; four middle rectrices dark metallic bronze or greenish bronze, the next pair similar but with inner webs greenish black; two outer pairs of rectrices greenish black or black faintly glossed with bluish green or greenish blue, the outer web of next-to-outer pair slightly bronzed; remiges dark brownish slate or dusky, faintly glossed with violaceous; underparts brilliant metallic green (yellowish emerald green); femoral tufts and under tail-coverts white, the latter sometimes with a few small spots or streaks of grayish on lateral feathers; maxilla dull black; mandible pinkish with tip dusky; iris dark brown; feet dusky.

Adult female. Above similar in color to adult male; beneath brownish gray (between drab gray and smoke gray); the sides, from neck to flanks inclusive, metallic green, with feathers gray beneath surface; anal tufts white; a grayish white postocular spot; bill, etc., as in adult male.

Identification	(See Plate 8B.)

In the hand. The only large hummingbird likely to appear in the southeastern United States (peninsular Florida) that has a strongly forked blackish or violet tail, a partially exposed nasal operculum, a wing length of at least 48 mm, and a small white spot behind the eye.

In the field. Appreciably larger than the ruby-throated humming-bird and extensively and uniformly green above and below. The tail is blackish and deeply forked in males and less so in females, and the under tail-coverts are white or mostly white. Both sexes have a small white spot behind the eye, and females have whitish underparts, becoming greenish on the sides. It is normally found in wooded areas and copses, and in Florida has been observed mostly during fall and winter months in southern areas.

Habitats This species is widely distributed on Cuba, apparently occupying a variety of lowland habitats, but probably primarily open forests of both humid and arid types. It may also occur in the mountains of Cuba. On Great Bahama the birds frequent brushy undergrowth of open pine woods, and generally occur where there is any considerable growth of bushes on both of the larger and smaller islands. Barbour (1943) has stated that they occur in parks, gardens, and wild, open country, and George Watson (personal communication) found them widely distributed in mixed forests in the Sierra Crystal in Oriente, coastal scrub forest at Playa Giron, and garden parkland in Soledad.

Movements This species is resident in Cuba and the northern Bahama Islands. However, it is an occasional vagrant to New Providence Island, and has appeared in southern Florida on several occasions. The first of these was in 1943, when an individual was seen by numerous observers from October 20 to November 8. It was next seen on June 12 and 15, 1953, about 16 kilometers south of Cocoa (Sprunt, 1954).

The most recent observations reported individuals at Naranja in January 1961 and at Stock Island on March 27 of that year (*Audubon Field Notes* 15:323). In 1964 the species was again seen at Cocoa Beach between October 10 and 19 (*Audubon Field Notes* 18:26), and a female was observed at Hypoluxo on August 10, 1977 (*American Birds* 31:991).

Foraging Behavior and Floral Ecology No specific information is available on these subjects. The species seems to be a generalist forager, "occurring wherever there are flowers" (Barbour, 1943).

Breeding Biology Chapman (1902) found a nest on the branch of a coffee bush in southern Cuba in March. It was composed of green mosses, bound about with strips of bark, which hung in flowing streamers 12–13 centimeters below. Two eggs were present. According to Barbour (1943), nests may be found in any month. Renesting or multiple nesting is evidently frequent, since one bird that lost her initial nest in a hurricane built a new one on a chandelier. Four broods were raised from this single nest, and never once was her mate observed during this period. The incubation and fledging periods are unreported, but studies of a related species—the fork-tailed emerald—indicated a fledging period of 24–25 days (Wolf, 1964). Courtship and mating displays are also unknown, but have recently been described for the related blue-tailed emerald (Elgar, 1980).

Evolutionary and Ecological Relationships

This species' nearest relative is the Hispaniolan emerald, which Ridgway (1911) included with it in the genus *Riccordia*, mainly because their outer tail feathers are relatively wide as compared with those of more typical species of *Chlorostilbon*.

There have been no descriptions of any hybrids involving the Cuban emerald, or of its ecological relationships with other hummingbirds and plants.

Genus *Cynanthus* Swainson 1827

Synonyms: *Hylocharis* Boie 1831, *Basinna* Boie 1831, *Phaeptila* Gould 1861, *?Eucephala* Reichenbach 1854, *?Chrysuronia* Bonaparte 1850

*T*his genus includes at least nine species of Middle and South American hummingbirds that are medium-sized (wing usually 40–60 mm) and have a reddish bill with a darker tip, longer than the head, very slightly decurved, broader than deep, and becoming broader basally. The broad nasal operculum is completely unfeathered, the frontal feathers forming a transverse line across the base of the forehead. The wing is about three times as long as the exposed culmen, and the outermost primary is the longest. The tail is rounded, square-tipped, or slightly forked, with the rectrices all fairly broad with rounded tips. The sexes are alike or dimorphic, the adult male with or without a definite gorget, usually green above, with a broad tail that is dark and iridescent or chestnut-colored. Females are mostly coppery green above, and often have white on the head, underparts, or tail.

2. Residential distribution of white-eared hummingbird (races b = *borealis*, l = *leucotis*, p = *pygmaea*). Stippling indicates probable area of nonbreeding movements.

WHITE-EARED HUMMINGBIRD

Cynanthus leucotis (Vieillot)
(Hylocharis leucotis of AOU, 1957)

Other Names	None in general English use; Orejas blancas, Chupaflor orejiblanco (Spanish).
Range	Breeds casually in the mountains of southeastern Arizona, and south through the forests of both eastern and western Sierras from Sonora, San Luis Potosi, and Tamaulipas, Mexico, south to Nicaragua (Friedmann et al., 1950). Northern races winter in Mexico and Guatemala. (See map 2.)
North American Subspecies	*C. l. borealis* (Griscom). Breeds casually in southeastern Arizona (Huachuca Mountains) and in the temperate zone of northern Mexico from 1170 to 3000 meters on both slopes of the Sierra Madre Occidental and the Sierra Madre Oriental, wintering up to 1920 meters from Sonora and Chihuahua to northern Sinaloa and northern Durango. Also reported from Tamaulipas, but birds from this area may be closer to *C. l. leucotis* (Friedmann et al., 1950).
Measurements	Wing, males 52.5–59.5 mm (ave. of 17, 55.3 mm), females 49–55 mm (ave. of 15, 51.9 mm). Culmen, males 14.5–18.5 mm (ave. of 17, 16.6 mm), females 16–18.5 mm (ave. of 15, 17.4 mm) (Ridgway, 1911). Eggs, ave. 12.5 × 8.0 mm (11.9–12.7 × 7.9–8.3 mm).
Weights	Breeding females average 3.25 g (Wagner, 1959). The average of 158 males was 3.6 g (standard deviation 0.3 g); that of 51 females was 3.2 g (standard deviation 0.2 g) (Lyon, 1976).
Description	(After Ridgway, 1911.)

Adult male. Forehead, loral and malar regions, chin, and upper throat rich metallic violet or violet-blue, passing into velvety black on suborbital and auricular regions and into duller black, faintly glossed with bluish or greenish, on crown; occiput and hindneck dark metallic bronze or bronze-green; back, scapulars, wing-coverts, and rump varying from bright metallic green to bronze-green or golden green; upper tail-coverts similar but usually more bronzy (sometimes golden bronze), and, together with feathers of rump, more or less distinctly margined with rusty; middle pair of rectrices bright bronze-green, bronze, or golden bronze; the next pair similar but darker; the remaining rectrices bronzy black, tipped (more or less distinctly) with bright bronze or bronze-green; remiges purplish dusky, the inner secondaries glossed with bronze-green; a broad white postocular stripe, extending backward and downward above and behind upper margin of au-

93

ricular region to side of neck; middle and lower throat brilliant metallic emerald green (more yellowish green posteriorly) abruptly defined against the dark violet or violet-blue of upper throat and chin; chest, breast (except medially), sides, and flanks metallic bronze or bronze-green, interrupted by grayish margins to the feathers, the basal grayish also showing where feathers are disarranged; median line of breast and abdomen dull grayish white, sometimes tinged with brownish buffy; femoral tufts dull white; under tail-coverts grayish brown, faintly glossed with bronze, centrally, broadly margined with dull whitish; basal half (more or less) of bill coral red, terminal portion dull blackish; iris dark brown; feet dusky.

Adult female. Above similar to the adult male, but pileum dusky brown, the feathers (especially on forehead) sometimes margined with pale rusty brown, and lateral pair of rectrices broadly tipped with brownish gray; a broad black suborbital and auricular patch and white postocular stripe, as in adult male; underparts pale brownish gray or dull grayish white, spotted with metallic bronze-green, this predominating laterally; median line of breast and abdomen plain dull grayish white or pale brownish gray; under tail-coverts grayish centrally (the shorter ones bronzy or bronze-green) broadly margined with dull grayish white; maxilla dull black, mandible reddish, with terminal portion dusky; iris and feet as in adult male.

Young male. Pattern of coloration as in adult, but no blue on head, and brilliant emerald-green of throat merely indicated; pileum dull dusky greenish, the feathers margined with dull tawny, this prevailing on occiput; chin and upper throat dull grayish white spotted with dusky; lower throat metallic emerald-green, the feathers distinctly margined with grayish white; prevailing color of rump, superficially, dull tawny, the upper tail-coverts distinctly margined with the same; outer pair of rectrices broadly tipped with light brownish gray, the second pair more narrowly tipped with the same.

Young female. Like adults, but duller, the feathers of pileum margined with rusty, and spotting of underparts much duller and less metallic.

Identification   (See Plate 8C.)

In the hand. Most likely to be confused with the broad-billed hummingbird, since it too has a reddish base to the bill, which is somewhat broader than deep basally. A long white eye-stripe is present in both sexes, below which a black ear-patch extends forward to the lores. In females this is more dusky, and their throat and underparts are spotted with greenish, rather than uniformly grayish as in females of the broad-billed hummingbird.

In the field. the same criteria as noted above (reddish bill, white eye-stripe, and dark black ear-patch) serve as good fieldmarks, and the females' greenish tail and greenish flanks and throat are useful in separating this species from females of the otherwise similar broad-billed hummingbird. This species is found in pine-oak woods near streams, and especially in oak woodlands of mountains. Males utter a clear, repeated *tink* call that sounds like a small bell, delivered constantly from perches.

Habitats   Little is known of this species' habitats in the United States, since it is seen only rarely north of the Mexican border. They include woodlands in Cave Creek Canyon of the Chiricahua Mountains and Ramsey Canyon of the Huachuca Mountains in Arizona, the Chisos Mountains of Big Bend National Park in Texas, and the Animas Mountains of New Mexico.

In Mexico the species generally occurs in the temperate zone between 1170 and 3000 meters, nesting at least between 2250 and 3300 meters and wintering up to at least 1900 meters. Schaldach (1963) reported it to be the most abundant breeding bird in open, grassy fields within the arid and humid zones of the pine-oak forests of Colima, and Rowley (1966) also noted that it was the most abundant hummingbird in the upper levels (cloud forest and boreal forest) of his study area in Oaxaca. Moore (1939a) stated that it was the most common hummingbird in the mountains of northwestern Mexico above 1500 meters. It was the dominant species in relation to others of its family there, maintaining control of its preferred food flowers even against larger species such as the Rivoli and blue-throated hummingbirds. According to Wagner (1959), the species' altitudinal range is from 1200 to 3900 meters, whereas at the southern end of its range in El Salvador it occurs between 1000 and 2400 meters (Dickey and van Rossem, 1938). In the Soloma region of Guatemala it occurs commonly between 1750 and 2850 meters in scrub oak thickets, pine forests, and along the edges of oak and cloud forests, nesting in adjacent cornfields (Baepler, 1962). More generally in Guatemala it occurs from 1200 to 3300 meters above sea level, preferring the more open woods of oaks, pines, and alders and the clearings and brushy mountainsides (Skutch, in Bent, 1940).

All sorts of scrubby growth, but especially the undergrowth of oak forests, seem to represent optimum habitat for this species. The diverse habitats also include pine woods, rather dense pine-oak forests, high mountain fir forests, partially open mountain country with scattered trees and shrubs, suburban gardens, and even vacant lots with scattered shrubs and flowers.

Movements   Texas records of this species extend from April 27 to August 13. Arizona records generally fall between June 9 and August 14 in the Huachuca Mountains, although two specimens were supposedly taken in Arizona on October 1 (Phillips et al., 1964) and one sighting occurred on September 13 (*American Birds* 25:88). Other than Arizona and Texas, the only other records for the United States are from New Mexico, where the species has been seen a few times in the middle elevations of the Animas Mountains during June and July (Hubbard, 1978).

In the Valley of Mexico, considerable seasonable population

variations occur, depending on temperature and rainfall. There maximum breeding occurs during the summer months from June through September, when both rainfall and insect life also reach a maximum. However, elsewhere in Mexico it occurs at other times of the year, such as during spring months in the Colima area and during the winter months in the high mountains of Guatemala. Thus, the timing and extent of seasonal movements obviously varies greatly throughout the species' range (Wagner, 1959).

In the vicinity of Mexico City a proportion of the high montane population migrates, with the weather determining the degree of migration. Although the species is capable of nesting there at any time of the year, during the dry season there is an absence of flexible plant materials needed for nest-building. Thus, there are variations between permanent residents and relatively migratory populations. If there is unusually cold and wet weather between the end of October and the beginning of December, the birds overwinter in the Mexico City area and do not leave for the higher mountain areas for breeding until May or June (Wagner, 1959).

Foraging Behavior and Floral Ecology

According to Wagner (1959), this species shows no special preference for red flowers. It extracts insects from a variety of flowers, and during the winter also captures insects in flight. In Guatemala, one of the principal food plants at the beginning of the nesting season is a burmarigold (*Bidens refracta*), which has yellow flowers and produces relatively little nectar. Later, the birds specialize on various species of mints, especially the red-flowered *Salvia cinnabarina*, but sometimes also the blue-flowered *S. cacalioefolia*. In Mexico they use the blue-flowered *S. mexicana* blossoms but avoid the larger and more elongated red flowers of *S. cardinalis*, which are regularly visited by the larger blue-throated hummingbird (Wagner, 1959).

In an Oaxaca study area, Lyon (1976) found that this species had the most flexible foraging behavior of the six major species of hummingbirds present. It visited a wide range of blossom sizes, and exhibited an unusual raiding pattern as well, involving secretive low approaches to stands of *Penstemon* within the territories of larger and more dominant blue-throated and Rivoli hummingbirds. As the average territory sizes of the blue-throats decreased during the summer months, their efficiency of territorial defense increased, thus excluding the white-ears from the *Penstemon* stands and forcing them to become more dependent on scattered or smaller-flowered species, especially *Cuphea jorullensis*. The size of male territories in this species averaged 430 square meters, as compared with 720 square meters in the Rivoli and 780 square meters in the blue-throated.

Breeding Biology

In Guatemala, male white-eared hummingbirds become sexually active near the end of the rainy season, just as plants that blossom during the dry season are starting to open. Males gather into "singing assemblies" of as many as seven birds. These

Salvia mexicana

groups are well spread out, but probably within hearing distance of one another. The actual distance between individual birds may be from 18 to 30 meters, and the total assemblage may spread out over an area of 180 meters. Some males also display solitarily, well beyond the hearing of all others. Typically the birds sit on exposed perches from less than 1 meter above ground to as much as 12 meters in the air. Each male utters a low, clear *tink* note that is usually bell-like and repeated endlessly, especially in early morning hours. The seasonal singing activity corresponds to the nesting period of the females; certainly its major purpose is to attract females, but probably also deters other males from intruding in the territory. Frequently the nearest flowers are at some distance from the singing-perch, and thus the territory serves mainly as a mating station rather than as a means of establishing dominance over a local food resource. In Guatemala these territories are defended for three or four months, from early September until the end of the year (Skutch, in Bent, 1940).

Around Mexico City, the birds sing to some degree during the winter months, but song intensity increases during spring, and by midsummer the males begin to congregate on their common singing grounds. There they call from morning to night in groups of as many as seven individuals, according to Wagner (1959). Only during a short period between late March and late May are the birds sexually inactive in the Mexico City area, but in Colima they apparently breed during that period, which suggests a year-round potential for breeding, depending on local conditions.

Courtship involves several stages, beginning with a female's selection of one individual from the group of males, which she lures to her nesting area. She lands on a tree branch and is immediately courted by the male, which whirs around, above, in front of, and beside her. Sometimes the female moves to a new location, only to be followed by the male; this procedure is followed several times, with the sitting intervals becoming shorter and the intervening flights longer. While in flight the partners sometimes hover, facing one another, and whenever the female lands, the male repeatedly "invites" her to rejoin him in the air. The ensuing nuptial flight is wild and darting, during which the birds alternate looping maneuvers and short periods of facing one another while hovering. Its final phase is a rapid curving flight during which the birds presumably fly to a mating site.

Nest sites are nearly always in shrubs or fairly low trees. In Guatemala, the usual site is a composite shrub (*Baccharis vacinoides*) that grows abundantly on the mountainsides. All but 1 of 17 nests found by Skutch (in Bent, 1940) were in bushes of this plant, at heights of 1.5 to 6 meters above ground. However, in Mexico a favored location is on oaks; all 28 nests found by Wagner near Santa Rosa were on oaks (*Quercus nitens*, less often *Q. reticulata*), as were 2 of 4 nests described by Moore (1939a) from northwestern Mexico.

Oaks make an attractive nest site probably because the undersides of oak leaves have a downy hairy covering that can be removed, especially where leaf-miner larvae have been active or where leaf galls are present. The nests are constructed mainly out of such materials, which are held down with spider webbing and covered exteriorly with greenish mosses and grayish lichens for camouflage. The nests are usually almost 50 mm in diameter, with the rim of the cavity noticeably incurved and about 25 mm in diameter; they range from 25 to nearly 75 mm in height (Skutch, in Bent, 1940).

From 15 to 20 days are required to build the nest, and 60 to 70 days may elapse from the onset of nest-building to fledging of the young. In the Santa Rosa area of Mexico, resident birds may raise three broods per year (Wagner, 1959). Skutch (in Bent, 1940) suggested that two broods may be raised in a season, and mentioned a female that built a second nest 12 meters away from the first, only a week after fledging the single offspring of her first nesting effort.

Nests of several females are sometimes located fairly close to one another, at times only 35 to 50 meters apart. Further, new nests are often constructed on the foundations of old ones. Incubation lasts from 14 to 16 days, with the longer periods typical of winter months. Likewise, in Mexico the fledging period varies from 23 to 28 days, with the growth of the young depending on weather and seasonal variations in day-length (Wagner, 1959).

In his report on incubation behavior and nesting development, Skutch (in Bent, 1940) noted that one female devoted nearly eight hours of one day to incubation, and about four hours were spent off the nest, presumably for foraging. By the time the young birds were 7 or 8 days old, their pinfeathers began to sprout, and their eyelids began to part at 9 or 10 days after hatching. Four days later the green portions of their contour feathers appeared, and at 16 days the flight feathers began to emerge from their sheaths. Two days later the tail feathers did the same. The young were brooded nightly until they were 17 or 18 days old, by which time they were well-covered with feathers, and in Skutch's observations fledging required 23 to 26 days. One youngster, 40 days old and two weeks out of the nest, was still fed occasionally by its mother, even though she was now incubating her second clutch of eggs. Wagner (1959) noted that by the time the young are 20 days old they may weigh about 25 percent more than the average adult weight. However, in spite of such maternal care, there is a high incidence of nest and nestling mortality. Skutch (in Bent, 1940) reported that of 18 eggs in 9 nests, only 3 youngsters survived to fledging, while Wagner (1959) found that among a total of 39 nests only the nestlings of 12 fledged.

Evolutionary and Ecological Relationships   In the judgment of Mayr and Short (1970), this species and the black-fronted hummingbird of Baja California comprise a superspecies, with the latter a relict form and the most strongly differentiated avian form of that area. I agree with the close relationships of these two species, and further believe that *"Basilinna"* and *"Cynanthus"* should both be considered congeneric with the typical "sapphires" of the genus *Hylocharis.*

In spite of the wide ecological and geographic range of the species, no hybrids involving the white-eared hummingbird are known. Probably a good part of its success can be attributed to the fact that this species seems to be a generalist forager, using a wide array of blossom sizes and flower heights (Lyon, 1976).

3. Breeding (stipple) and residential (cross-hatched) distributions of broad-billed hummingbird.

100

BROAD-BILLED HUMMINGBIRD

Cynanthus latirostris Swainson

Other Names None in general English use; Chuparrosa matraquita, Chupaflor piquiancho (Spanish).

Range Breeds from southern Arizona, southwestern New Mexico, and southwestern Texas south to Chiapas on the west coast of Mexico, including Tres Marias Islands, and to Tamaulipas and northern Veracruz on the east coast (Friedmann et al., 1950). Northern populations winter in Mexico. (See map 3.)

North American Subspecies *C. l. magicus* (Mulsant and Verreaux). Breeds in southern Arizona, southwestern New Mexico, and (rarely) southwestern Texas south on both slopes of the Sierra Madre Occidental to Colima and Aquascalientes, Mexico.

Measurements Wing, males 49–57 mm (ave. of 31, 51.6 mm), females 49.5–54 mm (ave. of 19, 51.6 mm). Culmen, males 18.5–22 mm (ave. of 31, 20.4 mm), females 19.5–23.5 mm (ave. of 19, 21.4 mm) (Ridgway, 1911). Eggs, ave. 12.6 × 8.5 mm (extremes 11.5–13.5 × 7.5–9.8 mm).

Weights The average of 7 males of *C. l. magicus* was 3.72 g (range 3.2–4.4 g); a single female weighed 3.4 g (specimens in Museum of Vertebrate Zoology, University of California).

Description (After Ridgway, 1911.)

Adult male.. Above metallic bronze-green, usually duller on pileum, where sometimes passing into dull grayish brown on forehead; tail glossy blue-black or dark steel blue, the four middle rectrices tipped (more or less broadly) with deep brownish gray, the remaining rectrices sometimes narrowly margined with the same; remiges dusky brownish gray or dull slate color, faintly glossed with purplish, the outermost primary narrowly edged with pale gray or grayish white; chin and throat bright metallic greenish blue or bluish green (the color more blue anteriorly, more green posteriorly), passing into metallic bronze-green on breast, sides, flanks, and abdomen; under tail-coverts dull white, usually more or less distinctly grayish centrally, the shorter ones sometimes with dusky, slightly metallic, spots; anal tufts and tuft on each side of rump white; bill purplish red or carmine, dusky terminally; iris dark brown; feet dusky.

Adult female. Above similar in color to adult male but duller, especially on pileum, which is usually dull grayish brown or brownish gray anteriorly; remiges paler grayish brown; middle pair of rectrices bronze-green passing into blue-black or greenish black terminally (the extreme tip sometimes green or bronzy); other rectrices with basal half (more or less) bronze-green, the remaining portion blue-black tipped with brownish gray (most broadly on lateral pair); underparts sooty gray or dark drab-gray (browner than mouse gray); the sides of chest glossed (more or less) with metallic green or bronze-green; under tail-coverts mostly dull white (grayish centrally); anal tufts and tuft on each side of rump white; a white or grayish white postocular spot, and below this a dusky area extending to beneath eye; maxilla dull black, sometimes brownish basally; mandible dusky for terminal half (more or less), reddish basally; iris and feet as in adult male.

Young male. Similar to the adult female but feathers of pileum, hindneck, back, scapulars, rump, etc., tipped or terminally margined with pale buffy brown or grayish buff; rectrices as in adult male; chin and throat (in older specimens) intermixed with metallic bluish green or greenish blue feathers, these margined terminally with pale grayish or buffy brown.

Young female. Similar to the adult female but feathers of upperparts margined terminally or tipped with pale buffy brown (sometimes more cinnamomeous on pileum and rump).

Identification   (See Plate 8C.)

In the hand. Likely to be confused only with the white-eared hummingbird, which also has a reddish bill widened near the base and a white stripe behind the eye. However, in this species the white eye-stripe is barely indicated, the black ear-patch is less definite, and the tail is bluish black and slightly notched in both sexes.

In the field. Found in rather arid country often dominated by mesquite or agaves, sometimes also in mountain canyons. Both sexes have reddish bills, separating them from Rivoli hummingbirds, and the male's lack of a long white eye-stripe separates him from the male white-eared. Females also have less white behind the eye than do female white-eared, and they have more grayish underparts and a bluish black rather than greenish tail. They utter chattering kinglet-like calls, and the male produces a high-pitched humming sound during aerial display.

Habitats   In the United States this species is mostly limited in summer to rocky canyons in desert-like mountain habitats, where streams or springs provide growths of sycamores or mesquites. In Arizona it is fairly common in mesquite-sycamore vegetation from Guadalupe Mountains westward to the Baboquivaris, and northward at least to the Santa Catalinas (Phillips et al., 1964). Nests in México have been found from slightly above sea level in Sinaloa to 435 meters in Sonora, and most specimens from northern Mexico have been collected between 150 and 3000 meters (Moore, 1939b).

Farther south, the species is found in nearly all habitats in Colima, from sea level to about 2100 meters, the upper limits in pine-oak forest. It is especially common there in thorn forest and on high grassy slopes in oak woodland (Schaldach, 1963).

Movements   In the United States, this species is clearly migratory. In the Rio Grande valley of Texas it has been reported from May 17 to October 20 (Oberholser, 1974). In Arizona, it is usually present from mid-March until mid-September, with occasional arrivals in early March and sometimes lingering until October 1 (Phillips et al., 1964). In Sonora, it is a permanent resident in the tropical zone northward to the vicinity of Guaymas along the coast and interiorly to the vicinity of Moctezuma (van Rossem, 1945). There is no good evidence of migratory movements farther south in Mexico.

Probable postbreeding wandering has resulted in some extra-limital sightings in the United States. Thus, there is a single recent record of the species from Utah (*American Birds* 33:201) and at least seven records from California (*American Birds* 31:374). Most of the California records are for San Diego County from September to April, but there is one record as far north as Pacific Grove, Monterey County (*Audubon Field Notes* 23:622)

Foraging Behavior and Floral Ecology   The observations by Moore (1939b) are almost the only ones available on the foraging of this species. He observed the birds at flowers of the ocotillo, a yellow-flowered *Opuntia*, and paint-brush, but noted that the favorite foraging plant in Sonora was a red-flowered shrub called the "tavachin" (probably of the genus *Caesalpinia* or *Poinciana*), which was growing in sandy arroyos. A nesting female visited this species approximately every 15 minutes during the late afternoon.

In the United States, these birds have been observed foraging on ocotillos, agaves, penstemons, and other blooming plants (Oberholser, 1974). Samples from the stomachs of four birds collected in Arizona provide some idea of their insect consumption, which included leafhoppers, jumping plant lice, root gnats, flower flies, spiders, daddy-longlegs, and miscellaneous bugs and hymenopterans (Cottam and Knappen, 1939).

Breeding Biology   Nesting in Sonora and Sinaloa apparently occurs over a wide span of time, probably from January to August, with nests being found in January, March, and May (Moore, 1939b). A series of 16 egg dates from Mexico extend from January 16 to May 21, and half of these fall between March 25 and May 11, indicating the peak of the season (Bent, 1940). Birds in breeding condition have been collected in Queretaro in late November and December, and nesting has been noted in December (Friedmann et al., 1950). Records for Arizona are rather limited, but Bent (1940) indicated that five egg records extended from April 14 to July 15. In Texas breeding apparently extends from early May to early August (Oberholser, 1974). There are no specific nest records for New Mexico.

Practically nothing has been written on display behavior, but notes by F. C. Willard (in Bailey, 1928) indicated that the male performs a "pendulum swing back and forth in front of the female," accompanied by a sound much like the "zing" of a rifle bullet that is higher in pitch than that of any of the other small hummingbirds.

Four nests found by Moore (1939b) in northern Mexico were all within 2 meters of the ground. All had some grass stalks in the body of the nest, were lined with white plant down, and were adorned with bits of leaves and bark on the outside surface, but none had any lichens. They all were very small as well, having an internal diameter of only about 19 millimeters. One was placed on a small tree overhanging the bank of an arroyo; another was attached to the stalk of a vine; a third was in a bush covered by dry vines; and the fourth was in an "espino" tree. Three of the nests contained two eggs each, which were laid two days apart in at least one case.

A nest found in Texas was situated on a triple fork of a small willow about 3 to 4 meters above the ground, almost overhanging the Rio Grande River. One Arizona nest was also found over water, about 1.5 meters up in a small willow, and another was found in a hackberry bush 1.2 meters above a creek. Of three nests from Sonora, two were in mesquites and the other was in an apricot tree (Bent, 1940).

Brandt (1951) described some Arizona nests found in Sabino Canyon. One was on a small willow twig about 1 meter above ground, close to a stream channel. Nearby was an old nest on a dead, drooping willow twig, also only about 1 meter above water. Close to this old nest was a newly built nest on a drooping sycamore limb, a little higher above a dry stream bed. All three nests were apparently situated in such a way as to mimic the compact little balls of leaves and vegetation formed during periods of high water, and were largely composed of such vegetational debris, which made them extremely inconspicuous.

According to Oberholser (1974), the outside of the nest may be variably decorated with bits of plant stems, leaves, or even white cotton thread or the blooms of plants; only rarely does it include lichens.

No information is available on incubation and brooding behavior or on incubation and fledging periods.

Evolutionary and Ecological Relationships

Short and Phillips (1966) have described a hybrid obtained in the Huachuca Mountains involving this species and the Rivoli hummingbird, and they commented on the similarities of the genera *Cynanthus* and *Eugenes*. They did not suggest that the genera should be merged, but believed that the two are not as distantly related as is implied in present classifications such as those of Peters (1945) and the AOU (1957).

Mayr and Short (1970) have concluded that the broad-billed hummingbird is a close relative of the dusky hummingbird of western and central Mexico, and hybridization between these two species has been reported (Friedmann et al., 1950). They did not consider these to comprise a superspecies, but regarded them as closely related to *Amazilia*. No other definite hybrids are known, although—as noted in the account of the violet-crowned hummingbird—the type specimen of *Amazilia "salvini"* has at times been considered a hybrid between the violet-crowned and broad-billed hummingbirds.

Too little is known of the species' foraging ecology to comment on possible interspecific ecological relationships.

Genus *Amazilia*
Reichenbach 1849

*T*his genus includes at least 32 species of Middle and South American hummingbirds that are of medium size (wing 50–60 mm in most species) and have a flesh-colored to reddish bill that is straight or slightly decurved, becoming blackish toward the tip, and much broader than deep at the base. The nasal operculum is thick and largely exposed. The wing is normal in shape with the outermost primary the longest, and the tail is usually more than half as long as the wing and ranges from square-tipped to slightly double-rounded. The sexes are alike or similar, with the female somewhat duller. There is often an extensive amount of emerald-green on the head, back, and underparts, but in a few species the underparts are entirely white. The tail ranges from chestnut to purplish-black or bluish-black, without white markings.

4. Breeding (stippled) and residential (cross-hatched) distributions of violet-crowned hummingbird (races e = *ellioti*, v = *violiceps*). Light stippling indicates probable migratory route.

VIOLET-CROWNED HUMMINGBIRD

Amazilia violiceps (Gould)
(*Amazilia verticalis* of AOU, 1957)

Other names	Azure-crown, Salvin's hummingbird; Chupamirto corona azul (Spanish).
Range	Breeds in extreme southeastern Arizona and northwestern and western Mexico from Sonora and Chihuahua south to Chiapas. Northern populations winter in Mexico. (See map 4.)
North American Subspecies	(After Friedmann et al., 1950.) *A. v. ellioti* (Berlepsch). Breeds locally in extreme southeastern Arizona (Guadalupe Mountains) and regularly between 300 and 1800 meters through northeastern and eastern Sonora, across Sinaloa and extreme southwestern Chihuahua from sea level to 2250 meters south on the Pacific slope of the Sierra Madre Occidental, through western Durango to Colima, and thence east to Hidalgo.
Measurements	Wing, males 53–59.5 mm (ave. of 9, 57 mm), females 52–57 mm (ave. 6, 54.9 mm). Culmen, males 21–23.5 mm (ave. of 9, 22.6), females 21.5–24.5 mm (ave. of 6, 23.1 mm) (Ridgway, 1911). Eggs, ave. 13.7 × 8.8 mm (Rowley, 1966).
Weights	The average of 10 males was 5.78 g (range 5.5–6.2 g); that of 6 females was 5.19 g (range 5.0–5.5 g)(Delaware Museum of Natural History).
Description	(After Ridgway, 1911.)

Adult male. Pileum bright metallic blue or violet-blue; hindneck, upper back, scapulars, and wing-coverts dull bronze-green or olive glossed with bronze-green, the first usually more or less tinged or intermixed with blue on upper portion and along junction with white of foreneck; lower back, rump, and upper tail-coverts grayish brown or olive faintly glossed with bronze-greenish, the feathers sometimes narrowly and indistinctly paler on terminal margin, especially the upper tail-coverts, which are usually slightly more bronze-greenish; tail rather dull metallic greenish bronze; remiges dusky, faintly glossed with violet; rictal and malar regions and underparts (including under tail-coverts) immaculate white, the sides mostly light olive glossed with bronze-greenish; bill light rosy or carmine red, dusky at tip; iris dark brown; feet dusky (in dried skins).

Adult female. Similar to the adult male and not always distinguishable, but usually with coloration slightly duller.

Young. Similar to adults, but feathers of upperparts (including pileum) narrowly tipped or terminally margined with buffy, these markings broadest on rump and upper tail-coverts, sometimes obsolete on back.

109

Identification   (See Plate 8D.)
In the hand. Reddish bill (20–25 mm), distinctly widened near the base, and the white underparts provide for simple recognition of this species.
In the field. Favors riverside groves in mountain canyons, the edges of forests, and various plantations. The pure white underparts provide an excellent fieldmark for both sexes; the bright red bill is also a helpful guide. The calls are similar to those of the broad-billed hummingbird, but are somewhat louder and less grating.

Habitats   In Mexico this species occupies a fairly broad vertical range, from 300 to 2250 meters. In Sonora it is most numerous in the foothills of the tropical zone above 300 meters, but it locally extends to about 1800 meters in the transition zone during summer months. Its favorite habitats in Mexico consist of scrubby riparian groves in deserts or foothills, forest edges, wooded parks or plantations, and scrub oak vegetation (from various sources).

In the United States, it has bred only in the Guadalupe Canyon area of extreme southeastern Arizona and adjacent New Mexico. Guadalupe Canyon drains southwestward from its source in New Mexico's Peloncillo Mountains, and then cuts across the corner of Arizona before entering Mexico. It contains water in years of normal moisture, and is lined by cottonwoods, sycamores, other trees, and various shrubs (Ligon, 1961). There the violet-crowned hummingbird has nested among fairly tall sycamores (*Platanus wrightii*) (Levy, 1958; Zimmerman and Levy, 1960).

Movements   Nothing is known of the seasonal movements of these birds, but certainly those in Arizona and New Mexico are migratory. Most U.S. records are for July and August. In adjacent Sonora, records are available from as early as March and April in the lowlands (about 90 meters) in the extreme southern part of the state (van Rossem, 1945). The latest record for the United States is probably the individual observed at a Tucson feeder from late November until late February, providing the first indication of overwintering in Arizona (*American Birds* 25:610). Also an individual visited a feeder at Santa Paula, Ventura County, California, from July 6 until September 19, 1976, representing the first California record of the species (*American Birds* 30:1004, 31:223). A second California record has been reported (*Western Birds* 9:91–92).

Foraging Behavior and Floral Ecology   Scarcely anything has been written on this subject. Levy (1958) observed an adult violet-crown that perhaps was feeding young as it appeared every five to ten minutes from a sycamore grove to feed on the blossoms of an agave. The birds often feed at flowering trees 6 to 9 meters above the ground (Edwards, 1973).

Breeding Biology   The first account of possible nesting of this species in the United States was provided by Levy (1958), who observed as many as six birds in Guadalupe Canyon during July 1957. At that time he collected an adult female with a recent brood patch, but did not find a nest. However, during 1979, fieldwork in the canyon by Zimmerman and Levy (1960) discovered nesting in both Arizona and New Mexico. The first nest was found under construction within Arizona on June 20, and on June 28 a completed nest was located nearby. On July 5 two more nests were discovered on the New Mexico side of the boundary. Another possible nesting pair was also seen repeatedly entering a large sycamore, but no nest was found. Of the four nests that were located, all were in sycamores at 7, 9, 10, and at least 12 meters above ground. In one case the nest was near the tip of a horizontal branch, and another was saddled on a horizontal branch about 1.5 meters from the tip and about 7.5 meters out from the trunk. A third was placed in the sharp angle of a "V" in a malformed, semipendant branch.

Few nests of this species have been described in detail, but Moore (in Bent, 1940) has provided one account. This nest was in the crotch of a dead twig 2 meters above the ground, at the end of the branch of a thorny bush overhanging a creek in Sinaloa. Most of the nest was composed of whitish cottony material from a paloblanco (*Celtis laevigata*?) tree. This was bound together by fine webbing resembling that of a spider-web, but also strongly resembling the same cottony material from which the body of the nest was made. Three small twigs were attached to the external surface, as well as a number of pale greenish lichens, which provided the chief means of camouflage. At least two of the Arizona nests were also decorated with a few green lichens, and appeared quite white (Ligon, 1961).

Two nests of this species were found by Rowley (1966) among scrub oaks in Oaxaca. One was a little more than 1 meter above ground, and the other about 2 meters up; both were placed in small sapling oaks. Both were relatively crudely made and, according to Rowley, might easily have passed for old nests of the previous year. One was about 38 mm in external diameter and about 25 mm in total depth, with a cup 12 mm in diameter. A photograph of one of the nests indicates that it was decorated externally with large lichens, and apparently held to the branch by webbing.

Evolutionary and Ecological Relationships

Clearly the closest relative of *Amazilia violiceps* is *A. viridifrons*, which ranges from central Oaxaca and central Guerrero south to Chiapas. It is thus apparently partially sympatric with *A. violiceps*, and cannot be considered conspecific on the basis of present knowledge. Phillips (1965) has provided a detailed review of morphological variation and ranges in both of these forms.

The only possible hybrids so far reported involving this species are two birds, an adult male and a probable young female. The male, originally described as a new species (*Cyanomyia salvini*), was later believed to represent a possible hybrid involving *Cynanthus latirostris* (Bent, 1940). More recently it has been interpreted as simply an extreme example of *A. v. ellioti* (Friedmann et al., 1950), but Phillips, Marshall, and Monson (1964) evidently still regard it as a hybrid with the broad-billed hummingbird. No identification could be made on the second specimen.

Ecological relationships between this species and other hummingbirds or plants are still unstudied.

5. Breeding (stippled) and residential (cross-hatched) distributions of buff-bellied hummingbird (races c = *chalconota*, ce = *cerviventris*, y = *yucatanensis*). Light stippling indicates area of postbreeding movements.

112

BUFF-BELLIED HUMMINGBIRD

Amazilia yucatanensis (Cabot)

Other Names	Fawn-breasted hummingbird, Yucatan hummingbird; Chupamirto yucateco, Chupaflor vientre castaño (Spanish).
Range	Breeds from the lower Rio Grande valley of Texas south through eastern Mexico, Yucatan, Chiapas, and Belize. (See map 5.)

North American Subspecies

(After Friedmann et al., 1950.)

A. y. chalconota Oberholser. Breeds from Cameron and Hidalgo counties of Texas southward to northeastern Mexico as far as San Luis Potosi and northeastern Veracruz.

Measurements

Wing, males 51–57.5 mm (ave. of 5, 53.8 mm), females 52–52.5 mm (ave. of 2, 52.2 mm). Culmen, males 19–21 mm (ave. of 5, 20.2 mm) females 21–21.5 mm (ave. of 2, 21.2 mm)(Ridgway, 1911). Eggs, ave. 13.2 × 8.65 mm (extremes 11.8–15.3 × 7.7–9.4 mm).

Weights

Seven males averaged 4.05 g (range 3.0–4.7); and 7 females averaged 3.67 g (range 2.9–4.5) (Paynter, 1955, and U.S. National Museum specimens).

Description

(After Ridgway, 1911.)

Adults (sexes alike). Above metallic bronze-green or greenish bronze, duller and darker on pileum; the upper tail-coverts more or less tinged or intermixed with cinnamon-rufous, sometimes mostly of the latter color; middle pair of rectrices mostly or with at least terminal fourth metallic bronze, the basal portion chestnut; remaining rectrices chestnut, margined terminally with metallic bronze; remiges dusky, faintly glossed with violet; chin, throat, and chest bright metallic yellowish emerald green, the feathers pale buff basally or (on chest) subterminally; underparts of body, including under tail- and wing-coverts and axillars, pale cinnamon buff; femoral tufts white; bill rosy reddish in life, dusky terminally; iris dark brown; feet dull brown.

First-winter (sexes alike). Similar to first nuptial, but pileum darker and duller; edgings of chin, throat, and jugulum dark buff (Oberholser, 1974).

Identification

(See Plate 8E.)

In the hand. Reddish bill, which is markedly widened toward the base, and chestnut tail separate this from all other North American species except the rufous-tailed hummingbird. In the buff-bellied species the central tail feathers are somewhat shorter and are distinctly bronze-colored toward the tip. Additionally, the flanks and underparts are more buffy or fawn-colored, as compared to grayish in the rufous-tailed hummingbird.

In the field. Associated with semi-arid lowlands dominated by woods or scrubby growth; sometimes occurs in citrus groves. Distinct from the very similar rufous-tailed hummingbird by the buff-bellied's slightly forked tail and more buffy underparts. It has rather shrill calls that have not been well described.

Habitats
In Texas, at the very northern limit of its range, this species is found in dense thickets and among flowering bushes and creeping vines along streams, resacas, and gullies. It also occurs among remnant patches of Texas palmetto (*Sabal texana*) (Oberholser, 1974). More generally it is associated with semiarid coastal scrub habitats along the Mexican coastline. In Tamaulipas Sutton and Pettingill (1942) observed the race *A. y. chalconota* to be common from river level to the highest points reached on adjacent mountains (about 600 meters), in brushy rather than deeply wooded areas. *A. y. yucatanensis* of the Yucatan Peninsula and Belize is most abundant in clearings within high deciduous forest and moderately heavy rainforests (Paynter, 1955). *A. y. cerviventris* is associated with shaded woodlands (Sutton and Burleigh, 1940).

Movements
Probably this species is relatively sedentary over most of its range. In Texas it appears throughout the year, but individuals apparently wander north after the breeding season, rarely reaching the central coast and the eastern edge of the Edwards Plateau (Oberholser, 1974). There is also a general movement out of the state during the coldest months, probably involving a migration to Tamaulipas and Veracruz, and the birds are less frequent between October and April (Bent, 1940). However, some birds do overwinter, and as many as six have been counted on a single Christmas count in Brownsville (Oberholser, 1974). In addition, there are single extralimital sight records for Midland (*Audubon Field Notes* 19:55), Taylor (*Audubon Field Notes* 19:400), and the vicinity of Beaumont (*Audubon Field Notes* 23:498). Lowery (1974) summarized the species' status for Louisiana, which at that time consisted of three records, including one specimen record. Since then, the species has been seen at least once more in Louisiana (*American Birds* 32:364,1020). There is also one astonishing and highly questionable record for Massachusetts (*Audubon Field Notes* 18:496).

Foraging Behavior and Floral Ecology
Buff-bellied hummingbirds use several native flowers in Texas during spring and summer, including Texas ebony (*Pithecellobium flexicaule*), mesquite (*Prosopis glandulosa*), and anaqua (*Ehretia anacua*). In fall and winter they share the flowers of the giant Turk's cap (*Malvaviscus grandiflorus*) with other hummingbirds (Oberholser, 1974).

Breeding Biology Breeding in Texas was once much more common than it is at present; 30 early egg records range from March 24 to July 15, with 15 records between May 9 and June 9, indicating the peak of the nesting season (Bent, 1940). In Mexico breeding has been reported during April in San Luis Rotosi and Tamaulipas and at the end of March in Nuevo Leon (Friedmann et al., 1950). On the Yucatan Peninsula the nesting season apparently begins in late January and extends at least until mid-April (Paynter, 1955).

Nests are often built near woodland roads or paths and placed only a meter or two above the ground (Sutton and Burleigh, 1940; Sutton and Pettingill, 1942). According to Bendire (1895), they are usually saddled on a small, drooping limb or on the fork of a horizontal twig, between 1 and 3 meters from the ground. Small trees and bushes are the usual nest sites, including anachuita (*Cordia boissieri*), ebony, and hackberry, but sometimes nests are in willows. The nests are composed of shreds of vegetable fibers and thistle down, and are distinctively covered by dried flower blossoms, shreds of bark, and small pieces of light-colored lichens. Most are lined with thistle down, but some contain vegetable material resembling brown cattle hair. They are about 40 mm wide and 32 mm deep; and the cup is usually about 22 mm wide and 16 mm in depth. Bent (1940) described an exception to this general configuration, involving a nest that evidently had been used for three seasons, which was thus much higher than normal.

No information is available on incubation periods, incubation behavior, or on brooding behavior and fledging periods. However, these are probably similar to the information reported for the rufous-tailed hummingbirds.

Evolutionary and Ecological Relationships Mayr and Short (1970) suggested that this species is part of a superspecies that includes *A. rutila*. I believe that *A. tzacatl* is at least as closely related to the former as is *A. rutila*, and might on morphological grounds be considered part of the same superspecies. The two forms are rather widely sympatric over the Yucatan Peninsula, however, and thus have clearly attained full species status. There are no known hybrids involving the buff-bellied hummingbird.

6. Residential distribution of rufous-tailed hummingbird (race *tzacatl*). The South American distribution extends to western Ecuador.

116

RUFOUS-TAILED HUMMINGBIRD

Amazilia tzacatl (De la Llave)

Other Names	Reiffer hummingbird; Chupamirto De la Llave, Chupaflor coli-rufo, Chupaflor pechigris (Spanish).
Range	Breeds from southern Tamaulipas in eastern Mexico southward through Middle America to Colombia, western Ecuador and Gorgona Island. (See map 6.)
North American Subspecies	(After Friedmann et al., 1950.)

A. t. tzacatl (De la Llave). Breeds from southern Tamaulipas south through eastern Middle America to Colombia (except southwestern) and east to the Andes of Merida, Venezuela. Accidental in southern Texas.

Measurements Wing, males 46–61 mm (ave. of 60, 58.3 mm), females 52–58 mm (ave. of 36, 54.9 mm). Culmen, males 18–23 mm (ave. of 60, 20.8 mm), females 20–24 mm (ave. of 36, 21.3 mm) (Ridgway, 1911). Eggs, ave. 14 × 8.7 mm (extremes 13.5–14.2 × 8.6–9.1 mm).

Weights The average of 12 males was 5.4 g; that of 10 females was 4.72 g (Hartman, 1954). Four females ranged from 4.1 to 5.2 g, averaging 4.9 g; six males ranged from 5.2 to 5.5 g, averaging 5.3 g (various sources). There are slight seasonal weight variations (Stiles, 1980).

Description (After Ridgway, 1911.)

Adult male. Above metallic bronze-green or greenish bronze, the pileum darker and duller; upper tail-coverts and tail chestnut, the rectrices margined terminally with dusky bronze, the coverts sometimes partly bronze or bronze-green; remiges dusky, faintly glossed with violet; lores chestnut; malar region, chin, throat, chest, upper breast, and sides of lower breast bright metallic yellowish emerald-green, the feathers of chin and upper throat pale buff or buffy white basally, this much exposed on chin; abdomen and median portion of lower breast brownish gray; sides and flanks bronze-green; under tail-coverts cinnamon-rufous; femoral tufts white; bill reddish, dusky terminally, the maxilla sometimes mostly (rarely wholly?) blackish; iris dark brown; feet dusky (in dried skins).

Adult female. Similar to the adult male and perhaps not always distinguishable, but usually with the green of underparts more broken by whitish margins to the feathers; gray of abdomen paler; and cinnamon-rufous loral streak less distinct, sometimes obsolete.

Young. Essentially like adults, but anterior underparts much duller metallic green; the chin and upper throat (at least) sometimes grayish brown or brownish gray, with little if any metallic gloss; and feathers of pileum, rump, etc., tipped (more or less distinctly) with rusty.

Identification   (See Plate 8E.)

In the hand. Best separated from the quite similar *A. yucatanensis* by the more grayish underparts of *A. tzacatl* and its brownish rather than iridescent greenish central tail feathers. Additionally, the lores of *A. tzacatl* are chestnut, whereas those of *A. yucatanensis* are more definitely greenish, and the central rectrices are distinctly shorter than the outermost ones.

In the field. Found in thicket-like edge habitats, somewhat overgrown clearings, planted areas, and humid forested lowlands; likely to be confused only with the very similar buff-bellied hummingbird, which has a more buffy or tawny abdomen and a somewhat forked rather than nearly square-tipped tail. The rufous-tailed hummingbird utters a descending trill of rapid *ts* notes, and its song consists of a series of piercing *tss* or *tsip* notes that are opposingly accented and uttered at the rate of about 12 notes per 5 seconds (*Condor* 59:254). It also utters a *tchup*, a somewhat reedy and nasal *ca-ca-ca*, and burred or buzzy morning song that is sometimes uttered in flight (Slud, 1964).

Habitats   In Mexico, this species occurs in relatively open lowland habitats, especially along forest edges or clearings. In Belize, it resides in both semi-open and wooded areas, except for pine ridges. It occurs in heavy rainforest, but is less common there than at its edges (Russell, 1964). In Costa Rica it is the most widespread hummingbird species, and is especially common in overgrown open and semi-open country and along thickety borders and woodland edges. Although uncommon in heavily forested areas, it is sometimes abundant at forest openings and in cultivated lands, often occurring around houses (Slud, 1964). In that country it is found from as low as sea level to at least 1800 meters, and is often prevalent around citrus or other orchards (Carriker, 1910). In Honduras it ranges up to the lower edges of montane rainforest at about 1200 meters, but is most common at lower elevations in open forest, forest edge, and second-growth habitats (Monroe, 1968).

In Panama, the birds occur along streams, beaches, and more open border habitats in general. Less often they are found in forests, foraging from near the ground to canopy-level. They also are commonly observed along the borders of cultivated fields, in flower beds around houses, and in town parks planted to flowers (Wetmore, 1968). Skutch (1931) also noted that in Panama and other parts of its range this species prefers open country to dark, humid forests, and is the only species of hummingbird in the region that is truly characteristic of lawns, gardens, orchards, and plantings.

Movements There is no evidence that this species undertakes any significant migrations or seasonal movements, which is not surprising considering the essentially tropical climate characteristics of its breeding range. Records of vagrants reaching the United States are very few. Two specimens, obtained (but apparently not preserved) at Fort Brown, Texas, in June and July 1876, constitute the only authenticated records for the species in this country AOU, 1957; Oberholser, 1974). There have been two more recent sight records for southern Texas: a sighting on November 11–12, 1969, of a bird at a hummingbird feeder at LaPorte, Texas (*American Birds* 24:68) and a sighting on a golf course in Brownsville on August 20, 1975 (*American Birds* 29:84).

Foraging Behavior and Floral Ecology Skutch (1941) has described the foraging of this species in some detail. He noted that the birds spend much time probing for insects or nectar in the large red blossoms of *Hibiscus simensis*, the blue trumpet-like flowers of *Thunbergia*, the blue-flowered *Clitoria*, and coral vines (*Antigonon*). They also hover beside the hanging flowers of banana (*Musa*) plants, where they probe among the white blossoms in company with stingless bees. In other areas they seem fond of citrus blossoms as well as those of guava (*Psidium*) and wild plantain (*Heliconia*) (Carriker, 1910). The species is evidently a generalist forager (Snow and Snow, 1980).

Stiles (1975) reported that in Costa Rica this species is one of nine that regularly visit the flowers of nine species of *Heliconia*. This species concentrates especially on *H. latispatha*, which is found in sunny habitats. Reproductive isolation among the species of *Heliconia* probably involves both spacial and temporal patterns of niche partitioning among the numerous available pollinators.

In Colombia, the rufous-tail is common in the city of Medellin, where it commonly forages on *Thunbergia grandiflora*. The banaquit (*Coereba flaveola*) also visits this plant, and the hummingbird typically obtains its nectar by using a hole in the corolla that was previously made by the bananaquit (Borerro, 1965).

Breeding Biology The breeding season of this species seems quite extended, and may include the entire year in some areas. In Mexico, active nests have been reported in April and July (Edwards and Tasian, 1959). In Belize occupied nests have been found in January, February, May, August, and September (Russell, 1964). Likewise in Panama the species probably nests from at least the middle of December to the middle of September, with an absence of records for June, October, and November (Borrero, 1975). In Colombia, nesting in the Cauca Valley and the vicinity of Medellin extends at least from April through December, and there is a February record for the Corillera Occidental. The birds probably breed twice a year at Medellin (Borrero, 1965, 1975).

In a study area at La Selva, Costa Rica, the breeding season was greatly prolonged, but peaked during the dry season when there was maximum flower availability. Fifteen nest records extend from February to December, with a peak in March and

April and with no records for August, September, November, or January. Singing by males was noted for all months except August (Stiles, 1980). Likewise in Panama the majority of the nesting apparently occurs during the dry season, which there extends from January to May (Skutch 1931).

The nest is an open cup, about 44 mm in diameter and about 32 mm in height. The exterior is composed of weathered grass strips, leaves, and bits of vegetation, and decorated on the surface with lichens and mosses, which sometimes hang down festoon-like beneath it. The interior is lined with soft plant down, and the entire structure is bound together with cobwebbing (Skutch, 1931).

Nest locations are highly variable, ranging from 1 to 6 meters above ground, almost invariably on a rather slender support. Sometimes the nest lies between an upright branch and the base of a large thorn, in the angle between a horizontal and vertical stem, or in the axil of a slender leaf-stalk. Occasionally a lone leaf may be used as a foundation. The only apparent requirement is a horizontal support slender enough for the bird to grasp with its feet, from which building operations can begin on some nearby vertical or oblique surface. Frequently the nest is located close to or above a footpath (Skutch, 1931).

The nests are normally constructed so that they blend closely with the foliage around them. One nest, started on the 19th of December, was not completed until 12 days later, when the first egg was laid in it. In a second case, a week elapsed between the start of the nest and the first egg's appearance. On another occasion, a female spent 31 days attempting to produce a nest, only to have the attempts fail repeatedly. At least 12 fresh beginnings were made, involving 8 different locations. Most of these efforts were spoiled by the stealing of nesting materials by other rufous-tailed hummingbirds or tody flycatchers (*Todirostrum cincereum*). Generally when a nest is destroyed, a new one will be begun a short distance away, sometimes less than a week after the destruction of the first one (Skutch, 1931).

Eggs are usually laid on alternate days, but sometimes two days may pass between the laying of the two eggs. Incubation apparently begins shortly after the laying of the first egg, and normally requires 16 days. The rate of growth of the nestlings is fairly rapid. By the 6th or 7th day after hatching the eyes have opened and the pinfeathers are breaking open. By the time the young are 13–16 days old they are well-feathered, and their combined weight causes a collapse of the nest cup. Fledging periods have ranged from 18 to 23 days, frequently to 19 days (Skutch, 1931). A. F. Skutch (*Pub. Nuttall Ornithol. Club* No. 19:37–58, 1981) has recently provided additional observations on the reproductive biology of this species.

The mother continues to feed the young for a time after they leave the nest, but the exact period of such parental dependence is not known.

Evolutionary and Ecological Relationships

This species is obviously a very close relative of *A. yucatanensis,* and the two forms may comprise a superspecies. Mayr and Short (1970) consider *A. yucatanensis* and *A. rutila* to comprise a super-species, with *A. txacatl* a "closely related" species that replaces *A. yucatanensis* in wetter regions. The only reported hybrid combination seems to be a possible wild hybrid with *A. amabilis* (Butler, 1932).

Stiles (1975) has reported on the relationship of nine Costa Rican hummingbird species to the flowering phenology and pollination of eight *Heliconia* species. He found that this and other nonhermit hummingbirds are habitat-separated and pollinate *Heliconia* species that bloom fairly early in the rainy season. Besides such spacial and temporal isolating mechanisms, structural and ethological (flower-choice differences among pollinators) factors facilitate reproductive isolation. In the temperate zone of eastern Colombia the rufous-tail occurs with at least 13 other species of hummingbirds. There it is a generalist forager, defending favored flowers and also gleaning and hawking insects (Snow and Snow, 1980).

7. Residential distribution of berylline hummingbird (races v = *viola*, b = *beryllina*, l = *lichtensteini*, d = *devillei*). Dot indicates location of extralimital breeding.

BERYLLINE HUMMINGBIRD

Amazilia beryllina (Lichtenstein)

Other Names	None in English use; Chupaflor de berilo, Chupaflor colicanelo (Spanish).
Range	Breeds in Mexico from southeastern Sonora and southern Chihuahua east to Veracruz and south through most of Mexico to western Honduras and El Salvador (Friedmann et al., 1950). Accidental in Arizona (Animas and Chiricahua Mountains). (See map 7.)
North American Subspecies	(Presumed.) *A. b. viola* (W. de W. Miller). Resident in the Sierra Madre Occidental from southeastern Sonora to Guerrero and east to eastern Michoacan.
Measurements	Of *A. b. viola*: Wing, males 52–57.5 mm (ave. of 14, 55.5 mm), females 50.5–55.5 mm (ave. of 10, 53.9 mm). Culmen, males 18–20.5 mm (ave. of 14, 19.1 mm), females 19–21 mm (ave. of 10, 20 mm) (Ridgway, 1911). Eggs, 13.5–13.7 × 8.5–8.8 mm (Rowley, 1966).
Weights	The average of 13 males was 4.87 g (range 4.4–5.7 g); that of 8 females was 4.37 g (range 4.0–4.8 g) (Delaware Museum of Natural History).
Description	(After Ridgway, 1911).

Adult male. Above bright metallic green or bronze-green, passing into duller purplish bronzy on rump, the upper tail-coverts rather violet to violet-purple; middle rectrices metallic purplish, violet, to bronzy purple; the remaining rectrices chestnut, tipped, or broadly margined at tip, with purplish bronze (this sometimes wanting or obsolete on outermost rectrix); secondaries chestnut, or dull rufous-chestnut, broadly tipped with dusky, the innermost ones (tertials) mostly of the latter color; primaries chestnut or dull rufous-chestnut, with terminal portion extensively dusky, faintly glossed with purplish; malar region, chin, throat, sides of neck, chest, breast, sides, flanks, and upper abdomen bright metallic green (brighter and more yellowish than grass green), the feathers of chin and throat abruptly grayish white, those of underparts of body dusky brownish gray, beneath surface; lower abdomen pale buffy gray, grayish cinnamon, or isabella color; femoral and lumbar tufts white; under tail-coverts pale chestnut broadly edged basally and (usually) narrowly margined terminally with white; maxilla dull black; mandible reddish basally, dusky at tip; iris dark brown; feet grayish brown or dusky.

Adult female. Similar to the adult male, but slightly duller in color, especially the underparts, nearly the whole abdomen being dull cinnamon-buffy, the feathers of chin and throat showing more or less the basal or subterminal white.

Identification   (See Plate 8E.)

In the hand. Differs from the two similar *Amazilia* species in that the bill is not strongly broadened at the base. Further, the green flanks and underparts set it apart from the other species, although in females these areas are duller and more brownish.

In the field. Associated with forest edges, banana groves, and coffee plantations in Mexico; in drier areas, associated with wooded streams. Although similar to the rufous-tailed and buff-bellied hummingbirds, these two species never have bright green underparts. Males are also more chestnut-colored on the rump, and especially on the upper wing surface. Only the lower mandible is reddish, compared to reddish upper and lower mandible color basally in the other two species. Females are duller and more like these in that the lower abdomen is grayish or brownish, but generally are somewhat brighter below than either of the two other species. The male's call is a surprisingly loud *bob-o-leek*!, audible for some distance (Ruth Green, personal communication).

Habitats   In Mexico the berylline hummingbird is common and widespread among the wooded highlands between 900 and 3000 meters, especially in rather dense pine, oak, or pine-oak woodlands, fir forests, open areas having scattered trees or shrubs, and suburban gardens or vacant lots (Edwards, 1973). It is abundant in Colima, and its ecological range includes the thorn forest, parts of the tropical deciduous forest, oak woodlands, and both arid and humid pine-oak forests (Schaldach, 1963).

Movements   Except at the northern edge of its range, this species is probably essentially a permanent resident, subject only to seasonal altitudinal movements. However, in Sonora it is evidently only a summer visitor in the oak-pine zone of the southeastern mountains at about 1500 meters (van Rossem, 1945).

   The few United States records of this species are all for Arizona from June 20 to the end of September. The first sighting was in Ramsey Canyon in the Huachuca Mountains, when an individual was seen from late June to early August 1967 (*Audubon Field Notes* 21:593). In 1971 a female was observed in Cave Creek Canyon of the Chiricahua Mountains from June 30 to August 1 (*American Birds* 25:890), and in 1975 a berylline was observed from June 27 onward through the summer in Ramsey Canyon. Finally, on July 13, 1976, a pair was discovered nesting there, and at least one young had hatched by July 22; however, the nest was found abandoned on August 16. The species was again found nesting in Ramsey Canyon the following year (Anderson and Monson, 1981). Finally, in 1979 the species was seen in Carr Canyon, adjacent to Ramsey Canyon, for the only Arizona record that year (*Continental Birds* 1:108).

Foraging Behavior and Floral Ecology

According to Des Granges (1979), the berylline hummingbird is a wandering but not migratory species that defends feeding territories. In his study area, Des Granges noted that it was a relatively generalist type of forager. During the summer months the social dominance of the amethyst-throated hummingbird prevented it from foraging at the best tubular flower (*Malvaviscus arboreus*) in the arid pine-oak habitat, so the berylline fed at *Calliandra anomala* instead. During the winter months, however, the amethyst-throated hummingbird became less common, allowing the berylline access to the *Malvaviscus*. In the riparian gallery forest habitat the birds also fed on tubular flowers such as *Psittacanthus calyculatus*, whereas in the arid thorn forest they were attracted to *Ceiba aesculifolia* and *Lemairocereus*.

Breeding Biology

Very few observations on the breeding of this species have been published. Rowley (1966) located nine nests in Oaxaca between July and October, five of them during September. An apparently favorite nesting site there is the shrub *Wigandia caracasana*. Its outer dead seed stalks offer ideal nesting sites, especially where the plant's large leaves provide overhead protection from heavy rains. However, other nests were found in different flowering shrubs, one almost 5 meters up in an oak and another at least 15 meters above ground on the horizontal branch of a pine.

All the nests were abundantly covered by lichens, producing a nearly solid pattern. With a single exception they also always had a "streamer" of grass blades attached to the bottom with spider webbing, resulting in a very distinctive appearance. One of the nests measured nearly 50 mm in outside diameter, with an inside cup diameter of slightly more than 26 mm; it was about 50 mm in depth, exclusive of the streamer.

The first U.S. nesting in Cave Creek Canyon was in a riparian habitat at 1634 meters elevation; the nest was on a slender branch of an Arizona sycamore (*Plantanus wrightii*), about 7.5 meters above the ground. The second nest, was in a similar habitat, at 1722 meters elevation in Ramsey Canyon, again located about 5.5 meters above ground in an Arizona sycamore. Both nests were covered with green leaf-like lichens and measured about 40 by 50 mm, with a cavity depth of 15 mm. The Ramsey Canyon nest is believed to have hatched between August 10 and 13, and the two young fledged on August 20 and September 1, suggesting a fledging period of about 20 days (Anderson and Monson, 1981).

Evolutionary and Ecological Relationships

This species is obviously a close relative of the buff-bellied and rufous-tailed hummingbird, and also of such forms as the blue-tailed hummingbird. Land (1970) noted that a Guatemalan population of the last-named species seems to represent an intermediate form, and thus perhaps the two should be considered conspecific. No definite hybrids are known, but the form described as *Amazilia ocai* may represent one involving the berylline hummingbird and the red-billed azurecrown (Berlioz, 1932).

Not enough information is known of its foraging ecology to comment on interspecific relationships of this species.

Genus *Lampornis* Swainson 1827

Synonyms: *?Lamprolaima* Reichenbach 1854

*T*his genus includes at least six species of Middle American hummingbirds that are relatively large (wing 65–75 mm) and have a blackish bill that is longer than the head, very faintly decurved, and a culmen that is rounded except basally, where it is contracted into a narrow ridge. The edge of the maxilla is smooth or minutely serrate toward the tip, and the nasal operculum is partially to mostly hidden by frontal feathering, which reaches nearly or beyond the end of the operculi, forming a short point on each side of the culmen. The wing is about three times as long as the exposed culmen, and the outermost primary is the longest. The tail is from more than half to three-fifths as long as the wing, is square-tipped to slightly forked in males, and is usually double-rounded in females. The rectrices are moderately broad, with rounded tips. The sexes are dimorphic; the adult males have iridescent throats ranging from green to purple or rosy, and the females have grayish throats and dark tails, often with gray or white markings.

BLUE-THROATED HUMMINGBIRD

Lampornis clemenciae (Lesson)

Other Names None in general English use; Chupamirto garganta azul (Spanish).

Range Breeds from the mountains of southern Arizona, New Mexico, and Texas south through the mountains of Mexico to Oaxaca. (See map 8.)

North American Subspecies (After Friedmann et al., 1950.)

L. c. bessophilus (Oberholser). Casual to uncommon summer resident in the mountains of southern Arizona (Huachucas and Chiricahuas) and southern New Mexico (San Luis Mountains), becoming fairly common at elevations of 2400–3000 meters in the Sierra Madre Occidental of western Mexico to northwestern Durango and southeastern Sinaloa; winters at lower elevations.

L. c. clemenciae (Lesson). Fairly common summer resident in the Chisos Mountains of southern Texas and scarce in the Guadalupe Mountains of the same state, becoming common southward through the mountains of the Central Plateau and Sierra Madre Oriental to Oaxaca at elevations of 1800–3300 meters; winters at lower elevations.

Measurements Wing, males 72–79 mm (ave. of 23, 76.7 mm), females 68.5–71 mm (ave. of 8, 69.7 mm). Culmen, males 21.5–25 mm (ave. of 23, 23.3 mm), females 24–27.5 mm (ave. of 8, 25.8 mm) (Ridgway, 1911). Eggs, ave. 16.3 × 9.9 mm (Bent, 1940, reports 16.23 × 12.45 mm for a single egg).

Weights The average of 190 males in Oaxaca was 8.4 g (standard deviation 0.4 g); that of 62 females was 6.8 g (standard deviation 0.4 g) (Lyon, 1976).

Description (After Ridgway, 1911.)

Adult male. Above rather dull metallic bronze-green, passing into olive-bronze or bronzy olive on rump, where the feathers have narrow terminal margins of pale brownish gray or buffy grayish; upper tail-coverts dusky (sometimes faintly glossed with greenish or bluish), narrowly and indistinctly margined with paler; tail black, faintly glossed with bluish, the outermost rectrix with terminal third (or less) abruptly white, the second less extensively tipped with white, the third usually with a small median white streak or mark (usually more or less fusiform or diamond-shaped) near tip; remiges dark brownish slate color or dusky, very faintly glossed with purplish; a conspicuous white postocular streak, ex-

127

8. Breeding (stippled), wintering (hatched), and residential (cross-hatched) distributions of blue-throated hummingbird (races b = *bessophilus*, c = *clemenciae*). Light stippling indicates area of migration or postbreeding movements.

128

tending obliquely backward and downward behind upper posterior margin of auricular region, the latter, together with the suborbital and loral regions, plain dusky; a more or less distinct
malar streak of whitish (this sometimes obsolete); chin and throat
metallic blue (varying from a greenish to a slightly violet hue),
the feathers very narrowly and indistinctly margined with brownish gray and with concealed portion of the latter color; rest of
underparts plain deep brownish gray or brownish slate color, the
under tail-coverts broadly margined with white; femoral and anal
tufts and tuft on each side of rump white; bill dull black; iris
dark brown; feet dusky.

Adult female. Similar to the adult male, but blue of throat replaced
by the general dull brownish gray of underparts.

Young female. Similar to the adult female, but the pileum duller,
the lower parts paler and more brownish, particularly on chin
and upper throat, which are dull cinnamon (Oberholser, 1974).

Identification   (See Plate 8F.)

In the hand. The large size (wing 68–80 mm) and the long, blackish, rounded bill (at least 21 mm long) separate the blue-throat
from all other North American species except the Rivoli hummingbird. Compared to that species, the blue-throated hummingbird has a more greenish tail, which is rather square-tipped in
males and somewhat rounded in females, and in both sexes has
white markings at the tips.

In the field. Found in wooded streams of mountain canyons amid
rather lush vegetation. The birds often utter loud, piercing *seep*
notes while perched or in flight, and frequently fan the tail to
reveal its green coloring and white tips. Although the female Rivoli hummingbird also has whitish tips on the tail, the area in
the blue-throat is larger and more pure white than in the Rivoli.

Habitats   In Texas this species occurs in streamside vegetation of desert
mountains, especially the Chisos Mountains, at elevations of 1500
to 2280 meters. There, it occurs among cypress (*Cupressus arizonica*), pines, oaks, and bigtooth maples in Boot Canyon, and
moves out to drier canyon slopes to feed at agave plants (Oberholser, 1974). In Arizona it resides in moist canyons of the Huachuca and Chiricahua Mountains, and perhaps also the Santa Catalina and Santa Rita Mountains (Phillips et al., 1964). In New
Mexico it is occasional in the southwest (San Luis Mountains)
and the Guadalupe Mountains, and rarely reaches the northern
highlands.

In Mexico the birds have a wide altitudinal range generally between 1800 and 3300 meters during the breeding season, locally
descending to 300 to 900 meters during winter (Friedmann, et al.,
1950). Wagner (1952) noted that it sometimes reaches the limit of
tree growth at about 3900 meters, and only in the coolest part of
the year does it descend below 1800 meters at the southern end
of its range.

Movements   The blue-throated hummingbird is a summer resident in the
United States, with only rare winter occurrences north of Mexico.
In Texas its spring migration is from March 18 to May 22, and its
fall migration occurs between August 18 and October 24. There
are a few December and early January records for the Rio Grande
area (Oberholser, 1974). The earliest Arizona record is for early
April, but nests with eggs have been found only a few weeks
later.

Postbreeding vagrants probably account for most of the extralimital sightings of this species. These include several late summer or fall sightings along the coast of Texas, an early September
sighting near Denver, Colorado (*American Birds* 25:85), and a possible fall sighting in Utah (*American Birds* 27:94).

In various parts of Mexico the species is either a migratory or a
resident form; Wagner (1952) summarized the details of their seasonal occurrence. In the Mexican highlands and adjoining valleys
both sexes appear simultaneously between the last days of April
and the middle of May. Males immediately establish display territories, while females fly about until the rainy season begins in
late May or June and there is no longer a shortage of food in
breeding areas. The sexes are somewhat separated during the
breeding season: The males move into higher mountain levels
above the firs and among the pines and bushgrasses, where
flowering lupines are abundant; the females move to nesting territories with available overhanging nest sites, often in ravines or
valleys. These tend to be fairly well-separated, but when conditions require, the birds will associate with one another and other
hummingbirds' groves with an abundance of purple penstemons
(*P. campanulatus*) and forest rims where mints (*Salvia cardinalis, S.
elegans, S. genaereflora, Lamourouxia exerta*) occur.

Foraging Behavior   According to Wagner (1952), blue-throated hummingbirds live
and Floral Ecology   largely on insects, spiders, and plant lice. The particular color of
the plant is not important to them, but the form of the flower
determines to a great degree the kind of hummingbird that visits
it. Thus, the small *Salvia mexicana*, although visited often by
smaller hummingbird species, is utilized little by this one. On the
other hand, *S. cardinalis* has a considerably larger blossom and is
a highly favored food plant of the blue-throat in Mexico.

Marshall (1957) noted that in Arizona this species feeds at *Penstemon, Lobelia laxiflora*, and *Nicotiana*; in New Mexico it takes insects from the flowers of the shrubby honeysuckle, gilia, agave,
and other plants (Bailey, 1928). On the basis of an analysis of
three stomachs, Cottam and Knappen (1939) reported that the
animal foods include hemipterans, small beetles, flies, wasps,
spiders, and daddy-longlegs. The stomachs also contained pollen
grains and plant fibers.

In a study in the Chisos Mountains, Kuban and Neill (1980)
found that this species was the most abundant hummingbird in
the cypress-pine-oak habitat of their study area, and males defended elongated territories that paralleled Boot Creek. During

the mornings they often foraged outside their territories in sur-
rounding juniper woodlands, where nectar sources were more
abundant prior to late June. When foraging on their territories in
early June the birds ate only insects, which they captured by
gleaning from vegetation as well as hawking them in the sage.
When sage flowers became available in mid-July, the birds occasionally fed at them, but insects continued to dominate their diet
throughout the summer.

In the Oaxaca area, Lyon (1976) observed that the blue-throat
was the most successful of six major hummingbird species in
terms of the number and sizes of territories maintained and the
amount of preferred food plants (*Penstemon kunthii*) it dominated.
However, in a year when Rivoli hummingbirds were abundant,
they effectively displaced the blue-throats in all open meadows,
but were unable to do so in forest edge or open forest areas.

Breeding Biology   In Arizona, the breeding period of this species is relatively short;
available egg records extend from April 22 to July 17 (Bent, 1940;
Brandt, 1951). The timing of breeding in Mexico probably varies
considerably by area. Eggs have been found in Veracruz in February; young have been found in Colima in March; and in the
vicinity of Mexico City the eggs are laid between late June and
late September with a peak in July and August (Wagner, 1952).

To a greater degree than any other North American species of
hummingbird, female blue-throats seek out nesting sites that are
completely covered from above, such as in vertical-walled canyons, rock overhangs, or even under the roofs of such structures
as bunkhouses or old barns. Brandt (1951) described a remarkable
nest found in Ramsey Canyon, underneath a house built over a
running stream. What was presumably the same female had occupied this nest for at least 10 years, and produced up to three
broods per season in it. In 1944 the female began renovating it
on April 13. The first egg was laid on April 27, followed by a
second egg two days later. When completed, the nest measured
127 mm high by 63 mm in diameter; when Brandt collected it on
June 24 after the fledging of the young, he estimated that it consisted of some 24,000 kilometers of spider and insect thread! The
female immediately began to construct a new nest, and by July
10 had deposited two eggs in it. Although this apparent 10-year
lifespan is remarkable, even more impressive is a report of the
apparent survival for 12 years of a single distinctive but unbanded male (Edgarton et al., 1951).

In Arizona, as apparently also in Mexico, males and females
are not closely associated during the nesting period; the males
occupy higher levels of the mountains. The nests also are fairly
well spaced; Wagner (1952) diagramed the locations of five nests
along a stream. The total distance between the two most widely
separated nests was 250 meters, or an average inter-nest distance
of about 60 meters. Foraging areas of the females did not apparently overlap.

When defending feeding areas, males often exhibit both intraspecific and interspecific aggressive behavior, and they nearly always dominate smaller species such as violet-crowned, black-chinned, and even Rivoli hummingbirds. During such encounters the strongly patterned undertail surface is fanned and exposed, and this feature may be an important aspect of species recognition (Rising, 1965). The territorial call of the male is a loud *seep*, distinctly different from the *chip* call of the Rivoli (Marshall, 1957). Evidently males are able to make clear distinctions between species during interspecific encounters (Lyon et al., 1977).

The shape of the nest varies considerably in this species, especially in its total depth. Wagner reported that the dimensions of the nest cup and outer nest diameter were fairly consistent, but that the total depth of 10 nests measured by him ranged from 4 to 11.5 centimeters. Depending on the size of the nest, it may take the female from 15 to 30 days to construct it, based on Wagner's observations.

The materials used in nest construction, other than spider webbing, also vary considerably. They may include oak blossom hulls, mosses, coarse straws, stems of weeds, and other materials. Sometimes the nests are decorated externally with lichens or other vegetation. They are often supported mostly from one side or the rim, and rarely are suspended from above, with a nearly lateral opening. The two eggs, laid approximately 48 hours apart, average 0.74 grams each (Wagner, 1952).

Incubation requires from 17 to 18 days, and an additional 24 to 29 days are needed to bring the nestlings to fledging. By the 10th day after hatching the eyes are opening, and by the 12th day the feathers of the back are starting to emerge. The young are alternately brooded and fed until about the 12th day, and after 16 days the weight of the young is typically greater than that of the adult. The young are fully feathered after about 24 days, but at that age the bill-length is appreciably shorter than that of the parent bird (Wagner, 1952).

Evolutionary and Ecological Relationships

Mayr and Short (1970) did not identify the blue-throated hummingbird's nearest relatives. Ridgway (1911) placed the species in a monotypic genus (*Cyanolaemus*), separating it from the more typical *Lampornis* by its bill shape, which is relatively less depressed and narrower basally. Certainly the species can be easily included within *Lampornis*, and probably it is a close relative of the amethyst-throated hummingbird, which ranges from Mexico to Honduras. Apparently the only known hybrid is a still unidentified specimen involving the Costa or possibly the Anna hummingbird (Mayr and Short, 1970).

The very large size of this species effectively allows it to dominate most other hummingbirds with which it comes into contact (Kuban and Neill, 1980; Lyon, 1976). On the other hand, it is unable to use some of the smaller flowers, such as those of *Salvia mexicana* (Wagner, 1952). Nor can it exploit those that are low in nectar production, such as *Penstemon perfoliatus* and *P. gentianoides* (Lyon, 1976), even though these may be regularly used by smaller species of hummingbirds.

Genus *Heliodoxa* Gould 1850

Synonyms: *Eugenes* Gould 1856

*T*his genus includes about nine species of Middle and South American hummingbirds that are relatively large (wing 50–70 mm), with a stout blackish bill that is as long or longer than the head and slightly decurved, and with a culmen that is rounded except basally, where it is contracted into a narrow ridge. The edge of the upper mandible is smooth, and the narrow nasal operculum is hidden by frontal feathering that extends well beyond the front end of the nostrils, forming a distinct point. The feathering of the chin also extends well forward. The wing is three to four times the length of the exposed culmen, with the outermost primary the longest. The tail of adult males ranges from slightly to deeply forked, and is double-rounded or slightly forked in females. The sexes are dimorphic, and males of most species have a throat patch of blue, purple, or violet; likewise males of most (and females of some) have the forehead and crown iridescent. In females the underparts are grayish to whitish, often spotted with bright iridescent green, and with the lateral rectrices tipped with whitish or grayish. Although "*Eugenes*" has a less distinctly forked tail than do the typical species of *Heliodoxa*, it is clearly a member of this genus (Zimmer, 1951).

9. Breeding (stippled) and residential (cross-hatched) distributions of Rivoli hummingbird (races f = *fulgens*, v = *viridiceps*). Light stippling indicates area of postbreeding movements; dot indicates an extralimital breeding record.

RIVOLI HUMMINGBIRD

Heliodoxa fulgens (Swainson)
(*Eugenes fulgens* of AOU, 1957)

Other Names Magnificent hummingbird; Chupamirto verde montero, Chupaflor magnifico (Spanish).

Range Breeds from the mountains of southern Arizona and southwestern New Mexico south through Middle America to western Panama. Northern populations winter in Mexico. (See map 9.)

North American Subspecies (After Friedmann et al., 1950.)

H. f. fulgens Boucard. Breeds in the mountains of southern Arizona (north to the Grahams and Santa Catalinas), southwestern New Mexico (San Luis Mountains), and southwestern Texas (Chisos Mountains), south through the mountains of Mexico (usually from 1500–3300 meters) to the Isthmus of Panama. Has bred rarely in Colorado.

Measurements Wing, males 69.5–76 mm (ave. of 31, 73 mm), females 66.5–70.5 mm (ave. of 14, 68.7 mm). Culmen, males 25.5–31 mm (ave. of 31, 27.4 mm), females 27–30.5 mm (ave. of 14, 29.1 mm) (Ridgway, 1911). Eggs, ave. 15.4 × 10.2 mm (extremes 14–16.5 × 9.4–11.4 mm).

Weights The average of 119 males was 7.7 g (standard deviation 0.4 g); that of 24 females was 6.4 g (standard deviation 0.5 g), in Oaxaca (Lyon, 1976).

Description (After Ridgway, 1911.)

Adult male. Pileum rich metallic violet or royal purple, the forehead (at least anteriorly) blackish, usually glossed with green or bluish green; hindneck sides of occiput, and auricular region velvety black in position *a* (see note at beginning of Part Two for position descriptions), metallic bronze, bronze-green, or golden green in position *c*; rest of upperparts metallic bronze, bronze-green, or golden green, including tail, the latter sometimes with rectrices passing into pale grayish at tip; remiges dark brownish slate or dusky, faintly glossed with purple or purplish bronze; chin and throat brilliant metallic emerald green (more yellowish in position *a*, more bluish in position *b*), this brilliant green area extending much farther backward laterally than medially; chest and upper breast velvety black in position *a* (bronze or bronze-green in position *c*), passing into dusky bronze or bronze-green on lower breast, this into grayish brown or sooty grayish on abdomen and flanks; femoral and anal tufts white; a small white postocular spot or streak (sometimes a whitish malar streak also); under tail-coverts light brownish gray (sometimes glossed with

135

bronze or bronze-green), margined (more or less distinctly) with whitish; bill dull black; iris dark brown; feet dusky.

Adult female. Above, including four middle rectrices, metallic bronze, bronze-green, or golden green, the pileum duller (sometimes dull grayish brown anteriorly); three outer rectrices (on each side) with basal half more or less bronze-green, then black, the tip brownish gray or grayish brown, this broadest on outermost rectrix, much smaller on third; remiges as in adult male; postocular streak of white and below this a dusky auricular area; underparts brownish gray or buffy grayish, glossed laterally with metallic bronze or bronze-green, the feathers of chin and throat margined with paler or with dull grayish white, producing a squamate appearance; femoral and anal tufts white; under tail-coverts brownish gray (sometimes glossed with bronze-green), margined with pale brownish gray or dull whitish; bill, etc., as in adult male.

Immature male. Intermediate in coloration between the adult male and adult female, the crown partly violet, the throat only partly green, and chest slightly intermixed with black, the tail exactly intermediate, both in form and color.

Young female. Similar to the adult female, but feathers of upperparts narrowly margined terminally with pale grayish buffy, and underparts slightly darker and suffused, more or less, with pale brownish buffy.

Identification

(See Plate 8G.)

In the hand. A large (wing at least 65 mm) hummingbird notable for its long, blackish bill (25–30 mm), which is rounded rather than widened at the base, and its fairly long, greenish-black tail, which is slightly forked in males and rather square-tipped in females. The similar-sized blue-throated hummingbird has a more bluish tail, which is squared-off in males and slightly rounded in females.

In the field. Associated with oak or pine forests and (in Middle America) cloud forests, especially near forest edges or thinned woods, where they perch low in shrubby or thickety growth mixed with trees. Male's small white postocular spot resembles a staring eye (Slud, 1964). It may be distinguished from the blue-throated hummingbird by its tail, which is blackish and slightly forked in males, and greenish with white corners in females. Its call is a thin sharp *chip*.

Habitats

In Arizona, Rivoli hummingbirds occur commonly during summer among the maples of the lower mountain streams, and extend upward from 1500 to 2250 meters on mountain slopes to the ponderosa pine zone, with males occasionally reaching the edge of the fir zone (Bent, 1940; Phillips et al., 1964). In the Huachuca Mountains the birds are probably most common at the lower edge of the pine belt, where flowering agaves are relatively abundant. Likewise in the Chiricahua Mountains they are common in more open parts of the ponderosa pine forest, such as where fire has killed some of the trees and where flowering plants such as penstemons and honeysuckles (*Lonicera involucrata*) are in blossom (Bent, 1940).

In New Mexico, the species has been found during summer at about 2000 meters in the San Luis Mountains (Ligon, 1961). It also locally summers in mountainous areas of the northern and western portions of the state, from the fir forest zone down into evergreen and adjacent riparian wooded habitats. During migration it also occurs in intervening lowland and residential areas (Hubbard, 1978). Very rarely the species also summers in the mountains of Colorado, and there is a single nesting record for Boulder County (Bailey and Niedrach, 1965).

In Texas it occurs uncommonly between 1800 and 2300 meters in the Chisos Mountains during summer and probably breeds there, although nests have not been found. In these mountains the species favors the pinyon-juniper-oak zone, and occurs in somewhat higher and drier habitats than those typical of bluethroated hummingbirds (Oberholser, 1974; Wauer, 1973).

In Mexico, Rivoli hummingbirds generally range from 1500 to 3300 meters, occasionally descending as low as 900 meters (Friedmann et al., 1950). In Guatemala they occur from 900 to 2600 meters in cloud forest and woodlands of oaks or pines (Land, 1970). In Honduras, they inhabit cloud forests above 1000 meters, and occasionally pine-oak vegetation or scrubby growth (Monroe, 1968). In El Salvador they occur between 2100 and 2400 meters among oaks, pines, and rocky areas containing agaves (Dickey and van Rossem, 1938).

In Costa Rica the species extends from timberline down to 2100 meters, and occasionally as low as 1500 meters. There it is mainly associated with forest edges, breaks in woodlands, parklike pastures, and thinned woods, and is scarce in dense forests (Slud, 1964). At the southern end of its range in western Panama it is found on volcanic slopes from 1550 to 2300 meters elevation (Wetmore, 1968).

Movements   In Arizona, Rivoli hummingbirds have been recorded as early as April 5 and as late as November 11 (Phillips et al., 1964), but they probably normally arrive in the state in the latter part of April. They usually occur in Texas from early April until late September, but have been reported from March 30 to October 12 (Oberholser, 1974). They have been observed in the New Mexico from May through October, but have also rarely been seen in the Sandia Mountains during winter months (Hubbard, 1978; Ligon, 1961).

Postbreeding movements of adults or immatures are probably responsible for many of the extralimital records of this species in the United States. Thus it has been reported at least once during late summer from Nevada (*American Birds* 30:103) and Utah (*American Birds* 25:885) and several times from Colorado throughout the summer months from late June to September 6 (Bailey and Niedrach, 1965).

Farther south in Mexico and Central America the species is probably not markedly migratory, but at least in some areas the birds evidently move to lower altitudes during the nonbreeding season (Land, 1970).

Foraging Behavior and Floral Ecology

According to Des Granges (1979), this species is "trapliner" rather than territorial. In Colima it was found to forage largely on thistles (*Cirsium* sp.), but visited isolated clumps of flowers along its trapline as well, especially the tubular flowers of *Penstemon roseus*. It also is apparently associated with *Lobelia laxiflora* in more arid environments.

In a study area in Oaxaca, Lyon (1976) found that males of this species occupied feeding territories that averaged about 720 square meters in area, compared with slightly smaller territories in females. These territories were second only in size to those held by male blue-throated hummingbirds, and collectively the two species dominated the areas containing the richest nectar sources. They partitioned such areas on the basis of habitat. In one year a large population of Rivoli hummingbirds managed to displace the slightly larger blue-throats from all their territories in open meadows, but were unable to do so in meadow-forest edge habitats or in open forest areas. Both species foraged primarily on *Penstemon kunthii*, which blooms from May to October and provides the richest single source of available nectar in the area.

In a Costa Rica tropical highland habitat, Wolf, Stiles, and Hainsworth (1976) found that individuals of this species spent 84 percent of their foraging effort at the blossoms of only two species (*Centropogon talamanensis* and *Cirsium subcoriaceum*); these plants accounted for 99 percent of the territoriality records. A small amount of foraging was done at the flowers of *Bomarea costaricensis* and *Fushsia splendens* as well. In this area, as in Oaxaca, the species was territorial rather than trapliner.

Marshall (1957) reported that this species often captures insects near tree foliage, especially sycamores and Apache pines. Although riparian woodland is its preferred habitat, Marshall observed that it is sometimes found quite far from water, and when necessary can be independent of nectar sources. It is especially attracted to agaves (*A. americana* and *A. parryi*), the flowers of which are rich in insect life. Moreover, it forages on penstemons, honeysuckles, scarlet salvias, irises, and planted scarlet geraniums, as well as blossoms of *Erythrina corallodendrum* (Toledo, 1974). A sample of three stomachs included a large variety of insect life, including leaf bugs, plant lice, leafhoppers, parasitic wasps, beetles, flies, moth fragments, and a considerable number of spiders (Cottam and Knappen, 1939).

When not actually feeding, the birds seem to spend an unusual amount of time perched relatively high in tall or dead-topped trees, where they are prominently outlined against the sky (Dickey and van Rossem, 1938). However, Slud (1964) stated that the birds often perch and forage fairly low in shrubby or thickety growth, and Edwards (1973) stated that they often perch on inner tree branches within 4 to 6 meters of the ground.

Breeding Biology   In Arizona the nesting season is fairly short. Bent (1940) lists 24 egg records extending from May 6 to July 28, with half of these between June 14 and July 14. Birds either breeding or in breeding condition have been found in Mexico from March to November (Friedmann et al., 1950). Similarly, in Guatemala the nonbreeding season extends from December to February (Land, 1970). In El Salvador, however, breeding probably occurs during the winter months, although year-round breeding is also a possibility (Dickey and van Rossem, 1938).

Rivoli hummingbirds place their nests fairly high in trees. Of six nest sites mentioned by Bent (1940), the total range was from 3 to 16 meters above ground, and the average was 9 meters. A variety of trees are used as substrates, including cottonwood, mountain maple, sycamore, alder, walnut, pine, and Douglas fir, with none seemingly preferred over the others.

The nests are usually saddled on horizontal branches that may be smaller in diameter than the nest itself. They are usually slightly more than 50 mm in outside diameter and 50 mm in total depth, with a cup slightly more than 25 mm wide. They resemble those of the ruby-throated hummingbird, but are generally larger, proportionately broader, and not so high. The nests are composed of mosses and other soft vegetation, lined internally with plant down or soft feathers, and externally decorated with lichens that sometimes nearly "shingle" the entire outer surface. In one observed case, the birds required a week to build a nest and lay two eggs (Bent, 1940).

There is no information available on the incubation period, the development of the young, or the fledging period.

Evolutionary and Ecological Relationships   Although the Rivoli is usually considered a monotypic genus (or sometimes of two species, with the Middle American form *H. f. spectabilis* separated specifically), Zimmer (1951) has urged the merger of *Eugenes* into the fairly large genus *Heliodoxa*. I have followed this procedure here, and it seems entirely consistent with a broad generic concept. However, Wetmore (1968) has suggested that such a merger is premature on the basis of available information.

In any case, it seems likely that the nearest relatives of *H. f. fulgens* are among the species of the genus *Heliodoxa*. Further, the genus *Lampornis* is probably not far removed from this cluster of species. Short and Phillips (1966) have also suggested that *Amazilia* and "*Eugenes*" are probably not as distantly related to one another as most current classifications suggest. The only known hybrid involving the Rivoli hummingbird is with the broad-billed hummingbird (Short and Phillips, 1966).

Nothing specific can be said about the ecological relationships of the Rivoli hummingbird. Certainly it locally overlaps with and presumably competes with the blue-throated hummingbird. But the blue-throat is a slightly larger species than the Rivoli, which would probably place the latter at a competitive disadvantage.

Genus *Heliomaster* Bonaparte 1850

*T*his genus includes four species of Central and South American hummingbirds that are medium to fairly large in size (wing 55–65 mm), with unusually long and straight to slightly decurved black bills, which become broader and more depressed at the base, and a rounded culmen that contracts basally into a narrow ridge. The mandible is smooth-edged, and the nasal operculum is mostly nude, with frontal feathering extending to or beyond the middle of the operculum. The wing is less than twice as long as the exposed culmen, and the outermost primary is the longest. The tail is about half as long as the wing and is square-tipped to slightly rounded, and the rectrices are sometimes tipped with white. The sexes are similar, being bronze, greenish bronze, or bronze-green above, or olive-colored with a bronze gloss, and often with a white spot or streak on the rump. The underpart coloration is highly variable, but males have a reddish to violet gorget, which is lacking in females or replaced with dusky spotting. In some species the pileum of the male is also bright metallic blue or green.

10. Residential distribution of plain-capped starthroat (races p = *pinicola*, l = *leocadiae*, c = *constantii*).

142

PLAIN-CAPPED STARTHROAT

Heliomaster constantii (DeLattre)

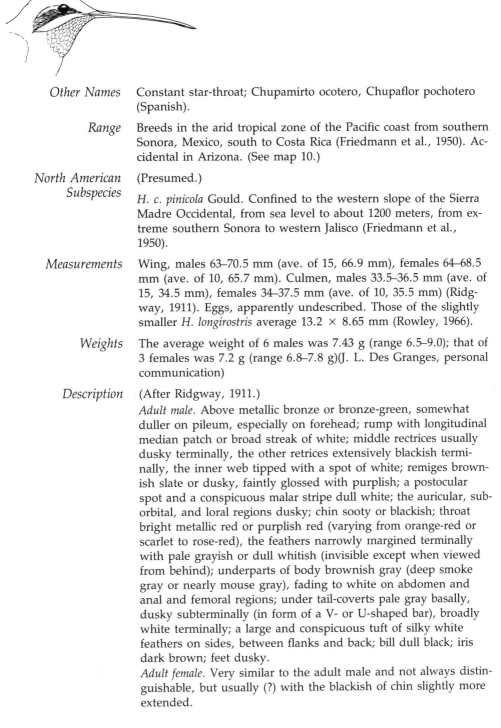

Other Names Constant star-throat; Chupamirto ocotero, Chupaflor pochotero (Spanish).

Range Breeds in the arid tropical zone of the Pacific coast from southern Sonora, Mexico, south to Costa Rica (Friedmann et al., 1950). Accidental in Arizona. (See map 10.)

North American Subspecies (Presumed.)

H. c. pinicola Gould. Confined to the western slope of the Sierra Madre Occidental, from sea level to about 1200 meters, from extreme southern Sonora to western Jalisco (Friedmann et al., 1950).

Measurements Wing, males 63–70.5 mm (ave. of 15, 66.9 mm), females 64–68.5 mm (ave. of 10, 65.7 mm). Culmen, males 33.5–36.5 mm (ave. of 15, 34.5 mm), females 34–37.5 mm (ave. of 10, 35.5 mm) (Ridgway, 1911). Eggs, apparently undescribed. Those of the slightly smaller *H. longirostris* average 13.2 × 8.65 mm (Rowley, 1966).

Weights The average weight of 6 males was 7.43 g (range 6.5–9.0); that of 3 females was 7.2 g (range 6.8–7.8 g)(J. L. Des Granges, personal communication)

Description (After Ridgway, 1911.)
Adult male. Above metallic bronze or bronze-green, somewhat duller on pileum, especially on forehead; rump with longitudinal median patch or broad streak of white; middle rectrices usually dusky terminally, the other retrices extensively blackish terminally, the inner web tipped with a spot of white; remiges brownish slate or dusky, faintly glossed with purplish; a postocular spot and a conspicuous malar stripe dull white; the auricular, suborbital, and loral regions dusky; chin sooty or blackish; throat bright metallic red or purplish red (varying from orange-red or scarlet to rose-red), the feathers narrowly margined terminally with pale grayish or dull whitish (invisible except when viewed from behind); underparts of body brownish gray (deep smoke gray or nearly mouse gray), fading to white on abdomen and anal and femoral regions; under tail-coverts pale gray basally, dusky subterminally (in form of a V- or U-shaped bar), broadly white terminally; a large and conspicuous tuft of silky white feathers on sides, between flanks and back; bill dull black; iris dark brown; feet dusky.
Adult female. Very similar to the adult male and not always distinguishable, but usually (?) with the blackish of chin slightly more extended.

143

Immature. Similar to adults, but greater part (sometimes whole) of throat dark sooty brown or dusky, the feathers margined terminally with grayish white.

Young. Similar to the immature plumage, as described above, but feathers of upperparts narrowly tipped or margined terminally with buffy.

Identification   (See Plate 8H.)

In the hand. Very large size (wing more than 60 mm) and long bill (culmen 33–38 mm) eliminate all other North American species; moreover, the tail feathers are broadly tipped with white.

In the field. Associated with arid scrubby lowlands, woodland borders, dry woods, plantations, and the like. Its very large size, long bill, and broadly white-tipped tail are distinctive. There is also a streak of white in the rump, a white malar stripe, and a throat that is sometimes glittering red (males) or spotted with dusky (females). Both sexes have dark grayish underparts. These birds often hawk for insects. While they are in flight, and sometimes while perched, a tuft of white flank feathers may be visible near the posterior edge of the wing.

Habitats   In Mexico this species occurs in scrubby, rather arid woodlands, woodland edges, partially open country with scattered trees or thickets, and scrubby riparian woodland, from sea level to 1500 meters (Edwards, 1973). In Colima it is found from the thorn forest zone to the upper edges of the tropical deciduous forest, but is most common in the denser thorn forest zone (Schaldach, 1963).

Movements   Since the plain-capped starthroat is essentially tropical in distribution, it probably undergoes relatively few seasonal movements. In Sonora it is essentially a resident species, but van Rossem (1945) suggested that there may be a partial exodus from there during the winter months.

Postbreeding wandering has perhaps accounted for the few records of this species in the United States, all of which have occurred in Arizona. The first reported individual visited a feeder in Nogales during late September 1969. In 1978 an individual was seen at a feeder in Patagonia, Arizona, between July 15 and 20. Earlier that year a possible sighting of the species was made on June 17 in Sycamore Canyon, west of Nogales, and on June 24 a similar sighting was made southwest of Patagonia. These sightings all occurred close to the Mexican border, about 500 kilometers north of the species' known range limits in Sonora. Finally, in Phoenix, well to the north of these observations, an individual frequented a yard feeder from October 17 to November 28, 1978 (Witzeman, 1979), and on June 28, 1980, an individual was observed near Sierra Vista (*American Birds* 34:919).

Foraging Behavior and Floral Ecology   Almost nothing is known of the foraging ecology of the plain-capped starthroat. According to Des Granges (1979), it resides in the Volcan de Colima area, and has exhibited feeding territoriality there. It showed a moderate degree of social dominance with other species, but almost throughout the entire year it fed nearly exclusively on aerial arthropods; during the short blooming period of *Ceiba aesculifolia,* however, nectar-feeding occupied nearly all of its time. This species frequently catches insects while flying close to the ground above roads or wide trails, and otherwise tends to perch quietly 4 to 6 meters above ground (Edwards, 1973).

Although his observations deal with the long-billed starthroat, Skutch (1972) has noted that starthroats are particularly fond of the flowers of the poro tree (*Erythrina*), which have long, slender red standards that the birds' long bills are particularly well adapted to probe. They also are attracted to the similarly long white corollas of bananas.

Breeding Biology
There is apparently no description available of the nest or breeding activities of this species, but Skutch (1972) has provided a fairly detailed description of the breeding biology of the closely related long-billed starthroat, which may provide a clue to the probable situation in the plain-capped starthroat: Breeding in the long-billed starthroat occurs during the early part of the dry season, between November and February. The nest is a shallow bowl, placed in a very exposed location. Nests have been found in shrubs and trees from 2 to 15 meters above the ground, usually attached to the upper side of a bend in a small horizontal branch about 25 mm in diameter. The nest is constructed of fine vegetational materials, fastened down to the branch with cobwebs, and decorated on the outside with a few lichens or small pieces of bark. One nest had an external diameter of nearly 50 mm and a cavity slightly more than 25 mm in width and depth (Rowley, 1966).

Skutch (1972) determined that in one nest the first egg was laid 8 days after the nest was finished, and the second egg was laid 2 days later. The incubation period was 18.5 to 19 days, with only the female incubating. The nestlings were hatched fewer than 24 hours apart, and they fledged when they were 25 and 26 days old. Nocturnal brooding ceased when the young were only 10 days old, but they continued to be fed for a surprisingly long period after they left the nest, at least until they were 48 days old.

Evolutionary and Ecological Relationships
The two Central American species of starthroats are so similar to one another that they may constitute a superspecies, with the plain-capped starthroat occupying more arid and westerly portions of Mexico and Central America and the long-billed starthroat adapted to more humid lowlands, extending southward to Brazil.

The unusually long and decurved bills of the starthroats approach those of the hermit hummingbirds, and perhaps these species compete locally to some extent. However, at least the plain-capped starthroat is strongly insectivorous, and does not normally defend feeding territories (Des Granges, 1979).

Genus *Calothorax* Gray 1840

Synonyms: *Doricha* Reichenbach 1854, *Philodice* Mulsant and Verreaux 1865, *Nesophlox* Ridgway 1910, *?Calliphlox* Boie 1831, *?Tilmatura* Reichenbach 1849, *?Thaumastura* Bonaparte 1850

*T*his genus includes at least seven and perhaps as many as ten species of Middle and South American and West Indian hummingbirds that are fairly small (wing usually less than 40 mm) and have a blackish bill that ranges from long, slender, and decurved to fairly short and nearly straight. The culmen is rounded except basally, where it forms a rather indistinct ridge; the edge of the maxilla is smooth; and the operculum is covered by frontal feathering, which extends beyond the end of the nostrils. The outer primary is the longest, and is sometimes narrowed in adult males. The tail is usually deeply forked in males and forked, rounded, or double-rounded in females, but with none of the rectrices narrowed or modified in shape. The sexes are dimorphic; the adult male usually has a red to purple gorget and a white breast, and the female is usually tinged with cinnamon below and with white or cinnamon tips on the outer tail feathers. The genus is probably closely related to the woodstars (*Acestrura*, in a broad sense), and the forked-tail condition is an unreliable indication of relationships.

11. Breeding (stippled) and residential (cross-hatched) distributions of lucifer hummingbird, and residential (hatched) distribution of Bahama woodstar.

LUCIFER HUMMINGBIRD
Calothorax lucifer (Swainson)

Other Names	None in general English use; Chupamirto morada grande (Spanish).
Range	Breeds in southwestern Texas (Chisos Mountains) southward through central and southern Mexico to Guerrero, mostly at elevations of 1200 to 2250 meters. Migratory at northern end of the range. Has bred in southern Arizona, and probably a regular breeder in adjacent Sonora. (See map 11.)
North American Subspecies	None recognized.
Measurements	Wing, males 36–39 mm (ave. of 10, 37.6 mm), females 39–44 mm (ave. of 8, 41.2 mm). Exposed culmen, males 19.5–22 mm (ave. of 10, 21.1 mm), females 20–22.5 mm (ave. of 8, 21.2 mm) (Ridgway, 1911). Eggs, ave. 12.7 × 9.7 mm (extremes 12.0–13.8 × 9.2–10.1 mm).
Weights	The average weight of 2 males was 2.75 g (range 2.2–3.3 g); that of 5 females was 3.08 g (range 2.7–3.5 g) (J. L. Des Granges, personal communication and specimen in Museum of Comparative Zoology).
Description	(After Ridgway, 1911.)

Adult male. Above metallic bronze, bronze-green, or golden green, usually duller on pileum, especially on forehead; remiges dull brownish slate or dusky, faintly glossed with purplish; four middle rectrices metallic green or bronze-green, the rest of tail purplish or bronzy dusky or blackish; a small postocular spot (sometimes also a rictal spot) of dull whitish; chin and throat brilliant metallic solferino or magenta purple, changing to violet, the posterior feathers of sides of throat much elongated; chest dull white; sides and flanks mixed light cinnamon and metallic bronze or bronze-green, the median portion of breast and abdomen pale grayish or dull grayish white; under tail-coverts dull white with central area of pale brownish gray; femoral tufts white; bill dull black; iris dark brown; feet dusky.

Adult female. Above as in adult male but lateral rectrices much broader, the three outermost (on each side) with basal half (approximately) light cinnamon-rufous, then (distally) purplish black, the two outermost broadly tipped with white, the black terminal or subterminal area on second and third separated from the cinnamon-rufous of basal portion by a narrow space of metallic bronze-green; fourth rectrix (from outside) mostly metallic

149

bronze-green but terminal or subterminal portion blackish and outer web edged basally with light cinnamon-rufous; a postocular spot or streak of cinnamon-buff, and beneath this a narrow auricular area of grayish brown; malar region and underparts dull light vinaceous-cinnamon or cinnamon-buff, passing into dull whitish on abdomen; the under tail-coverts mostly (sometimes almost wholly) whitish; femoral tufts white; bill, etc., as in adult male.

Young male (first winter). Similar to adult female including broader tail feathers, but darker above and below, size smaller, throat with some metallic purple feathers (Oberholser, 1974).

Young female (first winter). Similar to adult female (Oberholser, 1974).

Identification

(See Plate 8A.)

In the hand. Unique among North American hummingbirds in having a blackish (culmen 19–22 mm) bill that is more than half as long as the wing and distinctly decurved. The underparts are buffy to pale buff, the tail of the male is deeply forked; that of the female is rounded, with a tawny base and white tips.

In the field. Inhabits open desert-like country, often where agaves are abundant, and the long and decurved bill is the best field-mark for both sexes. The male is about the same size as the Costa hummingbird, but has a deeply forked tail and lacks red color on the forehead. The female resembles several other hummingbirds but, apart from the longer bill, the pale cinnamon-buff underparts and the tawny color at the base of the tail are fairly distinctive. The birds utter shrill, piercing shrieks when defending their nest; other calls have not been described.

Habitats

In the Chisos Mountains of the Big Bend area of Texas, lucifer hummingbirds occur from May through early July on the open desert or on the slopes of the mountains up to about 1500 meters. During late July and early August, after breeding, the birds begin to move upward into various canyons such as Boot Canyon at 1900 meters (Wauer, 1973). They sometimes occur at higher altitudes as well; as many as 10 individuals have been seen near the South Rim of these mountains at about 2200 meters in mid-July (Fox, 1954). Actual nests in the area have been found from 1100 to 1500 meters. The first Texas nests were found in a desert-like habitat dominated by agave (*A. lechuguilla*), sotal (*Dasylirion leophyllum*), and ocotillo (*Fouquieria splendens*) (Pulich and Pulich, 1963). Associated plants included candelilla (*Euphorbia antisyphilitica*), catclaw (*Acacia greggii*), mormon tea (*Ephedra*), yuccas (*Yucca* sp.), and cacti. Blooming cacti provided the principal source of food during the unusually late nesting observed by the Pulichs.

In northern Sonora, 30 females were found along a 3-kilometer stretch of Arroyo Cajon Bonito at about 1200-meter elevations. There they nested among sycamores and hackberries and foraged from streamside upward along the drier upper slopes where agaves were in flower (Russell and Lamm, 1978). More generally in Mexico the species is found in open country having scattered trees and shrubs and among brushy vegetation in arid areas. There is no special marked preference for any particular species of plant nor for any specific altitudinal zone (Wagner, 1946b).

Movements

In Texas, this species arrives as early as March 7 and has been reported as late as November 12 (one winter record for January 4). Typically it arrives during March, with males preceding females by a few days. By late August the birds are moving toward lower canyons, where they remain until about the second week of September. Betwen then and November the birds move back to their winter territories in the Mexican desert (Oberholser, 1974).

Vagrant birds in Texas sometimes reach the Edwards Plateau, more rarely the Gulf Coast (Rockport, Aransas County). Other than Texas, the species is essentially confined to Arizona, where it is very rare but where nesting has recently been reported (*American Birds* 27:804). There is also a single state record for Williamsburg, New Mexico (*American Birds* 33:796).

In the Valley of Mexico there are seasonal movements of these birds associated with variable availability of foods; there are few plants during the winter months (Wagner, 1946b).

Foraging Behavior and Floral Ecology

The relatively few observations of lucifer hummingbirds suggest that it consumes a fairly high proportion of insects in its diet, and its attachment to flowering agaves is probably in large part associated with the abundance of small insects usually found around these plants. In Texas, the overwhelming favorite plants from May through September are the yellow-green blossoms of several agaves (*A. americana*, *A. chisoensis*, *A. harvariana*, and *A. lechuguilla*). In early spring the birds also visit Chiso bluebonnet (*Lupinus havardii*) and ocotillo (*Fouquieria splendens*), and late fall migrants often concentrate on tree-tobacco (*Nicotiana glauca*) that has been planted along the Rio Grande (Oberholser, 1974). The species has also been observed foraging at the blossoms of *Erythrina coralloides* and *E. "corallodendrum"* (Toledo, 1974).

Wagner (1946b) reported that 11 stomach samples that he examined invariably contained insects, spiders, and other small animals, particularly dipterans. These insects are extracted from flowers of *Erythrina americana*, *Salvia mexicana*, *Loesalia mexicana*, *Lupinus elegans*, and other plants, including eucalyptus and *Opuntia* cactus. Sometimes the birds will also resort to removing entangled flies from spider webs (Bent, 1940), but they do not hawk them in flight.

Breeding Biology

Although few actual nests have been found in Texas, the breeding season there probably extends from May to July. Nests have been found from May 8 to August 2, and very recently fledged young have been observed between June 8 and the first week of August. There are now at least six nesting records for the Big Bend area (*American Birds* 32:1026). The single reported Arizona nesting of this species was in Guadalupe Canyon, Cochise

County, in May 1973 (*American Birds* 28:920).

In Mexico, breeding likewise seems to occur in the summer months. Bent (1940) reported six Mexican egg records from June 15 to July 4; most were from the state of Tamaulipas. In the Valley of Mexico, the principal breeding period is between May and September, with extremes of April and October (Wagner, 1946b).

Feeding territories in the Chisos Mountains are sometimes associated with the distribution of flowering agaves. The territory of one male contained two agaves along a cliff edge, and from them extended 6 meters on each side to some low trees, and 4.5 meters backward from the edge to another small tree (Fox, 1954). All but two of six observed males defended feeding territories, which usually consisted of circular areas having 12-meter radii. In one of the two exceptional cases, one male shared some agaves with black-chinned hummingbirds, and another male partially shared its territory with the first. Of two females, one showed partial possession of her area, while the other apparently visited undefended agaves. Two immature birds were evidently nonterritorial. Wagner reported that in Mexico the calculated size of a male breeding territory was 30 to 50 meters in diameter—considerably larger than the feeding territories reported by Fox.

The first two nests discovered in Texas were both placed in agave (*A. lechuguilla*) stalks, about 2 to 4 meters above the ground (Pulich and Pulich, 1963). Four nests found in Tamaulipas were all placed in shrubs, again only a few meters above ground (Bent, 1940). Four nests observed by Wagner were in low shrubs (*Senecio salignus*) about 1 to 2 meters above ground. The two nests found in the Chisos Mountains were similarly constructed. Both were placed on two or three dried pods that were attached to the stalk. On these pods the birds had made a foundation and constructed the nests of plant fibers, grass seeds, and pieces of leaves. Both were lined with plant down and feathers, and one was decorated externally with small leaves. The other nest, still unfinished, was undecorated. Neither contained lichen decorations, although this seems to be typical of nests found in Mexico (Bent, 1940; Wagner, 1946b). A third nest found in the Big Bend area was located almost 2 meters up in a dead shrub, but with flowering individuals of *Agave lechuguilla* in the vicinity (Nelson, 1970).

According to Wagner, the courtship of the male has two phases. The first is to attract the female and induce her into copulation, and the second is simultaneously performed by both partners. The first of these is a display flight by the male, performed daily in the same place, usually in the first 5 hours after sunrise. Its form is variable, but in part consists of repeated lateral flights between two perches on a tree or bush. At greater levels of excitement the male may ascend vertically upward in a spiraling flight and then pitch downward again to a perch. The more rarely seen second phase was observed once by Wagner a short time after dawn. In this case a male performed before a perched female, beginning his display with a sharply ascending and somewhat spiraling flight upwards for about 20 meters. At the peak of the ascent the bird hovered in place, and then began a rapidly descending swoop toward the female, pulling out of the dive while still some distance above her, and terminating the descent with a series of pendulum-like swings of decreasing amplitude as he slowly descended toward her. The flight terminated with the male again gaining altitude. The dive was accompanied by a sound resembling that of an electric fan, but apparently lacked vocalizations (Wagner, 1946b). This display has some components, especially the pendulum-like swinging, very much like that of the Bahama woodstar; it also resembles the display dives of *Archilochus* and *Selasphorus* to some degree.

Details of incubation and brooding behavior are not well known, but Wagner (1946b) estimated that the incubation period is 15 days from the laying of the second egg to the hatching of the first egg, or a total incubation period of 15 to 16 days. Incomplete observations indicated a fledging period of 22 to 24 days. Similarly, Pulich and Pulich (1963) estimated the fledging period at 21 to 23 days, also on the basis of incomplete information.

Evolutionary and Ecological Relationships

The unusually long and decurved bill of this species is not associated with obtaining nectar from unusually long tubular-blossomed plants, but instead may principally serve for extracting insects from plant blossoms and perhaps similar recesses. It thus seems somewhat comparable to the starthroats, which also have unusually long bills and apparently feed largely on insects rather than nectar. The starthroats often hawk insects during flight, however, which is rare for lucifer hummingbirds.

Taxonomists have generally maintained the genus *Calothorax* exclusively for the lucifer hummingbird and a very closely related species—the slightly shorter billed beautiful hummingbird of southern Mexico. These two forms clearly constitute a superspecies. They are also obviously very close relatives of the sheartails ("*Doricha*") of the same general area, differing from them only in the longer and more deeply forked tails of the males. I can see no reason for maintaining these two genera as distinct, nor for excluding some of the "woodstars" from the same genus. Other Central and South American genera such as *Acestrura*, *Chaetocercus*, *Philodice*, and *Calliphlox* may be part of the same assemblage, but no detailed comparisons of these types have been made in the present study.

The very small size of this species probably places it at a competitive disadvantage with many other sympatric species, and Fox (1954) noted that black-chinned and broad-tailed hummingbirds sometimes trespass on the territory of a male lucifer. However, a female drove away an immature Rivoli and some black-chinned hummingbirds from one agave, but another was driven away from an agave by a male black-chin. There are apparently no plants that this species has specifically become dependent upon, although several observers have commented on the attraction of lucifer hummingbirds to flowering agaves.

11. Breeding (stippled) and residential (cross-hatched) distributions of lucifer hummingbird, and residential (hatched) distribution of Bahama woodstar.

BAHAMA WOODSTAR

Calothorax evelynae (Bourcier)
(Nesophlox evelynae of Ridgway, 1911)

Other Names   None in general English use; God bird (Bahamas).

Range   The Bahama Islands. Accidental in North America (southern Florida).

North American Subspecies   *C. e. evelynae* (Bourcier). The Bahama Islands except for the southern-most islands (Inagua, Caicos, and Turks). (See map 11.)

Measurements   Wing, males 37–40.5 mm (ave. of 17, 38.9 mm), females 41.5–45.5 mm (ave. of 19, 43.3 mm). Exposed culmen, males 15.6–16.5 mm (ave. of 17, 15.9 mm), females 15.5–18 mm (ave. of 18, 16.6 mm) (Ridgway, 1911). Eggs, ave. 12 × 8 mm.

Weights   Two females in the U.S. National Museum weighed 2.2 and 2.6 g. No other weight data are available for the species.

Description   (After Ridgway, 1911.)

Adult male. Above rather dull metallic green or bronze-green, including middle pair of rectrices; remiges dark brownish slate or dusky, very faintly glossed with purplish; tail (except middle pair of rectrices) purplish black, the second and third rectrices with inner web cinnamon-rufous (except for a narrow space along shaft toward tip), the third (from outside) with basal portion of outer web (extensively) also cinnamon-rufous, the fourth with outer web (sometimes basal portion of inner web also) mostly cinnamon-rufous; a small postocular spot (sometimes a rictal spot also) of dull white; chin and throat brilliant metallic solferino purple, passing into violet or violet-blue posteriorly and laterally, the chin and anterior portion of throat decidedly reddish purple or purplish red; chest white, passing into light buffy grayish posteriorly; rest of underparts cinnamon-rufous, paler medially, the sides and flanks glossed with metallic bronze or bronze-green; under tail-coverts cinnamon-rufous medially, passing into cinnamon-buff or white laterally; femoral tufts white; bill dull black; iris dark brown; feet grayish brown (in dried skins).

Adult female. Above as in the adult male, but slightly duller metallic bronze-green, especially on pileum, where sometimes dull grayish brown, at least on forehead; three outer rectrices (on each side) extensively light cinnamon-rufous basally, broadly tipped with pale cinnamon-rufous or vinaceous-rufous, and crossed by a very broad subterminal band of purplish black, the latter separated from the rufescent basal portion on outer web by more or less of metallic green; third rectrix (from outside) mostly metallic

155

bronze-green, extensively black terminally, the concealed basal portion light cinnamon-rufous; chin and throat dull grayish white, sometimes tinged with pale cinnamon or cinnamon-buff; chest grayish white; rest of underparts cinnamon-rufous, paler medially, the under tail-coverts paler cinnamon-rufous or cinnamon-buff, sometimes indistinctly whitish along edges; femoral tufts white; bill etc., as in adult male.

Young male. Similar to the adult female, but lateral rectrices relatively longer and narrower and with the black relatively more extended; in older individuals the throat has a greater or less number of metallic reddish purple feathers.

Young female. Similar to the adult female, but feathers of upperparts (especially rump) indistinctly margined with rusty.

Identification   (See Plate 8B.)

In the hand. Identified by the combination of a fairly short, nearly straight bill (culmen 15–18 mm) and a tail that is either deeply forked (central tail feathers 13.5–17 mm) in males or rounded in females, with the central rectrices distinctly shorter (23–28.5 mm) than the outer ones. In both sexes the chest is white, becoming cinnamon-rufous posteriorly.

In the field. The strongly forked black and rufous tail of the male, together with the reddish to purplish gorget and crown, plus cinnamon underparts, identify this species. Females are much more difficult, but have a white throat and breast, with the rest of the underparts buffy and the tail buffy, with pale cinnamon tips and a blackish subterminal band. The birds are associated with scrubby woodlands, but in the Bahamas are also common around residential gardens.

Habitats   According to Brudenell-Bruce (1975) this species is common in the Bahamas wherever there are flowers, as in gardens, woods, copses, or open country.

Movements   The Bahama woodstar is apparently sedentary, to the extent that a distinct local race has developed in the Inagua group of islands. However, there are three North American records, warranting inclusion of the species in the current account. The first occurred in Lantana, Florida, between August 26 and October 13, 1971 (*American Birds* 26:52); the second was observed at Homestead, Florida, between April 7 and May 15, 1974 (*American Birds* 28:855); and the first actual specimen record was obtained in Miami, when a dead individual was found on January 31, 1961 (Owre, 1976).

Foraging Behavior   Little is known of the floral ecology of this species in the Baha-
and Floral Ecology   mas, although one early observer commented (*Ibis*, 1903, p. 292) on its preference for the flowers of sisal (*Agave sisalina*). In Florida it has foraged in a considerable variety of flowering plants including redbird cactus (*Euphorbia pedilanthus*), firecracker plant (*Russellia equisetiformis*), red pentas (*Pentas lanceolata*), yellow elder (*Steno-*

lobium stans), and Cape honeysuckle (*Tecomaria capensis*) (*American Birds* 28:855).

Breeding Biology

Northrop (1891) has provided an excellent early description of the male's display. The male hovered 15–20 centimeters in front of a perched female, with his tail and gorget fully exposed to her view. His wings were rapidly vibrating, and he swung quickly to and fro from side to side, at the same time rising and falling, like a ball suspended on an elastic thread that stretches and contracts as the ball sways. Suddenly the male expanded his tail and threw himself almost violently from side to side, making a rustling sound and uttering a few sharp notes. He then darted toward the female, seemed almost to touch her, and as quickly darted away. This was probably a precopulatory display.

The nests, little more than 25 mm in diameter, are made of a soft, wooly material similar to thistledown, camouflaged on the outside with tiny pieces of bark. Many different sites are used, but they are usually in or on the fork of a twig of a bush or tree, from 1 to 4 meters above ground (Brudenell-Bruce, 1975).

Breeding may occur year-round, but Brudenell-Bruce indicated that the main nesting season is in April. Miller (1978) observed nests with eggs or young in December on San Salvador Island of the Watling group; one of them contained three young. James Bond (in litt.) has found nests on Marguana in October, on Providencia in December, on Grand Turk from January through March, on Little Inagua in April, and observed nest-building on Great Inagua in May.

There is no information on incubation periods, nestling development, or fledging periods.

Evolutionary and Ecological Relationships

The genus *Nesophlox* was erected by Robert Ridgway in 1910, and was envisioned by him to include three species: *evelynae, lyrura* (now considered conspecific with *evelynae*), and *bryantae.* He considered this genus most closely related to *Calliphlox*, but distinguishable from it on the basis of tail and primary shapes. Later, Todd (1942) included *evelynae* within the expanded genus *Calliphlox.* I think there should be a combination of at least these genera as well as *Doricha* and *Philodice* with *Calothorax* as well.

No hybrids involving this species are known. Its probable nearest relative is the magenta-throated woodstar, and it is probably slightly less closely related to the purple-throated woodstar.

Genus *Archilochus* Reichenbach 1854

Synonyms: *Calypte* Gould 1856, *Stellula* Gould 1861, *?Melli-suga* Brisson 1760, *?Acestrura* Gould 1861, *?Chae-tocercus* Gray 1855

*T*his genus of Middle and North American hummingbirds consists of at least six species that are fairly small (wing 35–45 mm), with a blackish bill that is straight, slender, and about as long as the head (or somewhat longer), the culmen rounded except basally, where it is contracted into a ridge. The edge of the mandible is smooth, and the nasal operculum is hidden by frontal feathering that extends well beyond the anterior end of the nostrils. The wing is two to three times as long as the exposed culmen, and the outermost primary is the longest. The primaries are either normal in shape ("*Ca-lypte*" and "*Stellula*") or modified (in males of two species), with the six innermost ones abruptly narrower than the rest and having a prominent angle near the tip, and with the outermost primary strongly incurved terminally and distinctly narrowed and obtusely pointed in one species. The sexes are dimorphic, and the adult males have a red to purplish or blackish gorget (including in "*Ca-lypte*" the crown as well). The tail of adult males varies from forked to slightly forked or double-rounded, with the middle rectrices usually rather broad and the lateral ones often distinctly narrowed and sometimes incurved. The tail of females is rounded or double-rounded, with the outer rectrices less distinctly modified.

12. Breeding (stippled) and residential (cross-hatched) distributions of Costa
hummingbird.

COSTA HUMMINGBIRD

Archilochus costae (Bourcier)
(Calypte costae of AOU, 1957)

Other Names   Coast hummingbird, Ruffed hummingbird; Chupamirto garganta violeta (Spanish).

Range   Breeds in western North America from central California, southern Nevada, and southwestern Utah south to the Santa Barbara Islands, southern Baja California including all near-shore islands, southern Arizona, and southwestern New Mexico south to Sonora and Sinaloa, including Tiburon and San Esteban islands. Winters over most of the breeding range, from southern California and southwestern Arizona southward (AOU, 1957). (See map 12.)

North American Subspecies   None recognized.

Measurements   Wing, males 43–45.5 mm (ave. of 13, 44.4 mm), females 43.5–46 mm (ave. of 12, 44.7 mm). Exposed culmen, males 16–19 mm (ave. of 13, 17.2 mm), females 17–20 mm (ave. 12, 18.2 mm) (Ridgway, 1911). Eggs, ave. 12.4 × 8.2 mm (extremes 11.4–14 × 7.6–9.4 mm).

Weights   The average of 33 males was 3.05 g (range 2.5–5.2 g); that of 27 females was 3.22 g (range 2.5–3.4 g) (various sources, including specimens in Museum of Vertebrate Zoology).

Description   (After Ridgway, 1911.)

Adult male. Head, except postocular region, very brilliant metallic violet or amethyst purple, changing to violet-blue or even greenish and more reddish purple (magenta) in certain lights, the latero-posterior feathers of throat much elongated; rest of upperparts, including four middle rectrices, rather dull metallic bronze-green or greenish bronze; tail (except four middle rectrices) grayish brown or brownish gray, faintly glossed with bronze-greenish, the rectrices darker on shafts and toward tip; remiges brownish slate or dusky, faintly glossed with purplish; foreneck very pale brownish gray or grayish white, passing into more decidedly grayish on chest and median line of breast and abdomen; rest of underparts metallic bronze-green or greenish bronze, the feathers more or less distinctly margined with dull grayish; femoral tufts and conspicuous tuft on each side of rump white; under tail-coverts light brownish gray or bronzy centrally, margined with whitish; bill dull black; iris dark brown; feet dusky.

Adult female. Above rather dull metallic bronze-green or greenish

161

bronze, much duller on pileum, where (at least on forehead) sometimes dull grayish brown; middle pair of rectrices bronze-green; the next pair similar but with terminal portion black; third pair tipped with dull white or pale brownish gray, extensively black subterminally and dull brownish gray basally, the gray and black separated (at least on outer web) by more or less metallic bronze-green; fourth and outermost pairs with whitish tip broader, basal grayish more extended, and with little if any metallic greenish between the gray and black; remiges brownish slate or dusky, faintly glossed with purplish; underparts pale brownish gray, paler (dull whitish) on chin, upper throat, and under tail-coverts; femoral tufts and tuft on each side of rump white; bill, etc., as in adult male.

Young male. Similar to the adult female but feathers of upperparts more or less distinctly margined with pale grayish buffy; tail double-rounded instead of rounded; and throat with a central patch of metallic purple or violet feathers (in older individuals, similar feathers also on crown).

Young female. Similar to the adult female, but feathers of upperparts margined with pale grayish buffy.

Identification

(See Plate 16A.)

In the hand. Differs from typical *Archilochus* forms in that the males lack notches near the tips of the inner webs of the primaries, and the lateral rectrices are unusually narrowed (outermost rectrix only 1.5 mm in males, 3.5 mm in females).

In the field. Found in hot desert areas where water is often lacking, but sometimes also occurs in chaparral and woodland areas. The male is the only North American hummingbird with a purple gorget and crown that has a lateral extension down the side of the head. Females and immature males lack this, and at most have a few reddish flecks on an otherwise grayish throat. They cannot be separated with certainty from female black-chinned hummingbirds, but are slightly smaller and more grayish on the crown. The absence of cinnamon on the tail helps separate them from other western species, and the female Anna hummingbird often has a patch of red on the throat. The call-notes include soft *chip* or *chik* notes, and males utter two types of static (non-aerial) song: a single whistled note and a much shorter two- or three-noted whistle. The prolonged whistle is made during the diving display as the bird reaches the bottom of a deep U-shaped arc that may begin from a height of 30–60 meters. As the bird reaches the bottom of the dive, it begins to produce a shrill whistle that lasts about two seconds, after which it begins immediately to ascend and finally flies in a broad horizontal circle until it reaches its starting point. Beside these differences, the call is much longer than is the case with the Anna hummingbird. A similar but shorter call is produced while the male perches during static display (Wells et al., 1978).

Female Costas resemble black-chinned hummingbirds, but their *chip* call is very different—a very high, light and sharp *tik* or *tip*, which is often repeated to produce a rapid twitter. They are the palest in general coloration of the western hummingbirds, and the purest white below, usually having an immaculate white throat. Juvenile males likewise are very light below, with brownish feather-edgings above; often young males have some purple on the throat near the corners of the future gorget (Stiles, 1971).

Habitats   Throughout California, the breeding habitat consists of deserts or desert-like washes, mesas, or side-hills, particularly where sages, ocotillo, yuccas, and cholla cacti are abundant (Grinnell and Miller, 1944). In Joshua Tree National Monument, California, Costas are most commonly found during the nesting season along canyons or washes, where ocotillo, mesquites, or other flowering plants may be found (Miller and Stebbins, 1964). In Arizona the species favors habitats rich in ocotillos, chuparosa, and cacti (Phillips et al., 1964).

There is apparently no habitat separation of the sexes during the breeding season in this species (Pitelka, 1951a). Most observers stress the fact that the Costa is relatively independent of water at this time, and thus extends into more xeric habitats than do any other North American hummingbirds. Probably the same is true of the wintering period, although nothing specific has been written of this aspect of Costa biology.

Movements   Like the Anna hummingbird, Costas undergo only limited seasonal movements. In California, wintering occurs on the Colorado Desert northwest to Palm Springs, and birds rarely winter to Los Angeles. In Arizona, this species as well as some swallows is the first of the spring migrants, sometimes arriving in late January, and is frequent by late February and March. However, Costas breed early, and by the end of May they have disappeared from the desert areas, apparently having migrated to the Pacific coast of California and Baja California. They reappear in October, to spend the winter in western Pima County and southern Yuma County (Phillips et al., 1964).

In spite of these limited migratory tendencies, vagrant birds sometimes stray considerable distances. They have appeared on San Clemente, Santa Barbara, and Santa Catalina islands (Grinnell and Miller, 1944), have reached Oregon at least eight times (*American Birds* 34:924), occasionally reach New Mexico (*American Birds* 26:640; 31:1033) and Texas (*American Birds* 28:824, 29:709; Oberholser, 1974), and have even been reported from Utah (*American Birds* 29:722).

Foraging Behavior and Floral Ecology   Costa hummingbirds utilize a wide variety of flowering plants for foraging. On the Colorado Desert of California some of the important ornithophilous flowers include the early-blooming ocotillo and chuparosa, which begin to flower shortly after the arrival of Costa hummingbirds in that area (Grant and Grant, 1968). There are several other desert species of importance, including box-thorn (*Lycium* spp.), desert lavender (*Hyptis emoryi*), desert willow (*Chilopsis*), and sages (*Salvia mellifera* and *S. apiana*) (Grinnell and Miller, 1944).

In a study in Claremont, California, Grant and Grant (1968) observed territoriality behavior of male Costa hummingbirds among a population of larkspurs (*Delphinium cardinale*). Males occupied posts in nearby trees, defending their plants from intruders. They primarily fed on plants near their tree posts, but at times flew elsewhere to feed. Single males sometimes held posts for several days; in one instance they defended an area that included some 40 flowering stalks of larkspurs. During 6.5 hours of observation, this male made 42 foraging trips, visiting 1311 flowers, nearly 90 percent of which were located within its territorial limits. Intruder birds made only 12 feeding trips within the male's territory during this period, visiting 192 flowers, indicating the nearly exclusive use of the area by a single male.

According to Woods (1927), during the breeding season females of this species visit flowering plants less often than do males, perhaps because they must spend more time looking for nesting materials. Perhaps also they are then concentrating more strongly on obtaining minute insects and spiders that may be acquired incidentally during such searches. Woods believed that Costa hummingbirds are also less partial to the flowers of the introduced tree-tobacco shrub than are the larger species of California hummingbirds.

Breeding Biology   Nesting in Arizona begins fairly early, with well-developed young reported as early as mid-April, but others are still being fed by their mothers during June (Phillips et al., 1964). On the other hand, in the Santa Barbara area of California the Costa is a relatively late nester; together with the black-chinned hummingbird it begins nesting in middle or late April, raises a single brood, and nearly all the eggs hatch by the end of June. Bent (1940) reported a total period of egg records for California from March 11 to June 29, with a peak from May 12 to June 10; fewer records from Baja California ranged from February 24 to June 5, with a probable peak in late May. Bakus (1962) reported an unusual late January nesting for the San Diego area. Stiles (1972b) suggested that this species may raise one brood in the Borrego desert of southern California in early spring, and then move to the chaparral in April to breed a second time.

Territories are established almost as soon as males arrive on their nesting areas. In the Joshua Tree National Monument, males begin active display in early February, as soon as they become evident. Between aerial displays the males perch on lookouts at the tips of the highest available vegetation and periodically perform their diving displays. This usually consists of a very open U-shaped arc, with the male typically circling back to retrace the arc in the same direction rather than retracing it in the opposite direction, according to Miller and Stebbins (1964). These authors also noted a short swinging performance of not quite 1 meter in length, with the bird swinging slowly back and forth. The more typical display occurs throughout the day, and before sunup as well as after sundown. Woods (1927) likewise noted that the long U-shaped swoop may be performed repeatedly from the same direction or at a new angle. The usual sound produced is extremely prolonged and intense, something like the shriek of a glancing bullet; it is apparently of vocal origin, since a very similar sound may be produced by the bird while it is perched (Wells et al., 1978). At times, however, a more "booming" noise is made, and the dives are unusually narrow and steep (Short and Phillips, 1966).

Territories of males are very large, often 1–1.5 hectares, with no clearly defined core area. The vegetation is usually low and uniform in height, with scattered higher perching sites. Food is usually widely available, or present in large patches (Stiles, 1972b).

Miller and Stebbins (1964) reported copulation as occurring on a mesquite plant. The two birds were observed 1.5 meters above the ground on open twigs, when the male approached the female from in front and made short 50- to 75-mm darting flights toward her at various angles within an arc of about 90°. He then mounted her while she was perching, flew off, and again darted at her from the front. The two birds then flew off in close pursuit.

Nests are constructed in the typical hummingbird manner, and average 37.5 mm in outside diameter. There is usually a framework of fibers, stems, and other materials attached to the support by cobwebs and a lining of plant down or small feathers. The external surface is lined with a variety of items, including bark, paper, miscellaneous vegetable matter, and similar materials (Woods, 1927). Generally the nests are quite diverse in size, shape, and construction materials. The supporting vegetation is likewise highly variable; Bent (1940) listed 16 different types of trees used, as well as sage, yuccas, *Opuntia* and other cacti, and various weeds.

Nests have been found on vines clinging to rock faces, in citrus trees in open orchards, and in palm trees. The range of nest heights is also variable; Woods (1927) noted that it is usually less than 1 to more than 3 meters, but often about 1.5 meters. When a bush or small tree is selected, the nest is often at a height about halfway to the top of the tree; in larger trees the nest is usually on a small twig near the end of a projecting lower limb. Although the birds sometimes build nests near water, they typically occur at considerable distances from surface water. In favorable locations several nests may be closely situated to one another; there is one instance of six nests within a 40-meter radius in a thicket of dead cockleburs (Bent, 1940). Stiles (1972b) noted that a favorite location is at a break in the chapparal, either along an edge or in particularly tall bushes, providing the female with a clear view of the nesting vicinity.

The first stages of nest construction usually require two or three days, after which a similar period may ensue before the first egg is deposited. Almost invariably two eggs are laid, normally at an interval of about two days. Incubation apparently begins with the first egg, since the young usually hatch a day or so apart. The observed incubation periods range from 15 to 18 days, probably averaging about 16 days (Woods, 1927).

At hatching the young are almost totally devoid of feathers, but by the sixth day pinfeathers begin to appear. The young are fed at intervals of about half an hour, and according to Woods (1927) require from 20 to 23 days to fledge, based on eight observations. In Woods' experience no instances of successful raising of a second brood were known, and among a total of 29 nests both eggs hatched in 15 cases; in 4 other cases a single egg hatched, a total hatching success of 58.6 percent. Both young fledged in 7 of these instances, and in 5 additional cases a single young was fledged. Thus the fledging success was approximately one-third (32.7 percent) of the total number of eggs that were laid, and the largest single mortality factor was destruction by cultivation or by wind.

Evolutionary and Ecological Relationships

Costa hummingbirds have usually been placed along with *anna* in the genus *Calypte,* but various workers such as Mayr and Short (1970) have advocated the merger of *Calypte* with *Archilochus.* These authors believe that the Costa is a close relative of the superspecies *A. colubris,* which includes the ruby-throated and black-chinned hummingbirds. Wild hybridization has been reported with the broad-tailed and calliope hummingbirds (Banks and Johnson, 1961), and more recently with the black-chinned hummingbird (Short and Phillips, 1966).

Short and Phillips have commented on the similarity of the courtship dives of black-chinned and Costa hummingbirds, and the Costa at least at times performs a deep power dive similar to that of the black-chin. These authors have implied that the two species are closely related, and described several natural hybrids between them.

The center of the Costa hummingbird's breeding range is the Colorado Desert, where the ocotillo and chuparosa are among the most prevalent ornithophilous flowers, but several other flower species are commonly utilized, including desert willow and *Lycium* species. However, the Mojave Desert to the north is lacking in ornithophilous flowers, as well as in breeding hummingbirds (Grant and Grant, 1970).

I think that the nearest relative of the Costa is probably the Anna hummingbird; the two are now incompletely isolated from one another by the southern Sierra Nevada and the southern Coast Ranges of California, but they are effectively isolated ecologically and show considerable segregation in breeding seasons (Pitelka, 1951a). However, they are locally sympatric on the Palos Verdes Peninsula of California, where hybrids have been reported several times (Wells et al., 1978).

13. Breeding (stippled) and wintering (hatched) distributions of Anna hummingbird. Light stippling indicates area of migration or postbreeding movments.

ANNA HUMMINGBIRD

Archilochus anna (Lesson)
(Calypte anna of AOU, 1957)

Other Names None in general English use; Chupamirto cuello escarlata (Spanish).

Range Breeds in California west of the Sierra Nevada and southern coastal mountains from Humboldt, Shasta, and Tehema counties south to the Sierra San Predo Martir and San Quintin in northwestern Baja California. Also reaches Santa Cruz Island, California, and Guadalupe Island, Baja California. Winters over the breeding range, northward to Humboldt Bay and to the islands of the coast of California and Baja California, and southward on the mainland of Baja California. Also winters eastward from southern California across southern Arizona to northern Sonora, and northward to southern Oregon. In recent years breeds increasingly in Arizona (Zimmerman, 1973). (See map 13.)

North American Subspecies None recognized.

Measurements Wing, males 48.5–51 mm (ave. of 10, 49–7 mm), females 48–51 mm (ave. of 10, 49.6 mm). Exposed culmen, males 17.5–20 mm (ave. of 10, 18.2 mm), females 17–22 mm (ave. of 10, 18.8 mm) (Ridgway, 1911). Eggs, ave. 13.31 × 8.65 mm (extremes 11.3–14.3 × 7.7–9.4 mm).

Weights The average of 81 males was 4.31 g (range 3.3–5.8 g); that of 40 females was 4.07 g (range 3.3–4.7 g) (from various sources, including specimens in Museum of Vertebrate Zoology).

Description (After Ridgway, 1911.)

Adult male. Whole head except occiput and auricular region brilliant metallic rose red, changing to solferino and violet in certain lights—more golden or even greenish in position *b* (see note at beginning of Part Two for position descriptions)—the latero-posterior feathers of throat elongated; a small postocular spot or streak of white; occiput (except laterally, where at least partly metallic purplish red), hindneck, back, scapulars, wing-coverts, and rump metallic bronze-green, the upper tail-coverts and middle pair of rectrices similar but usually less bronzy, or more bluish, green; tail (except middle pair of rectrices) dark grayish, faintly glossed with greenish bronze, the rectrices blackish terminally and medially; remiges brownish slate or dusky, faintly glossed with purplish; chest pale brownish gray or dull grayish white, the feathers darker brownish gray beneath surface; rest of underparts deeper grayish, strongly glossed with metallic bronze-green laterally, the feathers more or less distinctly margined with paler grayish; femoral tufts and conspicuous tuft on each side of rump white; under tail-coverts brownish gray glossed with bronze-green or greenish bronze (especially on shorter coverts) and broadly margined with pale gray or grayish white; bill dull black; iris dark brown; feet dusky.

Adult female. Above metallic bronze or bronze-green, duller on pileum, the forehead sometimes dull grayish brown; middle pair of rectrices metallic green or bronze-green, sometimes dusky terminally; the next pair similar, but with terminal portion (broadly) blackish; third pair similar to second, but more extensively blackish terminally and narrowly tipped with white; two outer pairs with basal half (more or less) brownish gray, the tip pale brownish gray or dull grayish white (broader on outermost rectrix), the intermediate (subterminal) portion black; remiges brownish slate or dusky, faintly glossed with purplish; chin and throat pale brownish gray or dull grayish white, the center of throat usually with an admixture of metallic red or purplish red feathers, sometimes with a considerable patch of metallic reddish; the lower throat, at least, with mesial guttate spots or broad streaks of dusky grayish brown or dull bronzy; rest of underparts as in the adult male, but slightly paler and less extensively glossed with metallic greenish; bill, etc., as in adult male.

Young male. Similar to the adult female, but tail less rounded; lateral rectrices with dark subterminal portion duller blackish and less sharply contracted with dull grayish of basal portion; feathers of upperparts very narrowly and indistinctly margined with pale buffy grayish; and (at least older individuals) with metallic purplish red feathers on crown as well as on throat.

Young female. Similar to the adult female, but feathers of upperparts narrowly margined with pale brownish or dull buffy and throat without metallic red feathers.

Identification   (See Plate 16B.)

In the hand. Like the Costa hummingbird, differs from typical *Archilochus* forms because the males lack notches near the tips of the inner webs of the primaries, and the lateral rectrices are distinctly narrowed, although not so much as in the Costa (males 2.5–3 mm, females 5 mm). Females also have wider central rectrices (at least 8 mm in width) than do those of the Costa, and the wing length is slightly greater (48–51 mm vs. 43.5–46 mm).

In the field. Adult males are best separated from male Costa hummingbirds by their red rather than violet crown and gorget. Females of the two species are very similar, but females of the Anna hummingbird have a reddish patch on the throat and darker underparts than Costa females. When feeding the birds utter a heavy *chick*, which is repeated rapidly when alarmed; they produce a series of *ztikl* notes when chasing intruders. The song is a generally high-pitched assortment of squeaks, gurgles, and hissing noises, uttered while perched. The male also sings in flight: Typically he flies upward 22–44 meters, sometimes pausing to sing, and at the top of his climb he pauses a second time to sing before diving sharply downward over the female, making a sharp *peek* at the bottom of the dive. On Guadalupe Island the songs are distinctly different from those on the mainland (Mirsky, 1976). The *peek* dive-note may be vocal (Baptista and Matsui. 1979). Female Annas are distinctly larger than other western hummingbirds except for the broad-tailed, and the individual chip notes are very hard, sharp, and explosive *tzip* or *kip* sounds. These are often run together into an excited chittering, which like the chatter calls are fairly loud and harsh. Besides being generally grayer below, females also have less conspicuous black on the tail than do most other species, but juvenile males are sometimes fairly pale below and have little or no red on the throat. These birds usually have buffy-gray feather edgings on the upper surface, and when hovering birds of all ages tend to hold the tail down, nearly in line with the body, with little pumping, spreading, or flicking (Stiles, 1971).

Habitats   Essentially confined to California during the breeding season, this species then typically occupies broken chaparral or woodland, or mixed woodland and chaparral in open stands. During the breeding period the sexes show some habitat segregation, with males in more open habitats, such as on canyon sides, hill slopes, or level washes, and females in tracts of evergreen trees, especially live oaks. Outside the breeding period and when foraging the birds also occur in other habitats, often to 1800 meters elevation in the mountains during late summer, especially those rich in preferred flower species. Limited wintering also occurs in southern Arizona, especially in the areas where nighttime temperatures do not fall below freezing. Late summer habitats are quite diverse, with the birds tending to move to higher elevations, occasionally into boreal forest communities. Likewise, in August and September they use lower altitude areas, sometimes extending out into stubble-fields in search of plants such as blue-curls (*Trichostema*) (Grinnell and Miller, 1944).

Movements   Unlike most hummingbirds, this species is relatively sedentary, although the birds withdraw from the northern parts of the California breeding range in the colder months and migrate in small numbers into southern Arizona in September or early October, remaining there until December or (rarely) early March (Phillips, et al., 1964). They also do a fair amount of postbreeding wandering in California, with vagrant birds reaching the Farallon Islands, San Clemente, Santa Catalina, and most of the other islands of the Santa Barbara group during winter or spring months (Grinnell and Miller, 1944). In recent years the species has expanded its winter range considerably (Zimmerman, 1973).

There are a surprising number of extralimital records for Anna hummingbirds. For example, it has been reported several times in Alaska (*American Birds* 29:104; 31:211; 33:205), British Columbia

(*American Birds* 25:618; 29:718), and Washington (including one nesting record) (*American Birds* 27:89; 29:718; 30:881). It has also been seen at least once in Alberta (*American Birds* 31:193), Montana (*American Birds* 24:523), Idaho (*American Birds* 31:354), Colorado (*American Birds* 24:703), Oklahoma (*American Birds* 30:737), Louisiana (*American Birds* 34:171), and New Mexico (*American Birds* 28:804). It is rare but regular in western Oregon, mostly as a winter visitor, and nested there in 1981 (*American Birds* 35:855).

Foraging Behavior and Floral Ecology   The chaparral habitats of California include a number of hummingbird-adapted flowers and, although there is some ecological overlap in the foraging habitats of Anna and Allen hummingbirds, the Anna commonly exploits flower species such as bush monkey-flower (*Diplacus* spp.), Indian pink (*Silena laciniata*), and Indian paintbrushes (*Castilleja martinii* and *C. foliolosa*) especially in spring (Grant and Grant, 1968).

Bent (1940) described several observations of Anna hummingbirds feeding on the wing for midges and gleaning the trunks and branches of trees for invertebrates. They regularly visit sapsucker holes (Bent, 1940), as does the ruby-throated hummingbird; the birds evidently consume both the exuding sap and the insects attracted to the sap. According to Bent, the very favorite plant species of Anna hummingbirds is the red gooseberry (*Ribes speciosum*), which is abundantly in flower when the Annas begin nesting activities. Also of importance in southern California is the exotic tree-tobacco (*Nicotiana glauca*), and the fall blossoms of century plants (*Agave americana*) are widely available in the state as a result of planting. Likewise, the planted red-hot-poker (*Tritoma*) is common in gardens. Grinnell and Miller (1944) stated that perhaps the most important of the introduced plants are the many varieties of *Eucalyptus*, both for foraging and for nesting.

Stiles (1972b) stated that the tree-tobacco and *Eucalyptus globulus* are the most important introduced plants for hummingbirds in chaparral areas of California, and that citrus orchards also provide important spring nectar sources for breeding and migrating birds. However, the two most important native species in his study area (Santa Monica Mountains) were two species of *Ribes* (*malvaceus* and *speciosum*). In higher and somewhat cooler areas a species of manzanita (*Arctostaphylos glauca*) was frequently visited in early months. Stiles suggested that the reproductive strategies of the Anna hummingbird and *Ribes speciosum* have evolved together, resulting in an unusually early breeding season for the hummingbird.

Breeding Biology   In the Santa Monica Mountains, the breeding season of the Anna hummingbird begins in November or December, as males move onto breeding territories. The first heavy winter rains usually fall between November and January. The season ends in April and May when the males abandon their territories, and females cease their nesting activities between May and July. Thus, the female breeding cycle lags somewhat behind that of the male, sometimes by as much as a month (Stiles, 1972b).

Prior to breeding, adult and first-year males both hold feeding territories at localized rich sources of food, such as at eucalyptus or tree-tobacco plants. Females do not hold feeding territories during the prebreeding season, but either visit undefended flowers or poach from defended areas (Stiles, 1972b).

Breeding territories of males are larger and more energetically defended than are nonbreeding ones, and are typically established around rich, dependable, and easily exploited food resources. Males usually establish territories where *Ribes malvaceus* is in flower, and may later shift slightly as *Ribes speciosum* begins to replace the other species. Occasionally birds will also commute to local food sources well outside their territories, sometimes as far as 700–800 meters, rarely up to a kilometer away. Territories usually have from 5 to 10 regular perches within the core area, which is 900–1000 square meters in area and frequently about 50–100 meters in diameter. Although Stiles was unable to mark his birds, he had four cases of probable use of the same territory by the same individual in two successive years. Outside the core area is an ill-defined buffer zone, which may range from 2 to 6 hectares in size (Pitelka, 1951b, Stiles, 1972b).

Females begin nest-building a few weeks after the males have established their territories. They probably spend much more time than males in searching for insect food, but also need a reliable source of nectar. Thus, the location of suitable flowers is an important part of nest-site selection. Prior to nesting, females often restrict their activities to a single food source and will defend it, although less vigorously than will a male. The nest site is likewise probably chosen with reference to the food source, and that site is then also defended, becoming a nesting territory. Several perches are also chosen within the territory, for resting, preening, or using to sally forth to chase insects (Stiles, 1972b).

Nesting locations are extremely variable for Annas, ranging in height from less than 1 meter to 9 meters from the ground and on nearly every possible substrate, including electric wires, climbing vines, and many kinds of trees, such as citrus, eucalyptus, and many chaparral species, especially oaks. The nests are similar to those of the Costa, but average somewhat larger (nearly 50 mm in diameter), often have fibers or stemmy materials in the walls, and often are extensively ornamented with lichens. The lining frequently includes small feathers (Bent, 1940).

Nest-building usually takes 7 days, but the range may be from 3 days to at least two weeks (Legg and Pitelka, 1956). Probably most copulations occur during this time. Trousdale (1954) observed copulation during a period when a female was gathering tent caterpillar webs. The gathering was interrupted when the female flew to a clothesline and perched. A male that had been perching and singing on the clothesline then immediately left his perch to hover over and then mount the female. The male's wings fluttered during copulation, and as soon as it was completed the female returned to the oak tree and the male to his previous perch. According to Schuchmann (1979), copulation is preceded by the male flying back and forth before the perched female four to six times, producing a whistling sound with the bill slightly open. The female follows the male's movements with her bill, and when she opens her bill slightly the male alights beside her and copulation follows. Stiles (1982) has also recently described courtship and aggressive displays of this species in detail.

At the time of mating the nest is already at least partly built, but materials may be added to it well into incubation, which requires 14 to 19 days (Stiles, 1972b). Eggs are apparently laid a day apart, and sometimes the young hatch a day apart, suggesting that incubation may begin with the first egg (Kelly, 1955). Feeding during incubation occasionally occurs well away from the nest site, with weather regulating the periods that the adult bird is away from the nest. On cold or wet days, the bird remains on the nest longer and returns early. During incubation, the female does not go into torpor at night, but rather maintains normal body temperature (Howell and Dawson, 1954). Probably unusually long foraging periods in the evening hours are needed to compensate for this energy drain, which is also affected by the relative thickness and thermal conductivity of the nest itself (Smith et al., 1974).

By the time the birds are 6 days old they are well-covered with down, and their eyes typically open on the 5th day after hatching. Little or no brooding occurs beyond the 12th day. The nestling period ranges from 18 to 23 days, and the young remain dependent on their mother for a few days thereafter, but become independent within a week or two (Stiles, 1972b). If a nesting effort fails, the female usually begins to renest within about 10 days, and in many areas two broods are normally raised during a breeding season. In Stiles' (1972b) study area, the first eggs were found in December and the last eggs were laid in May, but Bent (1940) indicated a total span of 86 California nesting records that ranged from December 21 to August 17, with a peak between February 22 and May 18.

Juveniles begin to show territorial behavior at an extremely early age, sometimes only shortly after leaving the nest. The young birds often move about in pairs, presumably siblings, which may often chase one another in a manner resembling play. The young birds gradually become less "playful," and by fall young males frequently are holding feeding territories alongside adult males. In Stiles' study area Anna hummingbirds as well as rufous and Allen hummingbirds all occupied stands of tree-tobacco in large numbers, with Anna territories usually larger and more dispersed; the *Selasphorus* species territories tended to be smaller and more tightly packed. In individual encounters between the species, the Annas tended to be victorious, but they were unable to penetrate the areas occupied by *Selasphorus* because of the collective superiority of the latter.

Evolutionary and Ecological Relationships

According to Mayr and Short (1970), this species may be more closely related to the rufous superspecies (rufous and Allen hummingbirds) than to other species of *Archilochus*, including the Costa. Natural hybridization has occurred with black-chinned, calliope, and Allen hummingbirds (Banks and Johnson, 1961), and more recently it has been reported for the Costa (Wells et al., 1978).

Regardless of the closeness of their phyletic relationships, there is a considerable amount of ecological overlap and interactions between breeding Anna and Allen hummingbirds (Pitelka, 1951b). Their nesting cycles overlap considerably as well, although the Anna begins to breed earlier and often continues slightly longer in southern and central California (Pitelka, 1951a, 1951b). In the Berkeley area, the resident Anna hummingbird is territorial and breeding before the Allen males arrive; moreover, the Anna is larger in size, giving it a competitive advantage. Thus territories of Allen males tend to be peripheral to those of Anna, although (rarely) a male Allen is able to displace a territorial male Anna (Pitelka, 1951b).

The chaparral flora of California has several species adapted to winter growth and flowering (Grant and Grant, 1968), some of which have probably evolved in conjunction with the Anna hummingbird. As Stiles (1972b) noted, the *Ribes* species in particular is closely associated with the Anna, and the reproductive strategy of *R. speciosum* has probably evolved in association with it.

14. Breeding (stippled) and wintering (hatched) distributions of ruby-throated hummingbird. Light stippling indicates areas used during migration.

RUBY-THROATED HUMMINGBIRD

Archilochus colubris (Linnaeus)

Other Names   None in general English use; Mansoncito garganta de fuego, Chupaflor rubi (Spanish).

Range   Breeds throughout the eastern half of North America west to the middle of the Great Plains, from Southern Saskatchewan east to Nova Scotia, and south to southern Texas, the Gulf of Mexico, and Florida. Winters from middle Florida through southern Mexico and the rest of Middle America to Panama; casual in Cuba, Hispaniola, the Bahama Islands, and Bermuda (Friedmann et al., 1950). (See map 14.)

North American Subspecies   None recognized.

Measurements   Wing, males 37–40 mm (ave. of 10, 38.5 mm), females 43.5–45.5 mm (ave. of 10, 44.5 mm). Exposed culmen, males 15–17 mm (ave. of 10, 15.9 mm), females 17–19.5 mm (ave. of 10, 18.2 mm) (Ridgway, 1911). Eggs, ave. 13.0 × 8.4 mm (extremes 11.5–14.5 × 7.8–9.1 mm).

Weights   The average of 419 adult females (May-September) was 3.34 g (range 2.7–4.8 g); that of 202 adult males (April-September) was 3.03 g (range 2.5–4.1 g) (Clench and Leberman, 1978).

Description   (After Ridgway, 1911, with modifications.)

Adult male. Above metallic bronze-green, including middle pair of rectrices; remiges dark brownish slate or dusky, faintly glossed with purplish; tail (except middle pair of rectrices) dark bronzy purplish or purplish bronzy black; chin, malar region, suborbital region, and auricular region velvety black; a small postocular spot of white; whole throat brilliant metallic red (nearest geranium red in frontal light, changing to golden or even greenish in side light); chest dull brownish white or very pale buffy brownish gray, passing gradually into deeper brownish gray on breast and abdomen, the sides and flanks darker and overlaid by metallic bronze-green; femoral tufts and tuft on each side of rump white; under tail-coverts brownish gray (sometimes glossed with greenish bronze) centrally, broadly margined with dull white; bill dull black; iris dark brown; feet dusky.

Adult female. Above metallic bronze-green, golden green or greenish bronze, including middle pair of rectrices; three outer rectrices, on each side, broadly tipped with white (the white tip on third rectrix smaller and mostly confined to inner web), metallic bronze-green for basal half (more or less), the intervening portion black; remiges dark brownish slate or dusky, faintly glossed with purplish; a small postocular spot of dull white; auricular region deep dull grayish; lores dusky; malar region and underparts dull grayish white or very pale brownish gray (usually more decidedly whitish on chin, throat, and malar region); the flanks and shorter under tail-coverts usually more or less tinged with pale buffy brownish; femoral tufts and tuft on each side of rump white; bill, etc., as in adult male.

Young male. Similar to the adult female, but feathers of upperparts very narrowly and indistinctly margined terminally with pale grayish buffy, throat with small mesial streaks of dusky, and underparts usually more strongly tinged with buffy brownish, especially on sides and flanks. Also, the sixth primary is narrower (outer web 0.3 mm or fewer subterminally) and more abruptly angulated (Norris et al., 1957).

Young female. Similar to the young male, but throat without dusky streaks. Furthermore, the outer web of the sixth primary (counting from the inside) is at least 1 mm wide throughout most of its 20-mm length, rather than being very narrow toward the tip. Separation from adult females is difficult, but young females tend to have a brighter yellow to orange gape, more brown on the flanks, a more streaked throat, and unworn edges on the back and crown feathers (Leberman, 1972).

Identification   (See Plate 16C.)

In the hand. Adult males are best identified and separated from black-chinned hummingbirds by the combination of having inner primaries with small notches near the tips of the inner webs, the tail slightly forked, and a purplish red gorget. Females of both species have notched primaries, but the ruby-throated has a double-rounded tail, with the middle rectrices slightly shorter (22–24.5 mm) than the more lateral ones. The exposed culmen (17–19.5 mm) is also very slightly shorter than that of the black-chinned hummingbird, and the wing is also slightly shorter (43.5–45.5 mm vs. 46–48.5 mm).

In the field. A widely distributed species that occurs in deciduous woodlands during the breeding season, but also is found in suburban parks and gardens. Males produce humming sounds with their wings in flight, and utter a mouse-like squeaking call. The adult male's brilliant red gorget serves for identification in most areas, and except where the black-chinned hummingbird might be present the female's dull-white throat and otherwise greenish upperparts provide sufficient basis for recognition. Her tail is rounded and white-tipped, and lacks any rufous color at the base. The typical display flight of the male consists of a series of long arching flights in a pendulum-like manner, apparently without associated vocalizations.

Habitats   On its extensive breeding grounds of the eastern United States, this species is found in mixed woodlands and eastern deciduous forests rich in flowering plants; it sometimes also breeds in city parks or other areas planted with flowers. In Canada, its northern breeding limits approximately coincide with the southern limits of boreal forest; there it is generally associated with woodland clearings and edges, gardens, and orchards (Godfrey, 1966). Near the western edge of its breeding range in North Dakota it is associated with brushy margins or openings of tracts of deciduous forest, including river floodplain and upland forests (Stewart, 1975). At its southwestern limits in Texas it occurs in open coniferous and mixed woodlands, meadows with scattered groves and flowering vegetation, and urban areas (Oberholser, 1974). On their wintering areas of Costa Rica the birds have foraged where thickets and woodlands alternate with pastures (Wetmore, 1968). In El Salvador, the species winters in a wide variety of habitats, but appears to prefer open, sunny areas such as thin second-growth gallery forest and the edges of clearings (Dickey and van Rossem, 1938).

Movements   Ruby-throated hummingbirds are present in their wintering areas of Central America from late October until late March or early April (Dickey and van Rossem, 1938; Wetmore, 1968). In Texas spring migration occurs from middle or late March to mid-May, and fall migration lasts from late July or early August to late October. A few birds winter in coastal Texas, especially in and near the Rio Grande delta, and they occur casually to the eastern edge of the Edwards Plateau (Oberholser, 1974). The species sometimes winters as far north as southern Alabama, and has been reported at least twice as far north as North Carolina in December (Hauser and Currie, 1966).

Although early estimates of the energy costs of migration made ornithologists question the nonstop flight range of ruby-throats, newer data indicate that individuals carrying at least 2.1 grams of fat should be able to fly more than 950 kilometers, or easily far enough for a nonstop flight across the Gulf of Mexico (Norris et al., 1957).

During the spring migration, birds usually reach the southern parts of the Gulf Coast states in late February or early March. They generally move northward at the same approximate rate of movement as the 1.7°C isotherm, which closely correlates with the flowering times of several important spring foods such as *Aesculus pavia, Ribes odoratum, Aquilegia canadensis,* and similar species (Austin, 1975). As the birds reach their summer ranges, there is a gradual increase in the numbers of important flower species. Thus, in southern Florida, six important species are in bloom in January (and five continue through December), in the Carolinas five species bloom through April, and in the northeastern states nine species are flowering by May (Austin, 1975). Blooming in the northeastern states terminates in October, by which time the southern migration is well underway.

*Foraging Behavior
and Floral Ecology*

The most complete survey of ornithophilous flowers in the breeding range of the ruby-throated hummingbird is that of Austin (1975), who reported that this species forages on and presumably helps pollinate at least 31 plant species in 21 genera, including 18 plant families. This list excludes numerous introduced and cultivated species, as well as some plants that appear to be primarily adapted for pollination by other organisms. His list has been incorporated into the general list of hummingbird-adapted plants provided in Appendix Six. In Austin's view, at least 19 species of eastern North American plants have been influenced by selection for hummingbird pollination, and the birds also assist in the reproduction of at least 11 more species, many of which are of southwestern or West Indian affinities. R. I. Bertin (*Can. J. Zool.* 60:210–219, 1982) has concluded that the ruby-throat and its North American food plants are facultative mutualists, with the plants relatively more labile in that they are also adapted for pollination by various insects.

Ruby-throated hummingbirds are probably adapted to several primary foraging species in various parts of their extensive breeding range. Thus, in New York their nesting distribution has been reported to be locally governed by the occurrence of *Monarda didyma*, whereas in North Dakota *Impatiens* has been assigned equal importance. In most areas, at least, red is the predominant color of most hummingbird-adapted flowers, particularly in western states. Studies on the ruby-throated hummingbird in Saskatchewan, near the northern limit of the species' breeding range, have provided some information on color and feeding preferences in this species (Miller and Miller, 1971). This study found that foraging on artificial feeders occurred more or less equally throughout the day, beginning as early as half an hour after sunrise and terminating as late as an hour or more after sunset. Usually the birds concentrated on only one or two feeders, but at times they also explored other known or potential food sites as well as other colorful objects not associated with feeders. Apparently they quickly learned to recognize food sources by association with color and location, and often investigated potential food plants before they were in full flower. Experimental coloring of the feeding solutions indicated that the birds made fewer visits to blue fluids than expected by chance, but significantly more visits to clear fluids. No definite preference was shown for red fluids initially, but training the birds to associate red fluids with sugar and the others with unsweetened water quickly taught them to make the appropriate association; they soon were visiting the "correct" feeder with about 90 percent accuracy. Evidently a distinctive color is a definite aid in remembering the location of a food source.

In observations extending over two summers in a South Carolina garden, Pickens and Garrison (1931) noted that only 4 percent of the common wildflowers were red in color, but that hummingbirds predominantly visited plants of reddish colors. The authors also noted that, of 300 types of garden plants, red and orange colors occur among species of Western Hemisphere origin at a rate three times greater than those of the Eastern Hemisphere, suggesting the importance of hummingbirds in the evolutionary history of the Western Hemisphere flora. All of the eight species listed by James (1948) as the most important flowers for ruby-throated hummingbirds are red or partially red.

Breeding Biology   In general, male ruby-throats precede the females during spring migration, and usually migrate either singly or occur locally in groups of as many as several individuals gathered temporarily around favored food sources. However, the birds established territories as soon as they arrive on their breeding grounds. Territory sizes have not been accurately defined, but Pickens (1944) noted that in some cases nests may be located as close as about 63 meters apart. However, since males are promiscuous, this does not provide any indication of actual territorial limits of a single male. Pitelka (1942) reported that the feeding territory of a male in early summer consisted of about 970 square meters and was centered on a food supply, with mating a possible secondary function.

The usual aerial display has been well-described by a variety of early writers, all summarized by Bent (1940). It generally consists of flying back and forth along the arc of a wide circle, as if the bird were supported by a swaying wire, and with the swings "so accurate and precise that they suggest a geometric figure drawn in the air rather than the flight of a bird." Frequently the male passes very close to the head of the female at the bottom of the arc, with the wings and tail producing the loudest buzzing at that point. In another variation both the male and female hover in the air a short distance apart while facing one another, ascending and descending vertically over distances of from 1.5 to 3 meters. In one case these vertical oscillations were done out of synchrony, so that when the male was at the top of his flight the female was at the bottom of hers. Evidently the interest of the female in any male is limited to the few days immediately prior to egg-laying; likewise the male loses interest in a female after egg-laying is completed (Bent, 1940).

Copulation has not been well-described, but on one observed instance it occurred on the ground after a display flight by the two birds similar to the type just described (Whittle, 1937).

The construction of the nest is usually completed by the female alone and prior to egg-laying, with the exception of bits of lichens and additional lining that may be added later. It is typically constructed mostly of bud scales, about 25 mm deep and 25 mm in diameter, lined with plant down, and is covered on the outside with lichens. It usually resembles a knot saddled on a fairly small limb that slants downward from the tree. It is always sheltered from above by other limbs, and often is located directly over a brook or other open area. The height of the nest typically ranges from about 1.5 to 6 meters above the substrate, but rarely may be as high as 15 meters above ground.

Nest-building begins with leafy materials or bud scales, which are fastened to the limb by spider silk. Lichens are added around the outside before the lining of plant down is put in; in some cases the lining may not be added until the eggs have been laid and incubation has begun. Lining is added during the incubation period, and may even be added as late as two weeks after hatching. With the exception of a single observation by Welter (1935), there is no evidence that the male participates at all in nest construction.

A considerable variety of trees are used as nest sites. Pickens (1944) noted that the most commonly used sites in the upper piedmont and lower montane zones of South Carolina are lichen-covered post oaks (*Quercus minor*). However, in the lower piedmont where the oaks are more scrubby, pines and other tree species are more commonly used. In the Allegeny Park of New York, hornbeams commonly serve as nest sites, and in various other areas hickories, gums, tulip-poplars, junipers, and other species have been used. Probably those species having a fairly rough and lichen-covered bark are favored over relatively smooth-barked species.

The length of time required for construction of the nest seems highly variable. Hinman (1928) noted that a nest that was begun on May 29 was completed by June 5, and by June 8 incubation of two eggs was underway. On the other hand, Welter (1935) observed that in one observed nest 10 days elapsed from its initiation until the first egg was laid, while a later nest was essentially completed in a single day, with an egg being deposited four days later. In this unusual case the male reportedly assisted in nest-building.

Almost invariably two eggs are laid; Bent (1940) reported no exceptions to this rule, but Welter (1935) reported that only one egg was laid in one of the nests he observed. There is a one-day interval between the laying of the two eggs, and incubation begins with the laying of the second egg.

Although some shorter estimates have been reported by Bent (1940), the normal incubation period is probably 16 days. Egg dates extend from late March to June 15 in Florida, from late May to early July in New York, and from June 1 to July 17 in Michigan. It may be double-brooded in some areas (Nickell, 1948) and certainly is known to renest following an initial nesting failure. Old nests are sometimes reoccupied for subsequent use, even in subsequent years, but frequently a new nest is built, often in the same tree or a nearby one (Bent, 1940).

Fledging periods vary considerably in different areas; records from New England range from 14 to 28 days, and in a few carefully observed cases have been 20–21 days (Bent, 1940; Hinman, 1928). During the first few days after hatching the female inserts her tongue into the throat of the nestlings and squirts in nectar and tiny insects. During feeding, the female typically stands on the edge of the nest, braces her tail against its side, and some-

times thrusts her entire bill down into the nestlings' throats. As
the young birds become larger the bill may be inserted at right
angles, and even later the food may be directly passed from beak
to beak (Bent, 1940).

Evolutionary and Ecological Relationships

Mayr and Short (1970) concluded that the ruby-throated and the
black-chinned hummingbirds are very closely related geographic
representatives, comprising a superspecies. They also included
the Costa hummingbird in this species group as it is especially
similar to the black-chinned hummingbirds.

As summarized by Austin (1975), the plant relationships of the
ruby-throated hummingbird are complex; it or other hummingbirds have been effective in the selection and evolution of at least
19 species of eastern North American plants. Pickens (1927) noted
that *Macranthera "LeContei"* (= *flammea*) is the "most delicately
adjusted" species of ornithophilous plant that he was aware of in
its structural adaptations for pollination by the ruby-throat; it is
endemic in the southeastern states from Louisiana to Georgia.
Bené (1947) listed 28 species or genera of plants (including various garden or horticultural forms) reportedly visited by the species, several of which (cardinal flower, jewelweed, black locust,
horse chestnut, Oswego tea, etc.) were uniquely listed for the
ruby-throat.

Besides their relationships to these plants, ruby-throated hummingbirds exhibit a close association with sapsuckers and their
associated drilling behavior at various sap-producing trees. Foster
and Tate (1966) observed hummingbirds feeding more frequently
at sapsucker-drilled trees than the sapsuckers themselves. Although they came to these trees primarily to feed on sap, they
also fed on insects similarly attracted to the tree. Other hummingbird species (Anna, broad-tailed, and rufous) have also been
observed feeding at sapsucker drillings, but apparently mainly on
the sap itself.

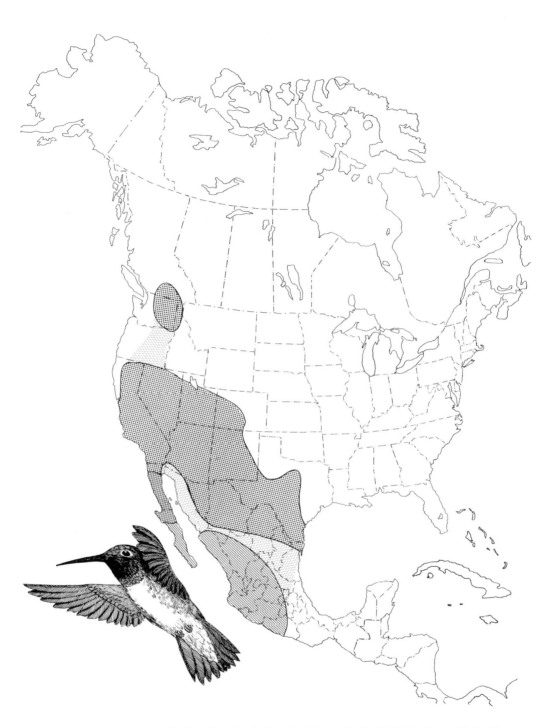

15. Breeding (stippled) and wintering (hatched) distributions of black-chinned
hummingbird. Light stippling indicates area used during migration.

BLACK-CHINNED HUMMINGBIRD

Archilochus alexandri (Bourcier and Mulsant)

Other Names Purple-throated hummingbird; Terciopelo barbanegro (Spanish).

Range Breeds from southwestern British Columbia and northwestern Montana south through western Montana, central Idaho, western Colorado, New Mexico, and south-central and southwestern Texas to northern Baja California, Sonora, and extreme northwestern Chihuahua (AOU, 1957). Winters from northern Baja California south to Guerrero, Distrito Federal, and Michoacan. (See map 15.)

North American Subspecies None recognized.

Measurements Wing, males 41.5–44 mm (ave. of 10, 42.7 mm), females 46–48.5 mm (ave. of 10, 47 mm). Exposed culmen, males 18–20.5 mm (ave. of 10, 19.2 mm), females 19.5–22 mm (ave. of 10, 20.6 mm) (Ridgway, 1911). Eggs, ave. 12.5 × 8.3 mm (extremes 11.68–13.72 × 7.87–8.89 mm).

Weights The average of 34 males was 3.09 g (range 2.7–4.1 g); that of 24 females was 3.42 g (range 3.3–3.7 g) (from various sources, including data from Museum of Vertebrate Zoology).

Description (After Ridgway, 1911.)

Adult male. Above rather dull metallic bronze-green, darker and duller on pileum, the forehead sometimes dull dusky; remiges dark brownish slate or dusky, faintly glossed with purplish; tail (except middle pair of rectrices) bronzy purplish black; loral, suborbital, auricular, and malar regions, chin, upper throat, and sides of throat uniformly opaque or velvety black; lower throat metallic violet or violet-purple, changing to black in position *b* (see note at beginning of Part Two for position descriptions); chest dull grayish white or very pale brownish gray; the underparts of body similar, but usually more decidedly grayish medially; the sides and flanks darker and glossed or overlaid with metallic bronze or bronze-green; under tail-coverts brownish gray (sometimes glossed with bronzy) centrally or medially, broadly margined with white; femoral tufts and tuft on each side of rump white; bill dull black; iris dark brown; feet dusky.

Adult female. Above rather dull metallic bronze-green, the pileum much duller, usually dull grayish brown or brownish gray, at least on forehead and crown; remiges dark brownish slate or dusky, faintly glossed with purplish; three outer rectrices (on each side) broadly tipped with white, the subterminal portion (extensively) black, the basal half (more or less) metallic bronze-green (sometimes grayish basally); underparts dull white or grayish white (more purely white on abdomen and under tail-coverts); the throat sometimes streaked or guttately spotted with dusky; femoral tufts and tuft on each side of rump white; bill, etc., as in adult male.

Young male. Similar to the adult female, but feathers of upperparts margined terminally with pale grayish buffy; underparts more or less strongly tinged or suffused with pale buffy brownish; throat streaked or spotted with dusky.

Young female. Similar to the young male, but throat usually immaculate or with the dusky spots or streaks smaller and less distinct.

Identification   (See Plate 16D.)

In the hand. Males best identified by the combination of the inner primaries having notches near the tips of the inner webs, a slightly forked tail, and a throat that is blackish, becoming violet posteriorly. Females also have notched primaries, but the tail is rounded, with the middle rectrices the longest (24–26 mm), and a dull-white throat. The exposed culmen (19.5–22 mm) of females is also very slightly longer than that of the otherwise similar female ruby-throated hummingbird; so is the wing (46–48.5 mm vs. 43.5–45.5 mm).

In the field. Occurs in mountain meadows and woodlands, canyons, and orchards. Males produce a dry buzzing sound with their wings when they fly, and utter a low *tup*. The blackish throat of the male is a distinctive fieldmark, but the female cannot be safely told from the female ruby-throat in a few areas (such as eastern Texas) where both might occur. Males do not sing while perched or in the air, but resemble the ruby-throat in that their courtship consists of long, swinging, pendulum-like swoops above the perched female, producing a long and drawn-out plaintive note at the bottom of the dive. They also perform a droning flight, resembling a horizontal figure 8 (Bent, 1940).

Females closely resemble those of the Costa hummingbird, but have longer bills, are generally grayer below, and have throat markings ranging from nearly immaculate to extensively marked with dusky. Young males are also rather heavily marked with dusky on the throat and are usually grayer below than Costa males. Perhaps the best distinction of these two species is their voice; the chip call of the black-chinned is low pitched, softer, and a slurred *tew* or *tchew*, rarely run together in a series, and the birds are generally much less vocal. While hovering, both species often nervously flick the tail open and pump it up and down (Stiles, 1971).

Habitats In breeding areas of California, breeding female black-chinned hummingbirds are characteristic of deciduous trees along stream bottoms, particularly in canyons, but they also occur in irrigated orchards. Evidently proximity to water is important in that area, and the associated trees include willows, cottonwoods, alders, sycamores, and valley oaks. Males frequent similar habitats, but often occur on drier canyon sides such as among live oaks and chaparral, or in desert washes where mesquite and catclaw thickets occur (Grinnell and Miller, 1944). In Texas the species is the most common nesting hummingbird, and is associated with agave-cactus desert and subhumid juniper-oak woods (Oberholser, 1974). In Arizona black-chins nest primarily among willows, cottonwoods, and sycamores along streams and in olive trees in towns (Phillips et al., 1964). Their favorite habitats there seem to be the mouths of canyons where sycamores occur in association with water, but they also extend to the dry washes where small patches of willows are present (Bent, 1940).

Movements Black-chinned hummingbirds winter almost entirely within Mexico, but have occasionally been reported during winter in southern California (once at Pacific Grove) and south-coastal Texas. Fall departure dates from Washington, Oregon, and California range from mid-August to late September. In Texas the majority of the birds are gone by mid-October, with a few persisting into December (Oberholser, 1974). Spring migration into Texas occurs from middle and late March to early May. The species usually arrives in Arizona in mid-March, and is common in some parts of southern California by late March. By mid-May it has reached northern Oregon, eastern Washington, and southern British Columbia (Bent, 1940). In Arizona the species is common through September, but apparently by midsummer most of the adult males have left the state, leaving only females and juveniles (Phillips et al., 1964).

There are a considerable number of extralimital records, including sightings in Nova Scotia (*Audubon Field Notes*, 18:495), Florida (*Audubon Field Notes* 18:457), Massachusetts (*American Birds* 34:140, 254), and Louisiana (*American Birds* 24:58; 31:341).

Foraging Behavior and Floral Ecology Much of the available information on the foraging behavior of black-chins comes from the work of F. Bené (1947). He found that the timing of the bird's arrival in its southwestern breeding areas coincides with the flowering of important food plants. In the vicinity of Phoenix, the advent of irrigation and introduction of exotic flora evidently was reponsible for the development of black-chin breeding in that area. When they arrive in late February or early March, the plants on which they feed are already in bloom, including agave, tree-tobacco (*Nicotiana glauca*), lantana, citrus trees, shrimp plant (*Beloperone guttata*), nasturtium, *Buddleia*, and others. The birds depart the area in June or July, presumably to move to higher elevations in the mountains where midsummer food is more abundant, and perhaps to undertake a second breeding cycle there.

Bené (1947) noted that black-chinned hummingbirds have been reported visiting at least 37 species or genera of flowers. He determined that they have no innate preference for red flowers, but that color preference could be conditioned by training. He also established that the form of a flower could serve as a conditioning stimulus, and that the memory of receptacle features or flower shape was apparently held for periods lasting several months. He also established that the birds could detect fairly small differences in concentrations of honey solutions, but judged that flower scent did not play any evident role in locating hidden nectar receptacles.

Bent (1940) summarized the many species of plants mentioned as foraging sites for black-chins, and noted that the exotic tree-tobacco (*Nicotiana glauca*) is very popular in California. Bené (1947) noted that the species is especially attracted to Hall's honeysuckle (*Lonicera japonica*); other species that have been specifically mentioned include *Delphinium cardinalis*, *Anisocanthus thurberi*, ocotillo, *Lycium andersoni*, palo verde, ironwood, Texas buckeye, Texas redbud, and Texas mountain laurel (Bent, 1940).

Breeding Biology   Although the data are not very clear, the sexes migrate separately in the spring, and there is an interval between their arrivals in the spring breeding areas, with males often arriving in advance. According to Bené (1947), black-chins establish three kinds of territories. One is a female nesting preserve in a breeding locality that includes a nest site, one or more perches, a roost site, and a feeding site. One is a mating area, visited by both sexes. Last is a male feeding preserve that includes guarding perches, a feeding site, and perhaps a roost. Males sometimes visit the female's nesting preserve, but do not feed on it. The male roosts near the female at the time of copulation and for a few days thereafter, but arrives only at nightfall, after his last meal of the day. On the preserve the nest and feeding sites are specifically defended, with the strength of defense growing as the breeding cycle progresses. Within the male preserve, only a relatively small area (from 3 to 6 meters in diameter) may be defended. After the breeding season the sphere of active defense may be an area as small as 7–15 meters in diameter, containing a couple of feeders.

Although birds probably initially establish territories on the basis of a local food supply, a later change in the territory may

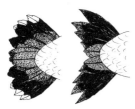

bring about a change in the nest site, perch, or roost, and thus a shift in the area guarded for food. For a male the roost is the central point in the territory, and he returns to it invariably except for the few days at the time of courtship, when he roosts beside the courted female. As the young birds become independent, they settle on the territories left by their parents at the end of the breeding cycle, and remain there until they depart for wintering areas (Bené, 1947).

With the appearance of females on the male's display areas, aerial display begins. It consists of a series of long, swooping, pendulum-like maneuvers about 30 meters in length, with the male passing very close to the female at the bottom of the arc, and ending about 5 meters higher (Bent, 1940). It sometimes takes the form of a narrow horizontal figure 8, and is accompanied by a loud whistling sound, presumably made by the wings or tail. According to Woods (1927), the dive may be accompanied by about four thin, vibrant notes, and the males utter a distinct courtship note as well, consisting of a long, drawn, pulsating, plaintive, liquid note. At the apex of each flight the bird may hover and call, or produce an apparently mechanical sound evidently caused by patting his wings together underneath him, sounding like the noises made by a bathing bird. Bené (1947) reported seeing as many as three swooping courtship sequences per day. These continued at least through the egg-laying period, but ceased shortly after egg-laying was finished, apparently through repeated rejections by the female. In the case of two females, the interval from the start of nest construction to the laying of the first egg was 5 days, whereas a third female probably laid her first egg 6 or 7 days after nesting was started. The eggs are usually laid one or two days apart, but Demaree (1970) observed a case in which two eggs were laid in a single day, only 3 days after nest-building had been initiated.

The nest is very similar in size to that of the ruby-throated hummingbird, but typically is not covered by lichens on the outside. It often is composed almost entirely of the yellowish downy material from the underside of sycamore leaves, resulting in a distinctive yellowish cast. However, the outside is sometimes covered by various small materials attached to spider webbing, including lichens. These often include bud scales, stamens, flower, bark, or leaf fragments, and the like. Nests are usually 1–3 meters above ground, and often overhang small or dry creek beds. They are located either in a fork or on a small, drooping branch of one of many trees, including alders, cottonwoods, oaks, sycamores, laurels, willows, apples, and oranges (Bent, 1940). All but 5 of the 26 nests tabulated by Pitelka (1951a) were in live oaks. Occasionally the nests are situated among woody vines or on taller herbaceous weedy plants. Rarely have they been found as high as 9 meters above ground, but the average height is less than 3 meters (Pitelka, 1951a).

Incubation is by the female alone, and has been estimated to last from 13 to 16 days. In a nest closely observed by Demaree (1970), incubation began the day after egg-laying was completed. One of the eggs hatched 16 days later; the other did not hatch. The young bird left its nest 21 days later, and remained in the ivy vines around the nest for 2 more days.

There have been several reported instances of females incubating eggs in one nest while feeding young in another (Cogswell, 1949), suggesting that double-brooding may be fairly frequent in black-chins. In one instance, a female was observed building a nest during the final week of brooding her earlier brood; thus, laying of the eggs in the new nest apparently occurred 2 to 7 days after the fledging of the first one. These observations were made in California, but double-brooding may also occur in Arizona (Phillips et al., 1964) and New Mexico (Bailey, 1928). In the Santa Barbara area of California the species is single-brooded, breeding from late April through June, at the same time that nesting occurs in the Costa hummingbird (Pitelka, 1951a).

The female continues to feed her young for several days after fledging, but the young birds gradually begin to learn the identity of suitable food plants. This occurs only gradually, after repeated visits to obnoxious species, probing fertilized flowers with dried nectaries, overlooking familiar fruitful species, and generally obtaining their food in an awkward fashion (Bené, 1947).

Evolutionary and Ecological Relationships

Hybridization in the wild has occurred with at least the Allen, Costa, Anna, and broad-tailed hummingbirds (Lynch and Ames, 1970; Mayr and Short, 1970); a possible hybrid with the ruby-throated hummingbird has also been suggested (*Bulletin of Oklahoma Ornithological Society* 2:14–15). As Mayr and Short (1970) have noted, this species is closely related to the ruby-throated hummingbird—the two having essentially allopatric breeding ranges—and they comprise a well-defined superspecies. They suggested that the Costa hummingbird is also a close relative of this superspecies and also mentioned that the broad-tailed hummingbird may be more closely related to this superspecies than to other species now included in *Selasphorus*.

Although it has a relatively wide total breeding distribution, the black-chinned hummingbird is common only in the southwestern United States, where a maximum abundance of bird-adapted flowers occurs. Bené (1947) listed nearly 40 species of flowers frequented by the species, many of which are southwestern in their distribution patterns. Those listed exclusively for the black-chinned hummingbird include chuparosa (*Beloperone californica*), shrimp plant (*B. guttata*), catmint (*Nepeta* sp.), myrtle (*Vinca major*), palo verde (*Parkinsonia microphylla*), *Poinciana*, rose of Sharon (*Althea* sp.), garden balsam (*Impatiens balsamina*), and iris (*Iris* spp.). Most of these plants are, of course, garden or horticultural forms rather than native North American flowers, but at least chuparosa is a typical hummingbird-adapted species with a number of specific adaptations that facilitate probing without damaging the ovaries (Grant and Grant, 1968).

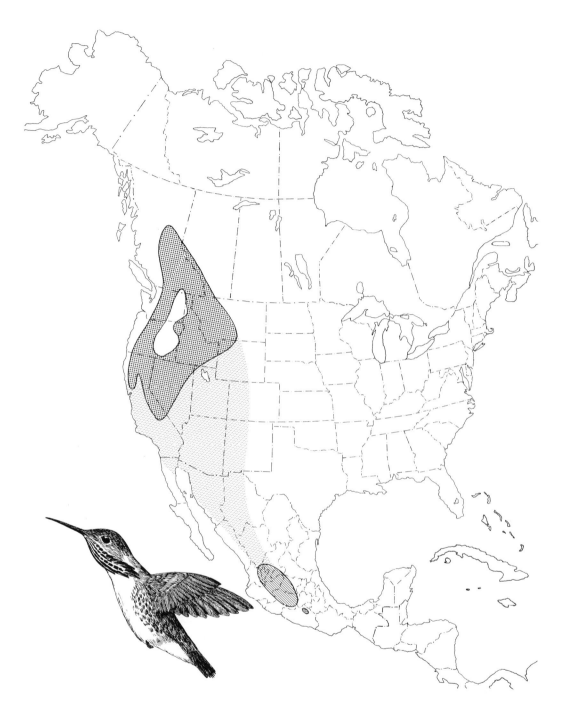

16. Breeding (stippled) and wintering (hatched) distributions of calliope hummingbird. Light stippling indicates areas used during migration; the small area of cross-hatching indicates *lowei*, an apparently residential race.

192

CALLIOPE HUMMINGBIRD

Archilochus calliope (Gould)
(*Stellula calliope* of AOU, 1957)

Other Names None in general English use; Chupamirto rafaguitas (Spanish).

Range Breeds in the mountains of western North America from central British Columbia and southwestern Alberta south through Washington, Oregon, Nevada, and California to northern Baja California, east to Utah and western Colorado, and probably in Guerrero, Mexico. Winters in Mexico (AOU, 1957). (See map 16.)

North American Subspecies *A. c. calliope* (Gould). Range in North America as indicated above, except for Guerrero, Mexico, where an endemic race occurs.

Measurements Wing, males 37–40 mm (ave. of 10, 38.7 mm), females 40–44 mm (ave. of 10, 42.8 mm). Exposed culmen, males 13.5–15 mm (ave. of 10, 14.3 mm), females 15–16 mm (ave. of 10, 15.6 mm) (Ridgway, 1911). Eggs, ave. 12.1 × 8.3 mm (extremes 10.7–13.0 × 7.4–9.6 mm).

Weights The average of 46 males was 2.50 g (range 1.9–3.2 g); that of 26 females was 2.83 g (range 2.2–3.2 g) (from various sources, including specimens in the Museum of Vertebrate Zoology).

Description (After Ridgway, 1911.)

Adult male. Above metallic bronze-green, usually rather duller on forehead; middle pair of rectrices subspatulate or with subterminal portion contracted, dull purplish black or dusky, edged basally (more or less distinctly) with cinnamon-rufous, and broadly tipped with dull brownish gray; remaining rectrices similar in coloration, but cinnamomeous basal edgings less distinct (sometimes obsolete) and grayish tip less distinct; remiges dull brownish slate or dusky, very faintly glossed with purplish; feathers of gorget narrow and distinctly outlined, much elongated posteriorly, pure white basally and metallic reddish purple (solferino) terminally, the basal white much exposed, especially on chin and upper throat; foreneck and chest white, or grayish white; rest of underparts more grayish, strongly tinged or suffused with cinnamon-buff laterally, the sides glossed, or overlaid, with metallic bronze-green, the under tail-coverts white, tinged with cinnamon-buff toward anal region; maxilla dull black or dusky; mandible dusky terminally, more flesh-color basally; iris dark brown; feet dusky.

Adult female. Above metallic bronze-green or greenish bronze (usually much more bronzy than in adult male); remiges brownish slate or dusky, very faintly glossed with purplish; middle pair of rectrices dull bronze-green or greenish bronze, sometimes with

193

terminal portion (more or less extensively) purplish dusky or blackish; next pair dull bronze-green with terminal third (more or less) black; the subbasal portion edged (on both webs), more or less distinctly, with cinnamon-buff; next pair similar but with the black relatively more extended and with an apical spot (usually small and wedge-shaped) of white; next similar but white apical spot larger and basal half mostly brownish gray; outermost rectrix like the last but only about the basal third grayish and white apical spot still larger; auricular region light brownish gray; a dusky triangular space in front of eye; chin and throat dull brownish white, usually more or less streaked or flecked with dusky or bronzy brownish; chest pale grayish cinnamon-buff or dull whitish, the median portion of breast and abdomen similar; sides and flanks cinnamon or deep cinnamon-buff; the under tail-coverts similar but paler; femoral tufts and tuft on each side of rump white; bill, etc., as in adult male.

Young male. Apparently not essentially if at all different from the adult female, but older individuals have some metallic purple or purplish red feathers on middle of throat.

Young female. Similar to the adult female but general color of upperparts more decidedly bronzy, with feathers very narrowly and indistinctly margined terminally with dull brownish or grayish buffy.

Identification   (See Plate 16E.)

In the hand. Unusually narrow and white-based feathers of the male's gorget are unique among North American hummingbirds; also, in both sexes the inner rectrices are expanded near the tips, rather than being gradually tapering. The very small size (wings 37–44 mm) of these birds is also a helpful criterion.

In the field. Usually found in mountain meadows near coniferous forests. The very small size of both sexes and the red-and-white striped gorget of the males are unique. When feeding the male sometimes utters a soft *tsip*, and also utters very chippy and squeaking noises; the most distinctive sound is a muffled *bzzt* or *pfft* produced near the bottom of each display swoop, which is a shallow U-shaped course. A high-pitched *see-ree* note is produced by the male as it approaches a female. Females closely resemble females of rufous and Allen hummingbirds, but are paler brown on the flanks, and the cinnamon of the tail feathers does not extend to the central feathers. The chip note of the calliope is very high-pitched and similar to that of the Costa, but it is relatively silent under most conditions. Females are distinctively small and short-billed, usually with a pale rusty wash on the sides, and rather little rufous in the tail. When hovering the birds hold the tail very still and unusually high above the plane of the body (Stiles, 1971).

Habitats   In California this species breeds in mixed brushland and forest, either of deciduous or coniferous trees or intermingled, in canyon bottoms, valley floors, and forest glades. Males are typically found in open areas, whereas females nest mostly in woods (Grinnell and Miller, 1944). Coniferous forest edges adjacent to meadow areas are also favored breeding locations. In the Grand Teton National Park area, territorial males frequented areas of low willows near grass- and sage-dominated meadows rich in scarlet gilia (*Ipomopsis*) and Indian paintbrush; females nested in nearby groves of lodgepole pines (personal observations). In Canada the birds are associated with openings in woodlands, glades, burntlands, and flowering meadows, and typically nest in open woodlands (Godfrey, 1966).

The species occupies a remarkably broad vertical range during the breeding season. In Washington it has been found nesting as low as 180 meters above sea level in the Columbia River valley; in California it is usually not found below 1200 meters and more commonly nests above 2400 meters. In the Sierra Nevada it often nests nearly to timberline, between 3000 and 3500 meters, and follows the advancing summer season to the limit of flowers. On the other hand, near the northern limit of its range in Montana, it probably nests at elevations of from less than 630 meters in the Kootenai Valley to perhaps as high as 2100 meters (Bent, 1940).

On migration, calliopes use a wider array of habitats. In Texas, where it is very rare, the birds are usually found along streams on mesas or in broad valleys where fringes of timber or tall thickets occur (Oberholser, 1974). In New Mexico it occurs from about 1500 to 3400 meters during the fall migration, and is probably most numerous on the high mountain meadows (Bailey, 1928).

Movements   During the winter months this species is largely confined to central Mexico, particularly the states of Michoacan, Mexico, and Guerrero. The species is rare east of Michoacan and Guerrero, and its migratory route is oval-like, similar to (but narrower than) that of the Allen and rufous hummingbirds. In the spring, the species migrates up the western portions of Mexico, arriving in southern California in early March. It apparently is limited in Arizona primarily to the southwestern and central deserts, and skirts most of Arizona, New Mexico, and Utah (Phillips, 1975).

The spring migration apparently passes slowly through California, with the birds arriving in Oregon during early May, in Washington from late April to mid-May, and in central British Columbia at about the same time. As with the rufous hummingbird, Idaho and Montana are reached last, usually not before the middle or latter part of May (Bent, 1940).

The fall migration likewise begins early, with adult males preceding females and immatures by a week or more. The birds are rare but regular in Colorado during late July and August; they sometimes summer in the state, although they have not been proven to nest there (Bailey and Niedrach, 1965). Late dates of departure for Washington, British Columbia, and Idaho are in late August, early to mid-September for Montana, and early September for Nevada. Similarly, late California dates are for early to mid-September (Bent, 1940). In northern Arizona the fall records are from July 14 to September 29 (Phillips et al., 1964), and the extreme dates in Texas are from July 25 to September 14 (Oberholser, 1974). There are no winter records for the United States, and probably the normal wintering limits are south of the central Mexican transverse volcanic belt (Phillips, 1975). Calliopes seem to wander from their normal migratory routes less than many of the other western hummingbirds, and there are few extralimital records. They sometimes wander out to the foothills and plains of Colorado during late summer (*American Birds*, 32:1192), and they have also reached western South Dakota, western Nebraska, and Kansas, as well as extreme eastern New Mexico (Clayton) and adjacent western Texas.

Foraging Behavior and Floral Ecology

This is the smallest of the hummingbirds that regularly occur in the United States, and as such is probably at a disadvantage in competing with the larger species. Migrant calliope hummingbirds during late May and June in Nevada sometimes have territorial encounters with the larger broad-tailed hummingbirds, and yet in the cases observed the calliopes were the victors when broad-tails entered their feeding territories. A male has also been reported diving at male black-chinned hummingbirds, and was defending a larger territory than either rufous or broad-tailed hummingbirds that were in the vicinity (Bailey and Niedrach, 1965).

In most areas of its range, the calliope breeds in company with various other western species, but tends to occur at higher elevations during summer than the others. Grant and Grant (1968) listed seven species of hummingbird-pollinated flowers (three of *Castilleja*, two of *Penstemon*, *Aquilegia formosa*, and *Ipomopsis aggregata*) that commonly occur in the higher Sierra Nevada and are regularly visited by this species during the breeding season. The birds forage almost to timberline on *Penstemon newberryi*, and occasionally have been seen above timberline (at 3300 meters) foraging on an introgressive population of *Penstemon menziesii davidsonii*.

According to Grinnell and Miller (1944), favorite flowers include gooseberries and currants (*Ribes*), manzanitas (*Arctostaphylos*), paintbrush, and penstemons. Bent (1940) indicated that they prefer red columbine and scarlet Indian paintbrush, but also use the yellow monkey flower (*Mimulus implexus*), as well as a lousewort (*Pedicularis semibarbata*) and a snow plant (*Sarcodes sanguinea*). Calliopes are also adept at hawking insects in flight, perhaps most often dipterans, hymenopterans, and coleopterans, but probably including almost any small insect (Bent, 1940).

In contrast to some of the larger hummingbird species, the calliope tends both to perch and to forage rather close to the ground; when foraging with larger species it feeds on flowers near the bottom of the plant, whereas other hummers more often forage on the topmost flowers (Bailey and Neidrach, 1965).

Breeding Biology

Males probably establish territories as soon as they arrive on their breeding grounds. No specific information on territory sizes is available, but there is one instance when four males maintained teritories within a 23,200-square-meter plot (Bent, 1940). By the first day of Calder's (1971) study on June 13 in the Grand Teton area the males were already actively engaged in territorial disputes; the territoriality continued until late July, when hatching occurred.

Bent (1940) summarized descriptions of the aerial display of the male. Like the other species, the display consists of a series of swooping flights along a U-shaped course that may be 7 to 9 meters across and begin from a height of 9 to 18 meters. It is perhaps a more shallow course than in some of the other species, and the accompanying sound is a mechanical buzzing, sounding like a *bzzt*. Evidently the wings are able to generate a more explosive and repetitive metallic *tzing* sound as well, which was produced by a male as it was hovering near a perched female (Wyman, 1920).

In one observation of copulation, the female was perched on a dead weed when a male shot past her close to the ground, flew about 7 meters upward along a hillside, then turned and darted back down in a narrow ellipse. On reaching the female he alighted on her and immediately copulated (Wyman, 1920).

Calliope nests are typically located below a larger branch or canopy of foliage, usually on a small branch that has small knots or cones on it. Frequently the tree is a conifer, and the nest is placed among a cluster of old cones in such a way as to resemble one of them extremely closely. When placed in aspens, the nests may mimic mistletoe knots. In height, they may range from 50 centimeters above the ground to as high as 21 meters. Of 9 nests in the San Bernardino Mountains of southern California, 6 were in yellow (ponderosa) or Jeffrey pine, 2 were in silver fir, and 1 was in an alder (Bent, 1940). However, in Montana they are commonly placed in Engelmann spruce, western hemlock, and arborvitae, or in alpine fir at higher elevations. Of 21 nests observed by Weydemeyer (1927), 9 were in Englemann spruce, 6 were in arborvitae, 3 in western hemlock, 2 in alpine fir, and 1 in Douglas fir. The nests ranged from 1 to 3 meters above the substrate (averaging a little more than 2 meters). Montana nests are often placed above a creek bank or along the edge of the forest, and invariably where there is a low branch hanging free of the rest of the foliage and providing a clear view in all directions (Weydemeyer, 1927).

Calder (1971) reported that in the Grand Teton area the nest is always located under a protective branch. Thus, it does not face the heat-sink of the cold nocturnal sky, and the overhead cover also provides protection from predators and precipitation. In this area the birds often nest at the eastern edge of wooded areas, in sites where the sunlight strikes the nest immediately as it clears the eastern horizon, and thus begins to warm the nest and incubating female.

Like some other hummingbirds, female calliopes often use the same nest site in subsequent years. Series of two-, three-, and even four-story nests have thus been reported, suggesting that at least a few individuals of this species may live as long as five years. Nests of the species are typically fairly small (about 31–44 mm in outside diameter), and invariably closely blended to the appearance of the nest substrate, with green to brownish lichens. When built among pine cones the outer surface is covered with bits of tree bark and small cone shreds, and usually rests against the side of a cone or is saddled between two cones. The shell of the nest is made of mosses, needles, bark, small leaves, and various miscellaneous materials, bound and covered with spider webbing and associated camouflage. The nest lining is composed of plant down, frequently the silk of willows or cottonwoods. Second-year additions to a nest are composed mainly of such materials, but at times the rim of the nest will also be heightened (Bent, 1940).

There is no good information on the timing of nest construction, but it is probably fairly rapid. In an Alberta nest, the first egg was deposited well before the sides of the nest were fully completed, and the second egg was deposited 3 days later. Nest construction continued well into the incubation period, which lasted 16 days. Calder (1971) reported a 15-day incubation period in the Grand Teton area, and in two nests noted that the number of foraging trips during incubation ranged from 87 to 111 times per day (about 3.6 hours per day). There was no relationship between duration or frequency of foraging flights and environmental temperatures, but the females did not feed the young after their last trip of the evening. Evidently this food was used for maintaining the body metabolism for the 8- to 9-hour period of nocturnal fasting, when the environmental temperature sometimes dropped nearly to freezing. Minimum night-time body temperatures were from 19.9 to 29.8°C above the corresponding minimum air temperatures, confirming the general view that incubating females do not become torpid at night.

The number of foraging trips after hatching was similar to that prior, but they were of longer duration; the total hours of absence per day (5–11) was also considerably longer. By the time the young were 8 days old they had attained a midday homeothermal condition, and brooding was discontinued after 11–12 days (Calder, 1971). In Alberta observations, the nesting period lasted 18 and 21 days in two different years, compared to a 21–23 day nesting period observed by Calder in Wyoming. The total nesting period (egg-laying to fledging) is about 37 days in British Columbia, and 34–38 days for western North America in general. In British Columbia the egg dates range from mid-May to mid-July, with a peak in mid-June (Brunton et al., 1979). Likewise, in California the egg dates are from late May to July 30, with a peak between June 10 and June 28, suggesting a very similar nesting cycle there. On the other hand, a few Utah egg records are entirely for July (Bent, 1940).

There is no indication that the calliope is double-brooded any-where within its range; the short nesting season typical of the western mountains probably would normally prevent such behavior. Weydemeyer (1927) found no evidence of a nest being used more than once in a single season.

Evolutionary and Ecological Relationships

Mayr and Short (1970) suggested that this species is a close relative of and probably should be considered congeneric with the forms currently separated in three other genera (*Selasphorus, Calypte,* and *Archilochus*). They did not suggest a possible nearest living relative. However, wild hybrids with the Costa and Anna hummingbirds have been reliably reported (Banks and Johnson, 1961), and one collected specimen (now lost) was a probable hybrid with the rufous hummingbird (Banks and Johnson, 1961). Thus, there are intergeneric hybrids with both *Selasphorus* and *Archilochus* (*"Calypte"*); the coloration and shape of the female's tail put the species somewhat intermediate between these two very poorly defined genera.

This species has a somewhat shorter bill than the other common western hummingbirds, and as a result is perhaps less able to reach the nectar of deeply tubular flowers. However, as Grant and Grant (1968) have noted, the very long tongue of hummingbirds helps to complement actual bill length, and the correspondence between bill length and corolla tube length is only a general one. On its breeding grounds, the calliope hummingbird often seems to be associated with *Ipomopsis aggregata*, which has a fairly short corolla tube, and with various species of *Castilleja*.

Genus *Selasphorus* Swainson 1831

Synonyms: *Atthis* Reichenbach 1854

*T*his genus includes eight or nine species of Middle and North American hummingbirds that are fairly small (wing 35–50 mm), with a bill that is blackish, slender, straight, and about as long as the head, a rounded culmen that is contracted into a slight ridge at the base, and with smooth edges on the upper mandible. The nasal operculum is hidden by frontal feathering that reaches beyond the nostrils. The wing is about three times as long as the exposed culmen, and the outermost primary (or two) is the longest, the outermost usually attenuated or sharply pointed in adult males. The tail is from two-thirds or three-fifths the length of the wing, and is rounded or nearly square-tipped in males, with the rectrices usually broad basally, but with pointed tips. In females and young the tail is rufous basally and rounded, and the individual rectrices are often tipped with white or rufous. The sexes are dimorphic; the adult males usually have a red to purple gorget, rufous coloring at least on the edges of some of the rectrices, and sometimes extensive rufous on the tail and body.

17. Residential range of bumblebee (cross-hatching) hummingbird; that of the (probably) conspecific wine-throated (stippled) hummingbird is also shown for comparison.

BUMBLEBEE HUMMINGBIRD

Selasphorus heloisa (Lesson and DeLattre)
(*Atthis heloisa* of AOU, 1957)

Other Names Heloise's hummingbird, Morcom's hummingbird; Chupamirto garganta violada (Spanish).

Range Breeds in the mountains of Mexico from southwestern Chihuahua and southeastern Sinaloa, Nuevo Leon, and Tamaulipas south to Oaxaca and Veracruz (Friedmann et al., 1950). The probably conspecific form *S. ellioti* (the wine-throated hummingbird) occurs from Chiapas south to Honduras. (See map 17.)

North American Subspecies *S. h. morcomi* (Ridgway). Breeds in the Sierra Madre Occidental of Mexico from southern Chihuahua southward (*Anales del Instituto de Biología, Univ. Mex.*, 32:338–9). Accidental in Arizona.

Measurements Wing, males 32.5–38 mm (ave. of 9, 34.6 mm), females 35.5–38 mm (ave. of 8, 36 mm). Exposed culmen, males 11.5–13 mm (ave. of 9, 12.1 mm), females 11.5–13 mm (ave of 8, 12.4 mm) (Ridgway, 1911). Eggs, no information.

Weights The average of 11 males was 2.13 g (range 1.95–2.7 g); that of 4 females was 2.33 g (range 2.2–2.5 g) (Delaware Museum of Natural History).

Description (after Ridgway, 1911).

Adult male. Above metallic bronze-green, greenish bronze, or golden bronze (sometimes tinged with copper-bronze on back); middle pair of rectrices metallic bronze-green or greenish bronze (sometimes dusky at tip), both webs edged for basal half or more with cinnamon-rufous; next pair of rectrices with basal half or more cinnamon-rufous, the terminal portion black, this usually separated from the cinnamon-rufous by a space of bronze-green or greenish bronze; other rectrices with basal half or more cinnamon-rufous, the subterminal portion extensively black (usually with more or less of bronze-green or greenish bronze between the black and the cinnamon-rufous portion), the tip broadly white; remiges brownish slate color or dusky, very faintly glossed with violaceous; sides of head brownish gray or grayish brown, passing into dull white (except in *S. ellioti*) on anterior portion of malar region and on postocular region; chin and throat brilliant metallic magenta purple, changing to bluish purple and even, partly, to greenish blue (but generally more reddish in *S. ellioti*), the more posterior feathers of the throat much elongated, especially laterally; chest, sides of neck, breast (medially), abdomen, and under tail-coverts dull white or grayish white; sides and flanks light cinnamon-rufous, overlaid, more or less extensively, by metallic bronze or bronze-green; bill dull blackish; iris dark brown; feet dusky.

Adult female. Above similar to the adult male, but tail with relatively much more black and less cinnamon-rufous, the latter also duller, especially on lateral rectrices, the middle pair of retrices without cinnamon-rufous edgings, the white tips also less purely white, those of inner rectrices sometimes cinnamomeous; chin and throat white, conspicuously spotted with metallic bronze; rest of underparts as in the adult male, but sides and flanks more extensively and uniformly cinnamon-rufous; and under tail-coverts more or less strongly tinged with the same.

Young male. Similar to the adult female, but tail, sides, and flanks as in adult male (the middle pair of rectrices, however, wholly bronze-green or greenish bronze).

Identification

(See Plate 8H.)

In the hand. Extremely small hummingbird (wing 32–38 mm) with very short bill (exposed culmen 11–13 mm), smaller than any other North American species. The male has an elongated reddish gorget, and both sexes have a rounded tail with cinnamon at the base. The outermost primary is narrower and more or less attenuated (but not sharply pointed) at the tip. The individual rectrices are normal in shape, and rounded at the tips.

In the field. Usually found in pines, pine-oak woodlands, or cloud forests (in Mexico). Its very small size helps to identify it; it is similar to the calliope hummingbird, but the male's gorget is not streaked with white, and the tail is rounded, with white tips. Females also closely resemble those of the calliope, but tend to have buff-tipped tails. In flight, the wings make little sound, and the movements are relatively sluggish. Males gather in loose groups to sing within earshot of one another; the song lasts 30–40 seconds and, although weak, is said to be beautiful. It has been described as a shrill whistle, changing rapidly in pitch, and the closely related (probably conspecific) wine-throated hummingbird of Guatemala and Honduras is said to utter a "sweetly varied outpouring" of sounds lasting for most of a minute (Skutch, 1973).

Habitats

In Mexico this species occurs mainly in the transition zone between 1500 and 2100 meters of the Sierra Occidental, and to as high as 2800 meters in the western portion of the State of Mexico (Friedmann et al., 1950). Its habitats include cloud forest edges, pines, and open pine-oak woodlands. Farther south, *S. ellioti* occurs in similar scrubby and open woodland habitats from the highlands of Chiapas southward to Honduras. In Guatemala it ranges from 900 to 2600 meters in open pine and oak woodlands, and also in bushy areas (Land, 1970). In El Salvador it has been found in low scrub at 2150 meters in the crater of the Volcan de Santa Ana (Dickey and van Rossem, 1938). In Honduras it occurs in and around cloud forests from 1500 meters upwards, especially in scrubby areas outside the forests that are rich in flowers (Monroe, 1968).

Movements

Bumblebee hummingbirds are probably fairly sedentary throughout most of their range, but perhaps the northwestern race *S. morcomi* is subject to some seasonal movements. This might account for the only records for this species in the Unites States. Two female specimens were obtained in Ramsey Canyon of the Huachuca Mountains in Arizona on July 2, 1896; otherwise the species has not been collected within several hundred kilometers of U.S. borders (Phillips et al., 1964). One other presumed early Texas specimen later proved to be a young calliope hummingbird (*Auk* 8:115).

Foraging Behavior and Floral Ecology

Little is known on this subject. Moore (1939a) described the species as one of several foraging on a large shrub in southeastern Sinaloa bearing thousands of grayish-lavender blooms. It also was observed foraging on a maroon-colored species of legume, and on some tawny flowers of a huge *Opuntia* cactus (Bent, 1940). Schaldach (1963) observed foraging on mints and sages (*Salvia*), and Wagner (1946b) reported foraging on *Erythrina americana*.

In a study area in Oaxaca, Lyon (1976) found that bumblebee hummingbirds were nonterritorial, but their small size enabled them to survive on the blossoms of unprotected plants located outside the territories of the larger species of hummingbirds found in the same area. Furthermore, they were able to utilize some bee-pollinated species of flowers (*Penstemon perfoliatus* and *P. gentianoides*) that produce only small amounts of nectar and thus are not exploited by the larger hummingbird. They also used another small species (*Cuphea jorullensis*) that otherwise was exploited only by white-eared hummingbirds. Furthermore, their curious bee-like flight apparently allowed them to forage for long periods in stands of a favored food plant (*Rigidella orthantha*) within white-ear territories without being evicted.

Breeding Biology

Although the behavior of the northern populations remains essentially unknown, A. F. Skutch (in Bent, 1940) has described finding singing assemblies of males of *S. ellioti* in Guatemala between 1800 and 3300 meters. He noted that these are not common anywhere, but where a single male is heard singing, one or more others are likely to be within earshot. In mid-October Skutch found one such assembly on a steep brushy slope at about 2700 meters. Each male had a singing site on the exposed twig of a bush or low tree, and was separated from the others by 22 to 27 meters. No others were found within 1.6 kilometers of these four, and the birds seemed to be oriented in a line, with those at the extreme ends apparently out of hearing range of one another. The group was located near a highway, but Skutch did not comment on the distribution of food plants in the area.

Each male would sing without pause for 30 to 40 seconds, with a weak but melodious voice that had rising and falling cadences similar to those of a small finch such as a seedeater (*Sporophila* sp.). As the bird sang it spread its gorget to form a shield-like appearance, and turned its head from side to side, shifting the apparent coloration of the gorget from magenta to velvety black. At times the bird would also vibrate its wings, or suspend itself in midair, while still singing, or it would make a long, looping flight, eventually returning to the perch from which it began, singing the entire way.

The only record of nesting is for the form *S. ellioti*. Baepler (1962) reported that this species was fairly common after late July in scrub oak thickets between 2100 and 2400 meters in the vicinity of Huehuetanango, Guatemala. On August 12, a nest containing two nestlings was located in a slender oak, about 1 meter above the ground, near the end of a branch. No description of the nest or the eggs was provided.

Evolutionary and Ecological Relationships

The southern form *S. ellioti* is probably no more than subspecifically distinct from *S. heloisa*, as Ridgway (1911) has treated it, but recent tradition has been to maintain the forms as two separate species (without any good reason).

Equally questionable is the practice of maintaining a separate genus (*Atthis*) for these populations. Ridgway (1911) considered that the birds were related to *Selasphorus*, but could be distinguished on the basis of the form and coloration of the tail in the adult male. If one follows the criterion of Brodkorb (in Blair et al., 1968) that a generic trait must not be limited to the condition typical of a single sex, then merger with *Selasphorus* seems reasonable. This had been done by Phillips, Marshall, and Monson (1964), although Brodkorb retained the genus, apparently on the basis of relative bill length and tail shape. Brodkorb placed the genus adjacent to *Archilochus* rather than *Selasphorus*. I believe that, together with "*Stellula*," "*Atthis*" occupies an intermediate position between the extremely specialized (in primary and rectrix condition) types of *Archilochus* and *Selasphorus*, and their intermediate state is an argument favoring the merger of all these species into a single large genus.

Unfortunately, too little is known of the ecology of this species to comment on its interspecific relationships with other hummingbirds or with plants, but it seems to occupy a similar ecological niche to that of the black-chinned hummingbird in the

United States. The unusual vocal abilities of the male should also receive some attention. Perhaps the relative absence of specialized primaries (the outermost primary of males of the northern population is slightly attenuated) or tail feathers of males has been a source of selection for more elaborate vocalizations.

18. Breeding (stippled) and wintering (hatched) distribution of rufous hummingbird.

RUFOUS HUMMINGBIRD

Selasphorus rufus (Gmelin)

Other Names	None in general English use; Chupamirto dorada (Spanish).
Range	Breeds in western North America from southeastern Alaska, southern Yukon, east-central British Columbia, southwestern Alberta, and western Montana south through Washington and Oregon to the Trinity Mountain region of northwestern California and southern Idaho. Winters in Mexico south to Guerrero and Veracruz (AOU, 1957). (See map 18.)
North American Subspecies	None recognized.
Measurements	Wing, males 38–41.5 mm (ave. of 18, 40.3 mm), females 43–45 mm (ave. of 11, 44.4 mm). Exposed culmen 15–17.5 mm (ave. of 18, 16.5 mm), females 17–19 mm (ave. of 11, 18 mm). Eggs, ave. 13.1 × 8.8 mm (extremes 11.4–14.0 × 7.7–10 mm).
Weights	The average of 22 males was 3.22 g (range 2.9–3.9 g); that of 20 females was 3.41 g (range 3.0–3.6 g) (from various sources, including specimens in the Museum of Vertebrate Zoology).
Description	(After Ridgway, 1911.)

Adult male. Pileum dull metallic bronze or bronze-green; rest of upperparts, including loral, orbital, and auricular regions, sides of occiput, and greater part of tail, plain cinnamon-rufous, the back sometimes glossed with metallic bronze-green; rectrices with a terminal median, more or less fusiform or cuneate, area of purplish or bronzy dusky; remiges dark brownish slate or dusky, faintly glossed with purplish; chin and throat brilliant metallic scarlet, changing to golden green in position *b* (see note at beginning of Part Two for position descriptions); chest white, passing through cinnamon-buff posteriorly into cinnamon-rufous on rest of underparts (paler medially); the under tail-coverts whitish basally; femoral tufts white; bill dull black; iris dark brown; feet dusky.

Adult female. Above metallic bronze-green, usually slightly duller on pileum; remiges dark brownish slate or dusky, faintly glossed with purplish; middle pair of rectrices metallic bronze-green (usually more dusky terminally), both webs broadly edged basally with cinnamon-rufous (sometimes with whole basal half or more of this color); next pair with more than basal half cinnamon-rufous, then metallic bronze-green, the terminal portion purplish black; three outer pairs broadly tipped with white, the subterminal portion (extensively) purplish black, the basal half (approximately) cinnamon-rufous, the latter usually separated from the black by more or less of metallic bronze-green; chin, throat, and chest dull white, the throat usually with tips of some of the feathers metallic orange-red or scarlet (changing to golden and greenish) sometimes with a large patch of this color; rest of underparts cinnamon-rufous laterally, fading into dull buffy whitish on breast and abdomen; femoral tufts white; under tail-coverts pale cinnamon-rufous or cinnamon-buff centrally, broadly margined with white or buffy white, the longer ones sometimes with the central area pale grayish or brownish terminally; bill, etc., as in adult male.

Young male. Similar to the adult female but upper tail-coverts cinnamon-rufous, with a terminal spot of metallic bronze-green; middle pair of rectrices cinnamon-rufous with terminal portion metallic bronze-green (sometimes partly blackish), the lateral rectrices with white tip smaller and cinnamon-rufous deeper and more extensive, and feathers of throat with a terminal mesial spot or streak of dusky metallic bronze or bronze-green.

Young female. Similar to the adult female, but feathers of upper parts (especially rump and upper tail-coverts) narrowly and indistinctly margined terminally with pale dull cinnamon or buffy, and throat spotted or streaked with dark bronzy, as in young male.

Identification   (See Plate 16F.)

In the hand. Like other *Selasphorus* species, the outermost primaries are attenuated and sharply pointed in males, and strongly incurved at the tips. The next-to-middle tail feather is also strongly notched in males. There is extensive rufous coloration on the back and rump of adult males, as well as a reddish gorget; in females and immature males the flanks and basal portions of the rectrices are rufous. Females may be separated from those of *S. sasin* by their wider fifth or outermost rectrices (at least 2.7 mm wide vs. no more than 2.6 mm in *S. sasin*); they also have slightly longer wings (43–46 mm vs. 39–45 mm in *S. sasin*). Female broad-tailed hummingbirds are slightly larger (wing usually over 45 mm) and less rufous below, with entirely green middle tail feathers; the rufous of the lateral feathers of less extent than the black, and the rufous of the next-to-middle tail feathers limited to the outer edge near the base rather than present on both sides. Although males can normally be separated from the Allen by back color, rufous males may rarely exhibit green backs (*Condor* 77:196).

In the field. Widespread in many western habitats, including forest edges, meadows, woodlands, and chaparral. The rufous back of males sets them apart from all other North American species. Females and immature males are very similar to those of Allen hummingbirds, except perhaps at extremely close range when the difference in the width of the outer tail feathers might be apparent. The calls include various low chipping and buzzy notes and an excited *zee-chupity-chup*. A musical buzz is also produced by flying males. In aerial display the males dive closely toward a female, with the feathers producing a loud whining sound near the bottom of the rather oval course that is followed. The chip-notes of rufous and Allen hummingbirds are almost identical, a fairly sibilant *chip* or *tchup*. In both species the females have white throats speckled with red centrally and greenish laterally; in immatures of both sexes the throat is rather uniformly colored with bronzy markings. Both species also are quite strongly marked with rufous below and on the tail; while hovering they hold the tail relatively high compared with the plane of the body and move it very little (Stiles, 1971).

Habitats In California this species occupies all sorts of terrains during migration, from lowland stream bottoms through foothill brushland and heavy chaparral to mountain ridges virtually at timberline (Grinnell and Miller, 1944). Similarly, in Canada it occurs over a great variety of habitats, from seacoast, coastal islands, and valley bottoms to meadows above timberline (Godfrey, 1966). High mountain meadows as well as lowland plains, urban gardens, and other diverse habitats are frequently used by birds on migration. While breeding, coniferous forest habitats are the primary nesting area, but locally the birds occupy forest edges and range out into mountain meadows.

Movements Because of its very large breeding range and tendency to wander, migration schedules are complicated. Rufous hummingbirds are gone from Alaska by late August, but there are a few September records. There are also some late September and early October records for British Columbia and Washington. Late departure dates for Oregon are in late October, and in California the species is a common migrant during late June, July, and August in the mountains; a few scattered individuals persist into late fall and rarely have been reported (in the Berkeley area) as late as January 1. In Montana the birds become rare in August and are typically gone by the latter half of September. In Idaho, the males begin to disappear in early July; very few immatures or females are left by August; and the latest state records are for early September. From mid-July throughout most of August the species is a common migrant in Colorado, with males appearing 7 to 10 days ahead of the females and immatures. By late August they are declining, and the latest records are for late September. In New Mexico the species is most abundant in early August, and is mostly gone by early September, although a few linger until the latter part of that month. Likewise in Arizona the few birds seen after August are in female and immature plumages, nearly all of which are gone by October. In Texas most of the fall migration is from late July to late September, with a few birds persisting until mid-October or (rarely) to the end of November.

A few birds are seen in winter months along the coast, in the Big Bend area, in the Rio Grande delta, and other localities (from various sources).

Similarly, in spring the species migrates entirely up the Pacific coast (Phillips, 1975), avoiding Texas, New Mexico, and Arizona, and passing through California from February to May. It arrives in Oregon by early March, and likewise reaches Washington in late February or early March and British Columbia by early April. By mid-April it has reached Alaska and usually reaches Idaho and Montana by the end of April or early May (Bent, 1940).

Vagrant birds often stray well away from their usual migration routes, especially in fall. Conway and Drennan (1979) summarized available records of rufous hummingbirds for the eastern states, and reported that for Florida alone there are more than 50 published records, involving 50–55 birds. According to them, birds have been reported in the eastern states from July 19 to May 1, but more than half of the records are for the months of November and December. The northernmost eastern record so far is from Nova Scotia.

In addition to the Conway and Drennan summary, there are more recent or other eastern records worthy of note. These include sightings in Georgia (*American Birds* 33:273), Alabama (*American Birds* 28:651), and Mississippi (*American Birds* 33:289, 30:730), plus several Louisiana records (*American Birds* 30:967) and scattered sightings in Ontario (*American Birds* 26:854), Michigan (*American Birds* 29:63), Wisconsin (*American Birds* 31:181), and Minnesota (*American Birds* 33:180). There is also a 1976 record for Big Diomede Island (*Ornithologiya* 14:197).

Foraging Behavior and Floral Ecology

Like choosing its diverse habitats, the rufous hummingbird uses a wide array of flowers. In California, favorite native species are the gooseberries, currants, and manzanitas; non-native plant species include eucalyptus, tree-tobacco, fuchsia, red-hot-poker, and the flowers of orange and peach (Grinnell and Miller, 1944). In Texas, plant species such as mints, columbines, penstemon, larkspur, bouvardia, tree-tobacco, and agave are all used at various seasons (Oberholser, 1974). In New Mexico the species is associated with currants, gooseberries, ocotillo, fireweed (*Epilobium*), Indian paintbrush, penstemon, and agave. In late summer it has been foraging almost exclusively on a red species of figwort (*Scrophularia*) growing in mountain valleys at about 2250 meters (Bailey, 1928). The birds have also been observed feeding in large numbers on Rocky Mountain bee plant (*Cleome*). Their fall arrival in southwestern New Mexico coincides with the blooming of agave in late July (Ligon, 1961). Likewise, during migration in Oregon and Washington the birds arrive just as crimson currant (*Ribes sanguineum*) is coming into bloom, and the birds feed heavily on this food resource. While in Oregon they also feed preferentially on red columbine and the blossoms of madrone (*Arbutus menziesii*). In Washington they often concentrate around the flowers of salmon-berry (*Rubus spectabilis*), thimble-berry (*R. parviflo-*

rus), and honeysuckles (Bent, 1940), but only the honeysuckle is
a typical nectar-producer.

This species defends feeding territories during migration as
well as on breeding grounds. Armitage (1955) observed defense
of areas of toad-flax (*Linaria vulgaris*) by fall migrant rufous hummingbirds (probably immature males) in Yellowstone National
Park; there the territories were very small (2–3 meters long by 2–
6 meters wide).

In the Grizzly Lake area of California, the birds hold territories
in late summer that include two primary food sources, *Aquilegia
formosa* and *Castilleja miniata*. Of these, the columbine produces
about four times the amount of nectar as the paintbrush, but the
feeding territories that are held have similar daily caloric produc-
tivity, and thus are size-regulated to adjust for differences in floral composition (Gass et al., 1976). In this area the individual
bird's abilities to hold territories is dependent on age, sex, and
the level of competition from conspecifics. The population is
more than half immatures, the adult males typically leaving
shortly after breeding is finished, perhaps to release food supplies for the young. The length of time they hold the territories
varies greatly, but adult females remained on territories longer
than did immatures of either sex (Gass, 1979). In an Arizona
study, adult males dominated all other age or sex classes of their
own species and all other species, tending to defend more
densely flowered areas than did adult females (Kodric-Brown and
Brown, 1978).

Breeding Biology   Males probably establish territories as soon as they arrive in their
breeding areas, several weeks in advance of most females. The
adult male's display flights normally comprise a complete oval,
with a slanted axis and broader at the bottom than at the top. In
the downswing the bird produces a mechanical sound starting
with an exaggerated wing buzz, followed by a staccato whining
note and ending with a rattle. These notes resemble sounds
made by the Allen, but there are several differences: One is the
absence of a "pendulum" sequence such as that of Allen males;
another is the whining note, broken three or four times in the
rufous display but continuous in the Allen's; a third is the several oval dives in a sequence by the rufous, as opposed to the
Allen's single pendulum sequence and a single dive at most
times. Spectrograms show the whining notes to be richer in over-
tones in the rufous, purer in the Allen, but this difference is not
apparent to the untrained ear. Apparently, however, the male's
displays are sufficiently species-specific to aid in separation of rufous and Allen immature males as well (F. I. Ortiz-Crespo, personal communication).

Nests are evidently built in a wide variety of locations, from
near the ground in low blackberry bushes to some 15 meters
above ground in tall firs. In Puget Sound a frequent location is
among huckleberry bushes, or at times among alders and blackberry vines. The drooping branches of conifers are also favored

locations, with the nest often on the lowest branch having a sharp downward bend (Bent, 1940). According to Kobbe (1900), most nests are placed between 2 and 5 meters above ground, with extremes of 75 centimeters and 9 meters, and are usually well hidden in evergreen foliage. Nearly all nests are placed above paths or gullies. All but 2 of 20 nests found by Kobbe were in spruce trees, and nearly all were decorated with lichens and lined with willow down.

Renesting in subsequent years on the old nest is apparently frequent, and occasionally a group of three nests stacked on top of one another has been found. Kobbe stated that the birds regularly renest if the first clutch is destroyed; usually the second nest is placed in a less exposed site and is often higher in the tree.

In coastal areas of Washington and Oregon overhead protection from rain is apparently also a prominent characteristic of most nest sites. Vines that overhang embankments, especially those having a southern exposure, or dry clusters of roots from upturned trees are also frequent nest sites in western Oregon (Bent, 1940).

Studies in British Columbia by Horvath (1964) indicate that there are seasonal differences in heights of nests, which are related to nest microclimate. Early nests are typically in conifers at low levels, whereas in summer they are in the crowns of deciduous trees. Low nests among conifers in the spring are protected from extremes of temperature better than higher ones, but by summer the nests in the tops of deciduous trees benefit from the temperature-reducing effects of evapotranspiration from the trees and avoid overheating the young.

Although the species has not been studied well in Alaska, the nests found there have similar interior temperatures to those of broad-tailed hummingbirds in the Rocky Mountains. Likewise food supplies during the breeding season in Alaska need intensive study, since the birds must at that time feed primarily on flowers adapted for pollination by insects, such as blueberries, salmonberries, and *Menziesia*. Only near the end of the nesting season is there a significant bloom of flower species adapted for hummingbird pollination (Calder, 1976).

In Washington, eggs have been found from April to July, indicating a fairly protected breeding season, but probably the month of May represents the peak of the season. There is no good information on the length of time required to build the nest, but Kobbe (1900) observed one nest that had a 3-day interval between the laying of the two eggs. There are likewise no good estimates of the incubation period; several early estimates of 12–14 days are clearly erroneous.

The total nestling period is approximately 20 days, and Dubois (1938) has carefully described the development of the young for the first 12 days. He noted that at 6 days the pinfeathers were becoming visible along the sides and edge of the wings, the eye-slit was noticeable, and slight ticking sounds were first heard. By the next day the pinfeathers had emerged on the sides, and at 8 days the eyes were partly open and there were filaments at the top of the head. On the 9th day there were prominent feather tracts visible along the sides of the belly, and the voice was becoming stronger. On the 11th day the young was well-covered with pinfeathers, the eyes were opened to an ellipse, and the feathers of the wings and tail were well sprouted. The eyes were well opened by the 12th day following hatching.

Although it must be regarded as extremely aberrant behavior, there is a single record of a male incubating eggs (Bailey, 1927). The female incubates almost constantly, and is usually off the nest for no more than about 20 minutes. However, by the time the young were 4 days old, the average interval was about 44 minutes in Dubois' study. After 7 days the female was absent for much of the morning, but would return in the afternoon to shield the nestling from the hot sun.

Evolutionary and Ecological Relationships

The rufous and the Allen hummingbirds apparently constitute a superspecies (Mayr and Short, 1970); probably only their allopatric breeding distributions prevent them from hybridization. The only reported hybrid combination involving the rufous is with the calliope hummingbird (Banks and Johnson, 1961).

Rufous hummingbirds have certainly evolved in association with a variety of plant species throughout their broad breeding range, and probably no single plant can be singled out as crucial to the success of this species. However, Grant (1952) described a remarkable instance of divergent evolution between two Sierra Nevada species of columbine (*Aquilegia formosa* and *A. pubescens*), associated with differing adaptations for pollination. In *A. formosa*, which is often pollinated by rufous hummingbirds, the flower is red and yellow, nodding, and has a relatively short (under 20 mm) spur. These traits facilitate feeding by hummingbirds but not by hawkmoths, which are less able to feed easily on nodding blossoms or to see the flowers in semidarkness. On the other hand, *A. pubescens* has yellow-to-white blossoms, erect flowers, and a much longer (at least 29 mm) spur. In this case, hummingbirds are unable to reach the nectar, which helps to avoid cross-pollination and reduces hybridization between these two closely related species.

In Alaska, only five plant species (*Aquilegia formosa* and four species of *Castilleja*) have floral characteristics associated with hummingbird pollination, and all are confined to southern Alaska (Grant and Grant, 1968). Probably the rufous hummingbird invaded Alaska fairly recently, and the spread of hummingbird-adapted flowers to this region has lagged behind that of the birds. Thus, the birds must get much of their food there from flowers usually adapted to bee pollination (Calder, 1976).

19. Breeding (stippled) and wintering (hatched) distributions of Allen hummingbird. Light stippling indicates areas used during migration; the small enclosed area indicates range of the residential race *sedentarius*.

ALLEN HUMMINGBIRD

Selasphorus sasin (Lesson)

Other Names	Red-backed hummingbird; Chupamirto petirrojo (Spanish).
Range	Breeds in coastal California from about the Oregon line southward to Santa Barbara County, and the islands off the coast of southern California. Winters south to the Valley of Mexico and Morelos (Phillips, 1975).(See map 19.)
North American Subspecies	*S. s. sasin* (Lesson). Breeds on the mainland of coastal California; winters south to the Valley of Mexico and Morelos.
	S. s. sedentarius Grinnell. Resident on San Clemente and Santa Catalina islands of the Santa Barbara group off coastal California, and on the adjoining California mainland (*Western Birds* 10:83–85, 11:1–24).
Measurements	Of *S. s. sasin*: Wing, males 36.5–38.5 mm (ave. of 10, 37.8 mm), females 41–42 mm (ave. of 9, 41.6 mm). Exposed culmen, males 15–16.5 mm (ave. of 10, 15.9 mm), females 17–18.5 mm (ave. of 9, 17.8 mm)(Ridgway, 1911). Eggs ave. 12.7 × 8.6 mm (extremes 11.7–14 × 7.6–10 mm). Measurements of *S. s. sedentarius* average larger (Stiles, 1972b).
Weights	The average of 38 males of *S. s. sasin* was 3.13 g (range 2.5–3.8 g); that of 18 females was 3.24 g (range 2.8–3.5 g) (from various sources). Averages of 19 males and 26 females of *S. s. sedentarius* were 3.52 and 3.73 g, respectively (Stiles, 1971).
Description	(After Ridgway, 1911.)

Adult male. Above metallic bronze-green, the feathers of rump with basal portion (mostly concealed) deep cinnamon-rufous; upper tail-coverts and tail deep cinnamon-rufous, the rectrices with a terminal, more or less fusiform streak of purplish black or dusky, the lateral ones with this dusky confined mostly to outer web; remiges dark brownish slate or dusky, faintly glossed with purplish; loral, orbital, auricular, and postocular regions deep cinnamon-rufous, sometimes brokenly extending across nape; chin and throat brilliant metallic scarlet or orange-red, changing in position *b* to golden and greenish, the latero-posterior feathers of the gorget elongated (see note at beginning of Part Two for position descriptions); chest white, passing gradually into pale cinnamon-rufous or cinnamon-buff on breast and abdomen, this into deep cinnamon-rufous on sides and flanks; femoral tufts white; under tail-coverts cinnamon-rufous, paler basally; bill dull black; iris dark brown; feet dusky.

Adult female. Above metallic bronze-green, the upper tail-coverts with basal portion light cinnamon-rufous (partly exposed); middle pair of rectrices with basal half (laterally, at least) cinnamon-rufous, the terminal half (more or less) metallic bronze-green; next pair similar, but terminal portion (extensively) black, the tip of inner web sometimes with a small spot of white; three outer rectrices (on each side) broadly tipped with white, crossed by a broad subterminal area of black, the basal portion cinnamon or dull light cinnamon-rufous, this separated from the subterminal black (at least on third rectrix) by more or less of metallic greenish; remiges dark brownish slate or dusky, faintly glossed with purplish; underparts dull white (sometimes slightly tinged with pale cinnamon-buffy), passing into light cinnamon-rufous on sides, flanks, and under tail-coverts; the throat usually spotted, more or less, with metallic orange-red or scarlet; bill, etc., as in adult male.

Young male. Similar to the adult female, but upper tail-coverts mostly (sometimes wholly) cinnamon-rufous, rectrices more extensively cinnamon-rufous, and throat strongly tinged with cinnamon-rufous and spotted or speckled with dark bronzy.

Identification   (See Plate 16G.)

In the hand. A typical *Selasphorus* species in that males have the outermost primary attenuated and sharply pointed as well as strongly incurved toward the tip. Adult males differ from *S. rufus* in that the rufous coloration does not include the back, but rather only the tail and rump, while the back is green. Females closely resemble those of *S. rufus*, but their outer rectrices are narrower (less than 2.7 mm vs. more than 2.7 mm in *rufus*), and the tail is usually less than 25 mm (23–26 mm) in contrast to the usual 26 mm or more (25–29 mm) in *S. rufus*.

In the field. Adult males can be readily recognized by their rufous tail and rump, interrupted by a greenish back and crown. Females and immature males cannot by separated safely from those of the rufous hummingbird, and both species have a similar call, a sharp *tchup*. However, the courting flight of the male is quite different: The male produces a series of pendulum-like arcs above the female, with each arc about 6 to 9 meters across; at the bottom of the arc the tail is bobbed to produce an interrupted buzzing, after which there are one or two final faster swoops from much greater height, with a veering follow-through. In this final phase it produces a ripping *vrrrrp* sound, probably mechanical in nature.

The wing-noise of the Allen hummingbird is very high-pitched and similar to that of the rufous, and females of both species tend to be more strongly marked with rufous below and on the tail than do other western hummingbirds. Their dorsal color is also quite golden in hue, and the throat of adult females is essentially white, with red specks centrally and bronze-green laterally. Immature birds have the entire throat rather uniformly marked with dusky to greenish spotting, and juveniles have cinnamon-buff feather edging dorsally. In flight both species hold the tail quite high, with little movement (Stiles, 1971).

Habitats   This species is essentially limited during the breeding season to coastal California, in humid ravines or canyons essentially within the summer fog belt. During this period the males occur in territories overlooking "soft chaparral"; the females are in willows, blackberry tangles, or beds of brakes along the bottoms of these slopes. By midsummer the birds sometimes visit the Sierras (Kings Canyon and Sequoia National Parks), and the migration route southward occurs along these mountain slopes (Grinnell and Miller, 1944). In the vicinity of Berkeley, male territories typically occur along canyon bottoms or stream courses where there are areas of massive, deciduous vegetation, including willows, poison oak, or dogwood. Areas between territories often consist of trees or open grassy slopes. Females typically occupy groves or more or less continuous woodland during the nesting period, frequently nesting in live oaks (Pitelka, 1951b). The nonmigratory race on the islands off the California coast is also found in canyons and ravines where there is a heavy growth of brush (Grinnell and Miller, 1944).

Movements   Allen hummingbirds are migratory only at the northern end of their range. Northward migration begins very early; in the San Diego district the birds begin moving northward by January, and spring migration is over by April (Grinnell and Miller, 1944). In the Berkeley area, males take up territories between mid-February and mid-March, and even at the northern limit of their breeding range probably arrive no later than late February (Pitelka, 1951b). The postbreeding southward movement occurs chiefly during July and August. However, in the Santa Monica Mountains of California, postbreeding birds begin to arrive in late May or June, with the earliest arrivals high in adult males; by late June and July most of the birds are juveniles. By early October Allen hummingbirds (and rufous hummingbirds) have begun to leave the area, and all *Selasphorus* hummingbirds are usually gone by the end of the month (Stiles, 1972b). However, on the Palo Verdes Peninsula, the race *S. s. sedentarius* breeds throughout the year (Wells and Baptista, 1979).

In Arizona the species likewise is a regular early fall transient. In July and August the birds pass through the mountains of central southern Arizona, apparently on their way to the Valley of Mexico (Phillips et al., 1964).

According to Phillips (1975), Allen hummingbirds migrate southward along an elliptical route that takes them all the way to the Valley of Mexico by August. Adult males precede the females, but young males linger in California for about a month after the last adult males have gone, and half a month after the last females have departed. In Phillips' view, there are only two local wintering concentrations of Allen hummingbirds: one in the Valley of Mexico during August and the other in Morelos in December. The return route in spring is apparently a more westerly one, resulting in an oval migration route for the entire year.

Extralimital records of this species are not numerous, but it has been reported from as far north as Victoria, British Columbia (*American Birds* 25:792) and as far east as Louisiana (*American Birds* 30:730, 32:1020). There have also been a number of sightings from Texas in recent years (*American Birds* 25:602; 30:741; 31:350; etc.). Although there have been a considerable number of summer sightings throughout Oregon, the species apparently breeds only in Curry County (AOU, 1957). It is a rare visitor in western Washington.

Foraging Behavior and Floral Ecology

Little of a specific nature has been written on the food and foraging behavior of Allen hummingbirds. Bent (1940) mentioned that among the popular food plants are tree-tobacco (*Nicotiana*), the blossoms of California lilac (*Ceanothus*), madrone (*Arbutus menziesii*), and the flowering stalks of the century plant (*Agave*). Also attractive are scarlet sage, mints, monkey-flowers (*Mimulus langsdorfi* and *M. cardinalis*), columbines, hedge-nettles (*Stachys albens*), and Indian paintbrush (*Castilleja grinnelli*). In late summer, the bush or sticky monkey-flower (*Diplacus*) is perhaps used more heavily than any other native plant, and during fall migration a great variety of flowering herbs, shrubs, and trees are utilized (Grinnell and Miller, 1944). Along the coast of south-central California this species frequently visits honeysuckles (*Lonicera involucrata ledebourii*) during the breeding season, and in the mountains of southern California an important late summer or fall plant is California fuchsia (*Zauschneria californica latifolia*) (Grant and Grant, 1968).

Legg and Pitelka (1956) listed a variety of plants used by Allen hummingbirds near Santa Cruz, and also observed them hawking insects in early morning and late evening hours. Two other observations noted probable foraging on ants on the ground, although the birds may have actually been obtaining grit.

Breeding Biology

In the Berkeley area, male territories are established between mid-February and late March, and typically are situated in shrubby areas along canyon bottoms or beside stream courses. Males guard their areas of shrubs, chasing intruders away, displaying above them, and performing circuit and advertisement flights aroung them. Yet, they defend only the shrubby areas and the airspaces 3–14 meters above them. Thus, territorial encounters are not so frequent in this species as in the Anna hummingbird, and there is no definite buffer zone between adjoining territorial core areas. There also are no challenge flights or patrolling of buffer areas, and boundaries of adjacent males seem to be recognized and respected by adjacent territorial holders (Pitelka, 1951b). There are often two types of territories: feeding territories, which are small and numerous and often contested, and mating territories, which are larger and more formally defined (Legg and Pitelka, 1956).

The aerial display of the male usually consists of a series of arcing pendulum-like flights some 6–9 meters across, typically with a pause near the end of each arc. At the bottom of each arc the male spreads the tail and bobs it, producing an interrupted buzzing and shaking movement of the body. This flight is also accompanied by mouse-like squeaking vocalizations. After several arcs the male climbs to a higher elevation and performs a power dive at great speed. A ripping sound, something like that made by rapidly drawing a fine-grained file over the edge of a steel sheet, is produced at the bottom of the dive and lasts for a second or longer (Bent, 1940).

In a photographic analysis, Pearson (1960) determined that at the middle of the power dive the male descends at an angle of about 45° from the horizontal at between 84 and 102 kilometers per hour. The entire dive, from a height of about 18 meters, requires slightly more than a second, and has an average speed of about 64 kilometers per hour. As the bird levels off at the bottom of the dive, when the tail feathers produce the loud sound, it is probably traveling between 54 and 72 kilometers per hour.

Females nest in areas other than those used by males for display. Males have been occasionally observed in such areas, sometimes displaying, but they remain only a short period and do not hold territorial posts. The nests are often located in oaks; 29 of 30 nests in Pitelka's (1951a) study were found in live oaks, and were usually located between 2 and 4 meters above ground (12 of 22 nests), with extremes of 60 centimeters and 7.5 meters. In another study, 21 nests ranged in height from 45 centimeters to 12 meters, averaging 5.5 meters, and were mostly in eucalyptus trees (Legg and Pitelka, 1956).

According to Aldrich (1945), nesting sites are usually those that provide many separate supports for the first nesting materials; thus females place the nest where lateral supports are present. Dense tangles of vines are favorite sites, and in eucalyptus trees the nests are usually near the tips of drooping, incurved branches where the nest can be saddled between two fruits or among the petioles of leaves. In such tree locations the nests may be up to 15 meters from the ground, and are typically on limbs less than 25 millimeters in diameter. At times the nest is built between pieces of loose bark on the main eucalyptus trunk. Cypress trees, when nearby, are favored over eucalyptus, apparently because of the rough surface provided by their branches and twigs. When nests are in vines, they are frequently among wild blackberries and ferns, shaded by live oaks. Then they are often at the intersection of several leafless stems, whereas on ferns they are usually supported by both the leaves and stems. In such locations they may be as close as 15 centimeters to the ground. Overhead shade is apparently an important part of nest-site selection, and patchy shade may be favored over unbroken shade.

The length of time required to build a nest varies, but may

range from 8 to 11 days, with shorter periods associated with nests at old nest sites. Most of the materials are gathered within 22 meters of the nest, and invariably include spider webs. Bits of shredded leaves, bark, and grass are also used, and the down from willow trees or composite seeds is used for nest lining, as are downy feathers. Hair is sometimes also used for lining, and lichens are invariably used for the outer nest surface. Typically, moss makes up the majority of the outer layer, giving the nest a distinctive greenish color, whereas the inner layer makes up the greater bulk and always consists of white downy materials. The first material to be deposited is usually down, and as a rim is gradually developed the two layers become distinct. Lichens are placed with the light green side outward and are attached with spider webs. Frequently lichens are added after the eggs are laid, and lining may also be added throughout the incubation period (Aldrich, 1945).

Almost invariably there are two eggs, deposited on alternate days—rarely laid on successive days; two freshly laid eggs weighed 0.323 and 0.388 grams (Aldrich, 1945). Incubation sometimes begins after the laying of the first egg, but becomes more intense after the second egg is deposited, so that the eggs typically hatch a day apart. By three days after the laying of the second egg incubation reaches a constant level, with the bird on the nest about 80 percent of the daytime hours. The longest periods of absence are in midday, when the temperatures are highest, and the last departure is apparently dictated by daylight levels rather than temperatures.

When incubating the bird keeps its back directed toward the source of light, and temperature strongly affects the posture of the bird in the nest. Incubation lasts from 17 to 22 days, during which time the females pay little attention to courting males (Aldrich, 1945).

During the first few days after the young hatch, the female probably spends nearly as much time brooding on the nest as she had previously spent incubating. However, brooding nearly ceases by the time the young are 12 days old. In one observed nest, the young were very darkly pigmented when 6 days old, but their eyes were still closed and juvenile feathers were not evident. On the 7th day a few feathers appeared along the spine, and by the 8th day the first tail feathers had emerged. By the 11th day all the feathers of the dorsal tracts had emerged, and on the 12th day the eyes of one nestling were opening. The flight feathers emerged on the 13th day; wing-fanning was observed on the 19th day; and fledging of one young occurred the 22nd day after hatching. The second-hatched bird left the nest 25 days after hatching (Orr, 1939).

In the Berkeley hills, it is typical for two nestings to occur per season, but almost all breeding activity is over by mid-July. Males abandon their territories by mid-June, and gradually move out of the area (Pitelka, 1951b).

Evolutionary and Ecological Relationships

Mayr and Short (1970) indicate that the Allen and rufous hummingbirds have apparently mutually exclusive ranges and in their opinion constitute a superspecies. Apparently the only recorded wild hybrids are with the black-chinned hummingbird (Lynch and Ames, 1970) and the Anna hummingbird (Pitelka, 1951b; Wells and Baptista, 1979).

Williamson (1957) has reviewed the criteria for the generic separation of the Anna and Allen hummingbirds, as well as their hybrid traits, and has suggested that the hybrids might be fertile. He thus questioned whether the two species should be retained in separate genera.

The Allen interacts with the Anna hummingbird during the breeding season and competes with it for resources. The territories of Allen hummingbirds are often peripheral to or within the upland territories of Anna hummingbirds, and areas of overlap favor the Anna. In such areas a mutual but unbalanced population depression of males was found, with about 80 percent occupancy of suitable sites by Annas and no more than 48 percent occupancy by Allens. The larger size of the male Anna probably helps to account for their dominance, but there have been several records of apparent displacements of Anna males by Allen males (Legg and Pitelka, 1956; Pitelka, 1951b).

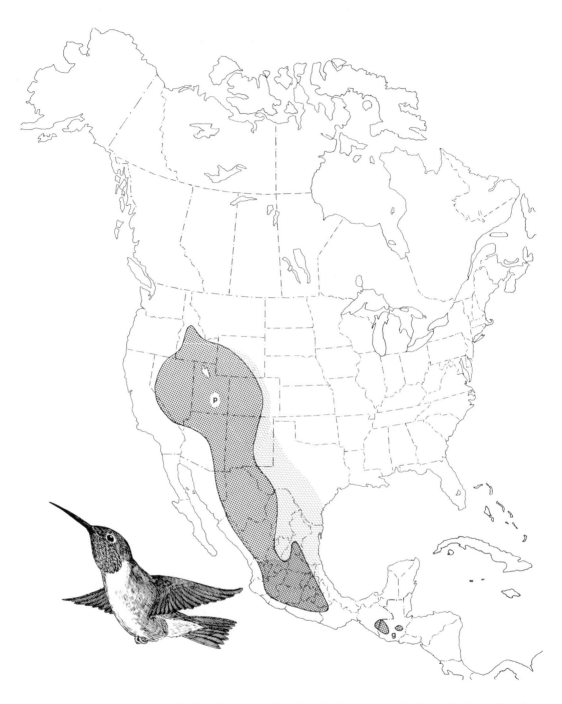

20. Breeding (stippled) and residential (cross-hatched) distributions of broad-
tailed hummingbird (races p = *platycercus*, g = *guatemalae*). Light stippling indicates areas used during migration.

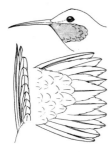

BROAD-TAILED HUMMINGBIRD

Selasphorus platycercus (Swainson)

Other Names	None in general English use; Chupamirto cola ancha (Spanish).
Range	Breeds in western North America from east-central California, northern Nevada, northern Wyoming, eastern Colorado, New Mexico, and southwestern Texas to southern Mexico and the highlands of Guatemala. Winters from central Mexico southward (AOU, 1957). (See map 20.)
North American Subspecies	(After Friedmann et al., 1950.) *S. p. platycercus* (Swainson). Breeds in the mountains of western North America from eastern California and Wyoming south through the mountains of Mexico, mainly from 2100 to 3600 meters, and southward at least to Oaxaca.
Measurements	Wing, males 46.5–50.5 mm (ave. of 19, 48.4 mm), females 45.5–52 mm (ave. of 16, 49.9 mm). Exposed culmen, males 16–19 mm (ave. of 19, 17.6 mm), females 17–20 mm (ave. of 16, 18.6 mm) (Ridgway, 1911). Eggs, ave. 13 × 8.8 mm (extremes 11.9–14.5 × 7.9–10 mm).
Weights	The average of 35 males was 3.16 g (range 2.5–4.1 g); that of 25 females was 3.60 g (range 2.6–3.8 g) (from various sources, including specimens in Museum of Vertebrate Zoology).
Description	(After Ridgway, 1911.)

Adult male. Above metallic bronze-green or greenish bronze; middle pair of rectrices metallic bronze-green (sometimes more bluish green); rest of tail dull purplish or bronzy black; the pair next to middle pair usually glossed, more or less, with bronzy green (sometimes mostly of this color), the outer web edged (except terminally) with cinnamon-rufous; the next pair sometimes also narrowly edged with the same; remiges dark brownish slate or dusky, faintly glossed with purplish; chin and throat bright metallic reddish purple (usually more reddish than solferino), the feathers crossed by a broad subterminal (concealed) bar of dull white, their basal portion dusky gray; chest grayish white, passing into very pale gray on breast and abdomen; sides and flanks darker grayish, tinged (especially the flanks) with pale cinnamon, the sides and sides of breast overlaid by metallic bronze-green; femoral tufts white; under tail-coverts white with a central area of pale cinnamon or cinnamon-buff (sometimes partly bronze-green); bill dull black; iris dark brown; feet dusky.

Adult female. Above metallic bronze-green, including middle pair of retrices, the latter sometimes blackish or dusky terminally; second rectrix (from middle) metallic bronze-green with terminal portion more or less extensively dusky; three outer rectrices, on each side, broadly tipped with white, cinnamon-rufous basally (more or less extensively), the remaining portion purplish or bronzy black with more or less of metallic bronze-green between the blackish subterminal and cinnamon-rufous basal areas; chin and throat dull white, the feathers with small mesial streaks or guttate spots of dusky or dusky bronze; chest dull brownish white or buffy grayish white; the breast and abdomen similar but, usually, more decidedly tinged with buffy; sides and flanks light cinnamon or pale cinnamon-rufous; under tail-coverts pale cinnamon or cinnamon-buff (sometimes partly grayish) centrally, broadly margined with white; femoral tufts white; bill, etc., as in adult male.

Young male. Similar to the adult female but feathers of upperparts (especially rump and upper tail-coverts) indistinctly margined terminally with pale brownish buff or cinnamon, and lateral rectrices with much less of cinnamomeous on basal portion.

Young female. Similar to the young male but retrices as in adult female.

Identification

(See Plate 16H.)

In the hand. Has a blackish bill about a third the length of the wing, which in males has the outermost primaries sharply pointed and the outermost slightly excurved. The wing is somewhat longer than in other *Selasphorus* species (minimum 45 mm), and the tail is generally rounded, with the individual feathers fairly wide and pointed (males) or wedge-shaped (females). Cinnamon color on the rectrices is limited to the edges of some in the inner rectrices (in males) or to the basal portions of the outer three rectrices (in females).

In the field. Usually found in mountain meadows associated with coniferous forests. Males are identified by their red throats and the loud buzzing noise made by the wings in flight. The only other sounds are occasional tinny *chip* notes. Where ruby-throated hummingbirds might also occur (as in Texas), the rounded rather than forked tail of the males will help to identify them, and the absence of cinnamon from the tail in males separates them from other *Selasphorus* species. Females closely resemble the other species of *Selasphorus* hummingbirds, and in general are almost impossible to identify in the field. They may sometimes be separated from the Anna, Costa, and black-chinned hummingbirds by their cinnamon at the base of the tail, but are not separable from female Allen or rufous hummingbirds.

There is a shallow 9- to 12-meter dive display by the male, and it produces a musical buzzing sound continuously while in flight. The sound is very high-pitched and is louder and shriller than most other species, but females produce only the normal humming sound in flight. The chip-note is very similar to that of the Allen and rufous hummingbirds, but slightly higher in pitch. The large size of the female, and its unusually large tail, with extensive black present, and the lack of rufous tinge below, is quite useful in recognition. The throat pattern of adult females consists of faint, dusky streaking or speckling, and young males often have a few magenta feathers (Stiles, 1971).

Habitats In California, the typical breeding habitat of this species is the woodland belt of pinyon pine, juniper, and mountain mahogany, especially where these trees are in their usual open stands, with interspersed xerophilous shrubbery. Proximity to thickets is particularly favored, such as of willow or silk-tassel bush (*Garrya*) associated with wet or dry stream courses (Grinnell and Miller, 1944). At the eastern edge of its breeding range in Texas, the species favors pine-oak woodlands and scrubby junipers on slopes or in canyons and gulches (Oberholser, 1974).

In Colorado the species is most abundant between 2100 and 2550 meters in the wooded transition zone. There it often nests along moist canyons in aspens, Douglas firs, or ponderosa pines (Baily and Niedrach, 1965). After the breeding season the birds move upward at least to timberline and often into the alpine meadows, which then are strewn with flowers. During fall migration the species also ranges well out into open country in the valleys and foothills (Oberholser, 1974).

Movements This is a highly migratory species, which winters primarily in the highlands of Mexico. In Texas it is scarce to rare in Big Bend National Park from late September to middle or late March; otherwise it is extremely rare during winter. Spring migration there occurs mainly during March and April, with breeding beginning very shortly after arrival (Oberholser, 1974). Likewise in Arizona the species occurs in the southern mountains from the end of February or early March, whereas in the northern part of the state the birds arrive in early April (Phillips et al., 1964). Early arrival dates for New Mexico and Colorado are for April; those for Wyoming and Utah are for May (Bent, 1940). Males typically arrive in advance of females during spring migration.

Fall departures in the northern part of the breeding range are during September in Wyoming and Colorado (Bent, 1940); the latest reported Colorado date is October 24 (Bailey and Niedrach, 1965). In Arizona the birds occur as late as the end of September, or perhaps early October, whereas in southern New Mexico (Carlsbad) they have been reported as late as early October. Most of the fall migration in Texas is from early August to middle or late October, with rare observations into November (Oberholser, 1974).

As might be expected with a highly migratory species, extralimital occurrences of broad-tailed hummingbirds are fairly numerous. They have been reported northwest of their breeding range to Washington (*Audubon Field Notes* 15:428) and Oregon (*Audubon Field Notes* 22:569; 23:617), and have reached east as far as Texas (*American Birds* 25:602, 30:864, 31:1021), Arkansas (*American Birds* 33:187), and Louisiana (*American Birds* 33:187).

Foraging Behavior and Floral Ecology

This species forages on a great variety of plants over its wide range, but in the San Francisco Peaks area of Arizona some of the important montane flowers on which it forages during the breeding season and in early fall include *Penstemon barbatus*, *Ipomopsis aggregata*, and *Castilleja miniata* (Grant and Grant, 1968).

In west-central Colorado, broad-tailed hummingbirds interact with four major plant species, including *Delphinium nelsoni*, *D. barbeyi*, *Castilleja miniata*, and *Ipomopsis aggregata* during the breeding season. Nesting begins soon after the onset of blooming by *D. nelsoni* and persists until *Ipomopsis* begins flowering in the same meadows. These two species of plants grow together in dry meadows and flower sequentially. The other two species of food plants are more associated with wetter habitats, and thus tend to be spacially separated from the first two. Studies by Waser (1978) indicate that *D. nelsoni* and *I. aggregata* compete with one another for hummingbird pollination, and during the brief period of flowering overlap some undesirable interspecific pollen transfer occurs. Thus, the two have tended to evolve or maintain sequential flowering periods in this area.

In Texas, this species feeds on a wide variety of plants, including agaves, yuccas, mints (*Salvia*), locusts (*Robinia*), lupines, and others, and to the insects attracted to their blossoms. The birds also glean insects from coniferous foliage, and sometimes hawk them from the air (Oberholser, 1974).

In the Chiricahua Mountains of Arizona, male broad-tailed hummingbirds establish breeding territories in open meadows that support heavy stands of *Iris missouriensis*, which is normally a bee-pollinated species. Most of the hummingbird foraging on this species is "illegitimate" (not resulting in pollination). The birds also forage to some extent on *Robinia neomexicana*, *Penstemon barbatus*, and *Echinocereus triglochidiatus*, the last two of which are more typical hummingbird-adapted species. Lyon (1973) noted that in this area the most important and abundant hummingbird-adapted plant is *Penstemon barbatus*, but it does not begin blooming until the end of June, or near the end of the blooming period of the iris. Thus, the iris provides an adequate early-season interim supply of food until the *Penstemon* is in full bloom, and allows for the establishment of breeding territories in dense stands of this plant. Similarly, in Colorado the breeding season of the species seems to be closely correlated with the flowering periods of the major plant resources (Waser, 1976).

Bent (1940) has summarized information on insect-eating by this species, which includes small flying insects captured in flight, spiders and small insects found in flowers, and probably also the insects that are attracted to the borings of sapsuckers. The flowers of figworts (*Scrophularia*) and ocotillo are especially favored for foraging, as are the insects associated with penstemons, larkspurs, agaves, gilias, gooseberries, and willow catkins.

Breeding Biology

In Texas, breeding occurs from late March or early April until mid-June (Oberholser, 1974). Egg records for Arizona are from May 8 to July 30, with a peak in mid-June to mid-July; those in Colorado are from May 22 to late July, with a peak in the second half of June. A small number of Utah records are from June 6 to July 23 (Bent, 1940).

In Colorado, as many as four nests have been found within an area of 24 to 32 square meters; all were about 7 meters above the ground in ponderosa pines (Bailey and Niedrach, 1965). Near Gothic, Colorado, nesting seasons are closely adjusted to the flowering periods of the major nectar-producing plants. These flowering periods lasted 70–80 days in two different years, whereas individual nesting cycles (from egg-laying to fledging) lasted 38–41 days. The total nesting season (from first egg laid to last egg hatched) lasted 64 days in both years studied (Waser, 1976).

In a study area in the Chiricahua Mountains of Arizona, Lyon (1973) observed eight male broad-tailed hummingbirds defending breeding territories that averaged about 2040 square meters in area. This is a larger territory than most other estimates, but it may have been a consequence of the birds' defending plants (*Iris*) normally associated with bee pollination and relatively low in nectar production.

By comparison, Barash (1972) observed three males displaying in Colorado while separated from one another by only 7 meters, forming a group that seemed to comprise a lek. On one occasion a female was present for a time in the display area, approaching to within 2 meters of one of the males. While the female was present, the rate of diplay activity increased (from 4.8 seconds per display circuit to 3.5 seconds per circuit). These small display territories, however, were apparently not centered on feeding areas.

The typical male aerial display consists of a U-shaped dive, often from 9 to 15 meters above ground and passing very close to a perched female. Sometimes females and males will hover nearly bill-to-bill in the air, as the male apparently displays his gorget to the female. Throughout the year the male produces a continuous musical buzzing sound while in flight, except perhaps during molt. Apparently no vocalizations are produced during the display dive, but the overall level of the vibration noises increases as the air passes rapidly through the slotted primaries (Edgarton et al., 1951).

Hering (1947) reported that during the diving performance the male produces a series of sharp clicking "notes," suggesting that vocalizations may be incorporated into the display. However, Marshall (in Banks and Johnson, 1961) simply noted that three "flups" are produced by the tail at the bottom of the dive. One observed copulation occurred while the female remained perched on a willow branch and the male alighted on top of her (Hering, 1947). This observation calls into question previous assertions that the birds might mate in flight.

According to Wagner (1948), the courtship has two phases: The first, associated with the attraction of the female, consists of the general display flights; the second, concerned with the synchronization of copulatory behavior, consists of the diving flights. Wagner believed that some individuals of this species might breed both on their wintering grounds in Mexico as well as in the United States, but Waser and Inouye (1977) have questioned that suggestion.

Females frequently build their nests in the same location for several consecutive summers. Bailey and Neidrach (1965) mentioned that a female (presumably but not definitely the same bird) nested for six consecutive seasons in a clump of small blue spruces. However, Waser and Inouye (1977) judged that the average life span was probably much shorter than this. One of the males they initially captured as an adult in 1972 was recaptured in 1975, indicating a minimum 4-year life span in that individual.

The nests are placed in a wide array of locations, from being saddled on large limbs to being situated on very small twigs. They are usually on low, horizontal branches of willows, alders, cottonwoods, pines, fir, spruce, or aspens, and are generally 1 to 4 meters above the ground. However, they have also been reported in tall sycamores and pines, from 6 to 9 meters above ground. Often they are above water, and they are usually decorated with lichens, shreds of bark, fine leaves, or other plant materials (Bent, 1940).

There does not seem to be any detailed information on the time required to build a nest, but Bailey (1974) mentioned a nest that had been built in 2 days. The incubation period has been reported as 16–17 days and the fledging period as 18 days (Bailey and Neidrach, 1965). Calder (1976) reported a 21- to 26-day fledging period for this species. Waser and Inouye (1977) indicated that the mean duration of a nesting cycle (laying to fledging) was 40 days. This would normally preclude second broods in the cool mountain areas inhabited by the species, although Bailey (1974) observed the simultaneous tending of two nests by a female: One nest contained young about 15 days old and a few days prior to fledging; the second nest contained the first egg of the second clutch. This egg was laid five days after the nest had been initiated, and the two eggs hatched 16 and 17 days later. Bent (1940) mentioned other earlier reports of second broods.

Calder (1976) described the energy relationships of incubating broad-tailed hummingbirds in the Rockies. He noted that during the nesting period the female initially leaves the nest to feed approximately 11–18 minutes before sunrise and makes her last trip at sunset. Throughout the day she may leave the nest about 60 times to feed, and about 30 times for shorter periods. On nights following a day of rain, the bird usually enters a state of hypothermia, and the nest temperature may drop from 32° to 11° C or even lower. This occurred at various times during incubation, hatching, and brooding periods, but did not seem to affect fledging success.

Evolutionary and Ecological Relationships

Mayr and Short (1970) suggested that this species might be more closely related to the ruby-throated superspecies than to any of the other North American species of *Selasphorus*, but they did not explain the basis for this position. Probable hybrids have been found with the black-chinned and the Costa hummingbirds (Banks and Johnson, 1961).

This species overlaps in its breeding range with the calliope hummingbird, but is substantially larger and probably outcompetes it in such areas. However, where broad-tailed hummingbirds occur in the same areas with rufous hummingbirds, the two species are not totally ecologically isolated, and they sometimes compete fiercely for the same food resources (Calder, 1976).

Several flowers interact with broad-tailed hummingbirds in west-central Colorado. At least two of them—*Delphinium nelsoni* and *Ipomopsis aggregata*—have apparently evolved or maintained sequential flowering periods that facilitate their pollination by the hummingbirds without seriously risking cross-pollination.

Origins of Latin Names of North American Hummingbirds

Amazilia Latinized form of the South American Indian name Amazili, with reference to the Amazon River.

beryllina—the color of beryl, bluish green.

tzacatl—probably from Aztec, grass (green). A man named Rieffer collected the first specimens of this species, which is sometimes called Rieffer's hummingbird.

violiceps—from the Latin *viola*, violet, and *ceps*, head.

yucatanensis—of Yucatan.

Archilochus Apparently after Archilochus of Paros, 7th century Greek poet; or from the Greek prefix *arch-*, chief, and *lochos*, a body of individuals: thus, first among the birds.

alexandri—after M. Alexandre, who discovered the species.

anna—for Anne de Belle Massena (c. 1806–1896), the wife of François Victor (see *Heliodoxa fulgens*).

calliope—from the Greek *kalliope*, beautiful-voiced; Calliope was the muse of eloquence; or from the Greek *kalle*, beautiful, and *ops*, face.

colubris—seemingly from the Latin *colubris*, a serpent, but more likely a Latinized form of *colibri*, a South American Indian name. The French *colibre* and the German *Kolibris* both refer to hummingbirds and are of the same origin.

costae—for Louis Marie Pantaleon Costa (1806–1864), Marquis de Beau-Regard, French nobleman who specialized in collecting hummingbirds.

Atthis Greek for an Athenian, possibly for Philomena, who was transformed into a bird; or after a mythical priest of the goddess Cybele.

Basilinna from Greek, a queen.

Calliphlox from Greek *kalos*, beautiful, and *thoras*, back.

lucifer—from Latin, light-bringing.

Calypte from the Greek *kalyptos*, covered or hidden.

Chlorostilbon   from the Greek *chloros*, green, and *stilbon*, flashing or glittering.

ricordii—after Philippe Ricord (1800–1889), French surgeon.

Coeligena   from the Greek, heaven-born.

Colibri   a South American Indian word of unknown meaning (see *Archilochus colubris*).

thalassinus—from the Greek *thalassios*, marine.

Cyanolaemus   from the Greek *kyanos*, cyan, and *loimas*, throat.

Cynanthus   perhaps from the Greek *kyanos*, dark blue, and *anthos*, bright.

latirostris—from the Latin *latus*, broad, and *rostris*, bill.

leucotis—from the Greek *leukos*, white, and *otos*, ear.

Eugenes   from the Greek prefix *eu-*, good, and *genos*, birth: thus, well-born.

Heliodoxa   from the Greek *helios*, the sun, and *doxa*, glory.

fulgens—from the Latin *fulgeo*, to shine or glitter. The vernacular name is after François Victor Massena (1798–1863), third Prince of d'Essling and Duc di Rivoli, a patron of natural history (Gruson, 1972).

Heliomaster   from the Greek *helios*, the sun, and from the Latin *magister*, double comparative from the root of *magnus*, great.

constantii—probably after C. Constant (1820–1905), Colombian taxidermist.

Hylocharis   from the Greek *hyle*, a wood or forest, and *charis*, delight or beauty.

Lampornis   from the Greek *lampros*, shining or beautiful, and *ornis*, bird.

clemenciae—for the wife of R.P. Lesson (1794–1849), French naturalist.

Nesophlox   from the Greek *nesos*, island, and *phlox*, flame.

Orthorhyncus   from the Greek *orthos*, straight, and *rhyncos*, bill.

cristatus—from the Latin, crested.

Philodice   from Greek mythology, the mother of Hilara and Phoebe.

Selasphorus   from the Greek *selas*, light, and *phoros*, bearing.

heloisa—named by R.P. Lesson and A. De Lattre for an unspecified woman, possibly the wife of De Lattre (Gruson, 1972).

platycercus—from the Greek *platys*, flat, and *kerkos*, tail.

rufus—from the Latin, reddish.

sasin—probably from the Nootka Indian name for this species. C.A. Allen (1841–1930) collected the species, and it was named *alleni* for him by H.W. Henshaw, but was later found to have been already described. The vernacular name Allen hummingbird has nonetheless been retained (Gruson, 1972).

Stellula from the Latin, a little star.

Trochilidae from the New Latin *trochilus*, a runner, and originally applied by Herodotus to a plover.

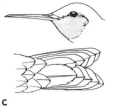

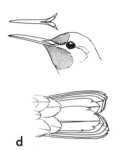

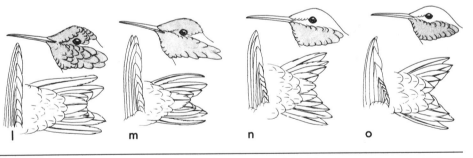

17. Male structural characteristics of (a) blue-throated hummingbird, (b) Rivoli hummingbird, (c) broad-billed hummingbird, (d) white-eared hummingbird, (e) lucifer hummingbird, (f) Bahama woodstar, (g) rufous hummingbird, (h) broad-tailed hummingbird, (i) Allen hummingbird, (j) calliope hummingbird, (k) bumblebee hummingbird, (l) Anna hummingbird, (m) Costa hummingbird, (n) black-chinned hummingbird, and (o) ruby-throated hummingbird. Stippling indicates areas of high iridescence. (Drawn to scale, after Ridgway, 1911)

APPENDIX TWO

Key to Identification of North American Hummingbirds

A. Larger, wing at least 60 mm
    B. Violet ear-patch present, tail with a black band near tip (*Colibri thalassinus*)
    BB. No violet ear-patch or black band near tip of tail
        C. Bill very long (culmen 33–36 mm), white rump patch present *(Heliomaster constantii)*
        CC. Bill shorter (culmen less than 32 mm), no white rump patch
            D. Tail bluish or black with white tip, that of male slightly forked (*Heliodoxa fulgens*, Figure 17b)
            DD. Tail green, with grayish tip, that of male somewhat rounded (*Lampornis clemenciae*, Figure 17a)
AA. Smaller, wing no more than 56 mm
    B. Bill reddish, at least on lower mandible, nasal operculum at least partly exposed
        C. Nasal operculum wholly exposed, a white eye-stripe present above a blackish ear-patch (*Cynanthus*)
            D. Ear-patch black, with a long white eye-stripe above (*C. leucotis*, Figure 17d)
            DD. Ear-patch grayish, bordered above with a short, dull whitish eye-stripe (*C. latirostris*, Figure 17c)
        CC. Nasal operculum partially concealed, not with combination of a white eye-stripe above a blackish ear-patch
            D. Tail forked and dusky violet to blackish, a small white spot present behind eye (*Chlorostilbon ricordii*)
            DD. Tail square or only notched, brownish; no white spot behind eye (*Amazilia*)
                E. Bill only slightly widened basally, only lower mandible reddish basally (*A. beryllina*)
                EE. Bill abruptly widened near its base, both upper and lower mandibles reddish
                    F. Chin and throat white (*A. violiceps*)
                    FF. Chin and throat metallic green
                        G. Central tail feathers brownish, abdomen brownish gray (*A. tzacatl*)
                        GG. Central tail feathers greenish, abdomen buffy (*A. yucatanensis*)
    BB. Bill blackish, not broader than deep at base, nasal operculum concealed by feathers

C. Bill either unusually short (exposed culmen less than one-fourth as long as wing) or long and decurved (exposed culmen more than half as long as wing)

    D. Bill short and straight, more than half of it covered by feathering (*Orthorhyncus cristatus*)

    DD. Bill long and decurved, tail deeply forked in males (*Calothorax lucifer*, Figure 17e)

CC. Bill straight or only slightly decurved, one-fourth to one-half as long as wing

    D. Plumage usually with considerable rufous, at least on tail, which is usually rounded in both sexes; outermost primary of male sometimes sharply pointed

        E. Abdomen pale rufous, bounded by a whitish breast, central tail feathers distinctly shorter than the rest and the tail forked in males (*Calothorax evelynae*, Figure 17f)

        EE. Abdomen and breast both whitish, with darker flanks, central tail feathers as long as the others (*Selasphorus*)

            F. Bill short (exposed culmen 10–13 mm), wing usually less than 36 mm (*S. heloisa*, Figure 17k)

            FF. Bill longer (at least 13.5 mm), wing usually at least 37 mm

                G. Lateral rectrices mostly blackish, wing 45–52 mm (*S. platycercus*, Figures 17h and 18d)

                GG. Lateral rectrices mostly rufous, wing 36–45 mm

                    H. Throat metallic red or purple (males)

                        I. Back metallic green (*S. sasin*, Figure 17i)

                        II. Back cinnamon-rufous (*S. rufus*, Figure 17g)

                    HH. Throat whitish, usually flecked with dusky (females)

                        I. Outermost rectrix no more than 2.7 mm wide (*S. sasin*, Figure 18b)

                        II. Outermost rectrix more than 3 mm wide (*S. rufus*, Figure 18c)

    DD. Plumage lacking any rufous, tail square or slightly forked in males and outermost primary never sharply pointed (*Archilochus*)

        E. Inner rectrices broadening subterminally, throat feathers of adult males very narrow and pure white basally (*A. calliope*, Figures 17j and 18a)

        EE. All rectrices more or less tapering toward tips

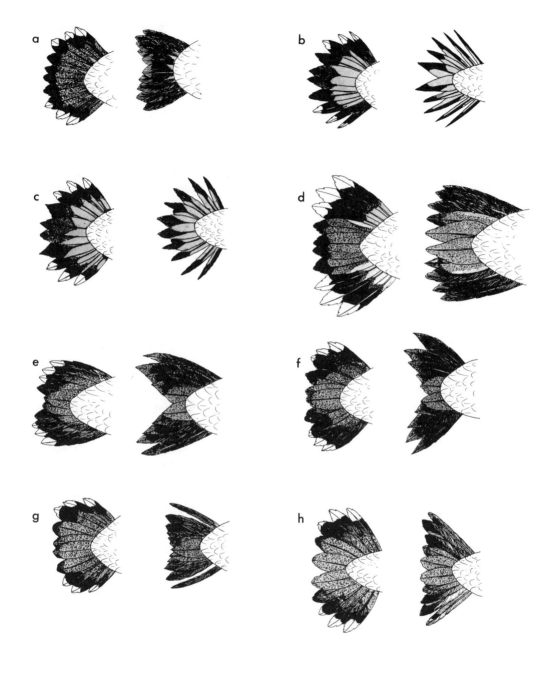

18. Tail shapes and color patterns of female (left) and male (right) hummingbirds, including (a) calliope, (b) Allen, (c) rufous, (d) broad-tailed, (e) ruby-throated, (f) black-chinned, (g) Costa, and (h) Anna. Dark stippling indicates green; light stippling indicates rufous to cinnamon. (Drawn to scale, after various sources)

    F.   Inner primaries with small notch near tip of inner web, lateral rectrices pointed
        G.   Throat metallic purplish or violet (males)
            H.   Throat purplish red (*A. colubris*, Figure 17o)
            HH. Throat black and violet (*A. alexandri*, Figure 17n)
        GG. Throat dull white, tail double-rounded or rounded (females)
            H.   Exposed culmen 17–19.5 mm, tail double-rounded (middle rectrices shorter than outer ones) (*A. colubris*, Figure 18e)
            HH. Exposed culmen 19.5–22 mm, tail rounded (*A. alexandri*, Figure 18f)
FF. Inner primaries not notched near tip of inner web, lateral rectrices mostly rounded
        G.   Gorget and crown metallic-colored (males)
            H.   Gorget and crown purplish red, outermost rectrices normal in width (*A. anna*, Figure 17l)
            HH. Gorget and crown violet, outermost rectrices distinctly narrowed (*A. costae*, Figure 17n)
        GG. Throat pale gray or dull whitish, no gorget (females)
            H.   Wing 48–51 mm, pale grayish underparts and tail corners (*A. anna*, Figure 18h)
            HH. Wing 43.5–46 mm, whitish underparts and tail corners (*A. costae*, Figure 18g)

APPENDIX THREE

Hummingbird Species of the World
Synopsis of
Family Trochilidae

(In part after Peters, 1945, and Morony et al., 1975, with modifications and additions. Authorities and dates are indicated for species described after 1945)

Genus and Species	1. Subfamily Phaethornithinae	
	Common Name	Range
Androdon		
aequatorialis	Tooth-billed Hummingbird	Panama to Ecuador
Ramphodon (Androdon)		
naevius	Saw-billed Hermit	Brazil (S.E.)
Glaucis		
dohrnii	Hook-billed Hermit	Brazil (S.E.)
aenea	Bronzy Hermit	Nicaragua to Ecuador
hirsuta	Rufous-breasted Hermit	Panama to Brazil
Threnetes (Glaucis)		
niger	Sooty Barbthroat	Cayenne, Brazil (Amapá)
loehkeni (Grantsau, 1969)	Bronze-tailed Barbthroat*	Brazil (Amapá)
cristinae (Ruschi, 1975)	Christina Barbthroat†§	Brazil (Amapá)
grzimeki (Ruschi, 1973b)	Black Barbthroat*	Brazil (S.E.)
leucurus	Pale-tailed Barbthroat	Guianas to Bolivia
ruckeri	Band-tailed Barbthroat	Guatemala to Ecuador
Phaethornis		
yaruqui	White-whiskered Hermit	Colombia to Ecuador
guy	Green Hermit	Costa Rica to Peru
syrmatophorus	Tawny-bellied Hermit	Colombia to Peru
superciliosus	Long-tailed Hermit	Mexico to Brazil
malaris	Great-billed Hermit	Cayenne to Brazil
margarettae (Ruschi, 1972)	Margaretta Hermit	Brazil (S.E.)
eurynome	Scale-throated Hermit	Brazil to Argentina
nigirostris (Ruschi, 1973a)	Black-billed Hermit†	Brazil (S.E.)
hispidus	White-bearded Hermit	Venezuela to Brazil
anthophilus	Pale-bellied Hermit	Panama to Venezuela
bourcieri	Straight-billed Hermit	Guianas to Peru, Brazil
philippii	Needle-billed Hermit	Peru and Brazil
koepckeae (Weske and Terborgh, 1977)	Koepcke Hermit	Peru
squalidus	Dusky-throated Hermit	Colombia to Brazil

continued on next page

*Known from only a few specimens.
†Known from one specimen.
§Taxonomic status uncertain.

241

Genus and Species	1. Subfamily Phaethornithinae Common Name	Range
augusti	Sooty-capped Hermit	Guyana to Colombia
pretrei	Planalto Hermit	Brazil to Argentina
subochraceus	Buff-bellied Hermit	Bolivia and Brazil
nattereri	Cinnamon-throated Hermit	Brazil and Bolivia
maranhaoensis (Grantsau, 1968)	Maranhão Hermit	Brazil (Imperatriz)
gounellei	Broad-tipped Hermit	Brazil (N.E.)
ruber	Reddish Hermit	Guianas to Bolivia
stuarti	White-browed Hermit	Peru and Bolivia
griseogularis	Gray-chinned Hermit	Venezuela to Peru
longuemareus	Little Hermit	Mexico to Brazil
idaliae	Minute Hermit	Brazil (S.E.)
Eutoxeres		
aquila	White-tipped Sicklebill	Costa Rica to Peru
condamini	Buff-tailed Sicklebill	Colombia to Peru

Genus and Species	2. Subfamily Trochilinae Common Name	Range
Doryfera		
johannae	Blue-fronted Lancebill	Guyana to Peru
ludovicae	Green-fronted Lancebill	Costa Rica to Bolivia
Campylopterus		
curvipennis	Wedge-tailed Sabrewing	Mexico to Guatemala
largipennis	Gray-breasted Sabrewing	Guianas to Brazil
rufus	Rufous Sabrewing	Mexico to El Salvador
hyperythrus	Rufous-breasted Sabrewing	Venezuela and Brazil
duidae	Buff-breasted Sabrewing	Venezuela and Brazil
hemileucurus	Violet Sabrewing	Mexico to Panama
ensipennis	White-tailed Sabrewing	Venezuela, Trinidad, Tobago
falcatus	Lazuline Sabrewing	Venezuela to Ecuador
phainopeplus	Santa Marta Sabrewing	Colombia
villaviscensio	Napo Sabrewing	Ecuador
Eupetomena (Campylopterus)		
macroura	Swallow-tailed Hummingbird	Mexico to Paraguay
Phaeochroa (Aphantochroa)		
cuvierii	Scaly-breasted Hummingbird	Guatemala to Colombia
Aphantochroa		
cirrochloris	Sombre Hummingbird	Brazil (E.)
Florisuga		
mellivora	White-necked Jacobin	Mexico to Brazil
Melanotrochilus (Florisuga)		
fuscus	Black Jacobin	Brazil (E. & Central)

| | 2. Subfamily Trochilinae | |
Genus and Species	Common Name	Range
Colibri		
delphinae	Brown Violet-ear	Mexico to Brazil
thalassinus	Green Violet-ear	Mexico to Bolivia
coruscans	Sparkling Violet-ear	Venezuela to Argentina
serrirostris	White-vented Violet-ear	Bolivia to Argentina
Anthracothorax		
viridigula	Green-throated Mango	Venezuela to Brazil
prevostii	Green-breasted Mango	Mexico to Peru
nigricollis	Black-throated Mango	Panama to Argentina
veraguensis	Veraguan Mango*	Panama
dominicus	Antillean Mango	West Indies
viridis	Green Mango	Puerto Rico
mango	Jamaican Mango	Jamaica
Avocettula (Sericotes)		
recurvirostris	Fiery-tailed Awlbill	Guianas to Ecuador
Eulampis (Sericotes)		
jugularis	Purple-throated Carib	Lesser Antilles
Sericotes		
holosericeus	Green-throated Carib	West Indies
Orthorhyncus		
mosquitus	Ruby-topaz Hummingbird	Guianas to Bolivia, Brazil
cristatus	Antillean Crested Hummingbird	Lesser Antilles
Klais (Abeillia)		
guimeti	Violet-headed Hummingbird	Honduras to Bolivia
Abeillia		
abeillei	Emerald-chinned Hummingbird	Mexico to Nicaragua
Stephanoxis		
lalandi	Black-breasted Plovercrest	Brazil to Argentina
Chlorestes (Chorostilbon)		
notatus	Blue-chinned Sapphire	Guianas to Peru
Chlorostilbon		
mellisugus	Blue-tailed Emerald	Costa Rica to Brazil
aureoventris	Glittering Emerald	Brazil to Argentina
canivetii	Fork-tailed Emerald	Mexico to Venezuela
ricordii	Cuban Emerald	Cuba and Bahamas
swainsonii	Hispaniolan Emerald	Hispaniola
maugaeus	Puerto Rican Emerald	Puerto Rico
gibsoni	Red-billed Emerald	Venezuela and Colombia
russatus	Coppery Emerald	Venezuela and Colombia
inexpectatus	Berlepsch Emerald§**	Colombia

continued on next page

*Possibly conspecific with *prevostii*.
†Known from only a few specimens.
§Known from one specimen.
‡Possibly a variant of *poortmani*.
#Probably an artifact.
¶Probably a hybrid.
**Taxonomic status uncertain.
††Possibly should be considered
 as two species.

§§Probably conspecific with *exima*.
‡‡Includes *sybillae*, sometimes considered a separate species.
##Includes *cinaereicauda*, possibly should include *calolaema*.
¶¶Includes *H. clarisse clarisse* of Peters.
***Probably conspecific with *heloisa*.
†††Probably conspecific with *flammula*.
§§§Probably conspecific with *ardens*.

	2. Subfamily Trochilinae	
Genus and Species	Common Name	Range
stenura	Narrow-tailed Emerald	Venezuela and Colombia
alice	Green-tailed Emerald	Venezuela
poortmani	Short-tailed Emerald	Venezuela and Colombia
auratus	Cabanis Emerald‡	Peru
iolaima	Natterer Emerald#	Brazil (Ypanema)
Cyanophaia		
bicolor	Blue-headed Hummingbird	Lesser Antilles
Thalurania (Cyanophaia)		
furcata	Crowned (Fork-tailed) Woodnymph	Mexico to Ecuador, Argentina
watertonii	Long-tailed Woodnymph	Brazil (Coastal)
glaucopis	Violet-capped Woodnymph	Brazil to Argentina
lerchi	Lerch Woodnymph¶	Unknown
Augasmall (Cyanophaia)		
cyaneoberyllina (Berlioz, 1965)	Berlioz Woodnymph†**	Brazil (Bahia)
smaragdinea	Emerald Woodnymph†¶	Brazil (S.E.)
Neolesbia		
nehrkorni	Nerkhorn Hummingbird¶††	Unknown
Damophila (Cynanthus)		
julie	Violet-bellied Hummingbird	Panama to Ecuador
Lepidopyga (Cynanthus)		
coeruleogularis	Sapphire-throated Hummingbird	Panama and Colombia
lilliae	Sapphire-bellied Hummingbird	Colombia
goudoti	Shining-green Hummingbird	Venezuela and Colombia
Cynanthus		
(Hylocharis)		
sapphirina	Rufous-throated Sapphire	Peru to Argentina
cyanus	White-chinned Sapphire	Peru to Brazil
pyropygia	Flame-rumped Sapphire†	Brazil (Bahia)
chrysura	Gilded Hummingbird	Brazil to Argentina
eliciae	Blue-throated Goldentail	Mexico to Panama
(Basilinna)		
xantusii	Black-fronted Hummingbird	Mexico (Baja California)
leucotis	White-eared Hummingbird	USA to Nicaragua
(Cynanthus)		
sordidus	Dusky Hummingbird	Mexico
latirostris	Broad-billed Hummingbird	USA and Mexico
(Eucephala)		
grayi	Blue-headed Sapphire	Panama to Ecuador
Chrysuronia (Cynanthus)		
oenone	Golden-tailed Sapphire	Venezuela to Brazil
Goldmania		
violiceps	Violet-capped Hummingbird	Panama and Colombia
Goethalsia (Goldmania)		
bella	Pirre Hummingbird	Panama and Colombia
Trochilus		
polytmus	Streamertail††	Jamaica

2. Subfamily Trochilinae

Genus and Species	Common Name	Range
Leucochloris		
albicollis	White-throated Humming-bird	Brazil to Argentina
Polytmus		
guainumbi	White-tailed Goldenthroat	Guianas to Argentina
milleri	Tepui Goldenthroat	Venezuela
theresiae	Green-tailed Goldenthroat	Guianas to Brazil
Taphrospilus (Leucippus)		
hypostictus	Many-spotted Hummingbird	Ecuador to Argentina
Leucippus		
fallax	Buffy Hummingbird	Colombia and Venezuela
baeri	Tumbes Hummingbird	Peru
taczanowskii	Spot-throated Hummingbird	Peru
chlorocercus	Olive-spotted Hummingbird	Ecuador to Brazil
Amazilia		
(Leucippus)		
chionogaster	White-bellied Hummingbird	Peru to Argentina
viridicauda	Green-and-white Humming-bird	Peru
(Polyerata)		
candida	White-bellied Emerald	Mexico to Costa Rica
chionopectus	White-chested Emerald	Guianas and Venezuela
versicolor	Versicolored Emerald	Venezuela to Argentina
luciae	Honduras Emerald†	Honduras
fimbriata	Glittering-throated Emerald	Guianas to Bolivia
distans (Wetmore and Phelps, 1956)	Tachira Emerald§	Venezuela
lactea	Sapphire-spangled Emerald	Venezuela to Brazil
amabilis	Blue-chested Hummingbird	Nicaragua to Ecuador
cyaneotincta	Blue-spotted Hummingbird†	Unknown
rosenbergi	Purple-chested Humming-bird	Colombia and Ecuador
boucardi	Mangrove Hummingbird	Costa Rica
franciae	Andean Emerald	Colombia to Peru
leucogaster	Plain-bellied Emerald	Venezuela to Brazil
cyanocephala	Red-billed Azurecrown	Mexico to Nicaragua
microrhyncha	Small-billed Azurecrown§	Honduras?
(Saucerottia)		
cyanifrons	Indigo-capped Humming-bird	Costa Rica, Colombia
beryllina	Berylline Hummingbird	Mexico to Honduras
cyanura	Blue-tailed Hummingbird	Mexico to Costa Rica

continued on next page

*Possibly conspecific with *prevostii*.
†Known from only a few specimens.
§Known from one specimen.
‡Possibly a variant of *poortmani*.
#Probably an artifact.
¶Probably a hybrid.
**Taxonomic status uncertain.
††Possibly should be considered as two species.

§§Probably conspecific with *exima*.
‡‡Includes *sybillae*, sometimes considered a separate species.
##Includes *cinaereicauda*, possibly should include *calolaema*.
¶¶Includes *H. clarisse clarisse* of Peters.
***Probably conspecific with *heloisa*.
†††Probably conspecific with *flammula*.
§§§Probably conspecific with *ardens*.

2. Subfamily Trochilinae		
Genus and Species	Common Name	Range
saucerrottei	Steely-vented Hummingbird	Nicaragua to Venezuela
tobaci	Copper-rumped Humming-bird	Venezuela, Trinidad, Tobago
viridigaster	Green-bellied Hummingbird	Guyana to Colombia
edward	Snowy-breasted Humming-bird	Panama and Costa Rica
(Amazilia)		
rutila	Cinnamon Hummingbird	Mexico to Costa Rica
yucatanensis	Buff-bellied Hummingbird	U.S. to Honduras
tzacatl	Rufous-tailed Hummingbird	Mexico to Ecuador
handleyi (Wetmore, 1963)	Escudo Hummingbird	Panama
castaneiventris	Chestnut-bellied Humming-bird	Colombia
amazilia	Amazilia Hummingbird	Ecuador and Peru
viridifrons	Green-fronted Humming-bird**	Mexico
violiceps	Violet-crowned Humming-bird	USA to Mexico
Eupherusa (Chalybura)		
poliocerca	White-tailed Humming-bird§§	Mexico
eximia	Stripe-tailed Hummingbird	Mexico to Panama
cyanophrys (Rowley and Orr, 1964)	Blue-capped (Oaxaca) Hum-mingbird	Mexico
nigriventris	Black-bellied Hummingbird	Costa Rica and Panama
Elvira (Chalybura)		
chionura	White-tailed Emerald	Costa Rica and Panama
cupreiceps	Coppery-headed Emerald	Costa Rica
Chalybura		
buffonii	White-vented Plumeleteer	Panama to Ecuador
urochrysia	Bronze-tailed Plumeleteer	Nicaragua to Ecuador
Microchera		
albocoronata	Snowcap	Honduras to Panama
Panterpe (Lampornis)		
insignis	Fiery-throated Hummingbird	Costa Rica and Panama
Lampornis		
clemenciae	Blue-throated Hummingbird	USA to Mexico
amethystinus	Amethyst-throated Hum-mingbird	Mexico to Honduras
viridipallens	Green-throated Mountain-gem‡‡	Mexico to Honduras
hemileucus	White-bellied Mountain-gem	Costa Rica and Panama
castaneoventris	White-throated (Variable) Mountain-gem##	Costa Rica and Panama
calolaema	Purple-throated Mountain-gem	Costa Rica to Panama
Lamprolaima (Lampornis)		
rhami	Garnet-throated Humming-bird	Mexico to Honduras
Adelomyia		
melanogenys	Speckled Hummingbird	Venezuela to Argentina

2. Subfamily Trochilinae

Genus and Species	Common Name	Range
Anthocephala		
floriceps	Blossomcrown	Colombia
Urosticte		
benjamini	Whitetip	Colombia to Peru
Phlogophilus		
hemileucurus	Ecuadorean Piedtail	Ecuador
harterti	Peruvian Piedtail	Peru
Clytolaema		
rubricauda	Brazilian Ruby	Brazil (S.E.)
Polyplancta (Clytolaema)		
aurescens	Gould Jewelfront	Venezuela to Brazil
Heliodoxa		
(Heliodoxa)		
rubinoides	Fawn-breasted Brilliant	Colombia to Peru
leadbeateri	Violet-fronted Brilliant	Venezuela to Bolivia
jacula	Green-crowned Brilliant	Costa Rica to Ecuador
xanthogonys	Velvet-browed Brilliant	Guyana to Brazil
schreibersii	Black-throated Brilliant	Ecuador to Peru
gularis	Pink-throated Brilliant	Colombia to Ecuador
branickii	Rufous-webbed Brilliant	Peru and Bolivia
imperatrix	Empress Brilliant	Colombia and Ecuador
(Eugenes)		
fulgens	Rivoli (Magnificent) Hummingbird	USA to Panama
Hylonympha (Heliodoxa)		
macrocerca	Scissor-tailed Hummingbird	Venezuela
Sternoclyta		
cyanopectus	Violet-chested Hummingbird	Venezuela
Topaza		
pella	Crimson Topaz	Guianas to Ecuador
pyra	Fiery Topaz	Venezuela to Peru
Oreotrochilus		
melanogaster	Black-breasted Hillstar	Peru
estella	Andean Hillstar	Ecuador to Argentina, Chile
leucopleurus	White-sided Hillstar	Bolivia to Argentina, Chile
adela	Wedge-tailed Hillstar	Bolivia
Urochroa		
bougueri	White-tailed Hillstar	Colombia and Ecuador
Patagona		
gigas	Giant Hummingbird	Ecuador to Chile
Aglaeactis		
cupripennis	Shining Sunbeam	Colombia to Peru
aliciae	Purple-backed Sunbeam	Peru

continued on next page

*Possibly conspecific with *prevostii*.
†Known from only a few specimens.
§Known from one specimen.
‡Possibly a variant of *poortmani*.
#Probably an artifact.
¶Probably a hybrid.
**Taxonomic status uncertain.
††Possibly should be considered as two species.

§§Probably conspecific with *exima*.
‡‡Includes *sybillae*, sometimes considered a separate species.
##Includes *cinaereicauda*, possibly should include *calolaema*.
¶¶Includes *H. clarisse clarisse* of Peters.
***Probably conspecific with *heloisa*.
†††Probably conspecific with *flammula*.
§§§Probably conspecific with *ardens*.

Genus and Species	2. Subfamily Trochilinae	
	Common Name	Range
castelnaudii	White-tufted Sunbeam	Peru
pamela	Black-hooded Sunbeam	Bolivia
Lafresnaya		
lafresnayi	Mountain Velvetbreast	Venezuela to Peru
Pterophanes		
cyanopterus	Great Sapphirewing	Colombia to Bolivia
Coeligena		
coeligena	Bronzy Inca	Venezuela to Bolivia
wilsoni	Brown Inca	Colombia and Ecuador
prunellei	Black Inca	Colombia
torquata	Collared Inca	Venezuela to Bolivia
phalerata	White-tailed Starfrontlet	Colombia
bonapartei	Golden-bellied Starfrontlet	Venezuela and Colombia
orina (Wetmore, 1953)	Dusky Starfrontlet†	Colombia
helianthea	Blue-throated Starfrontlet	Venezuela and Colombia
lutetiae	Buff-winged Starfrontlet	Colombia and Ecuador
violifer	Violet-throated Starfrontlet	Peru and Bolivia
iris	Rainbow Starfrontlet	Ecuador and Peru
Ensifera		
ensifera	Sword-billed Hummingbird	Venezuela to Bolivia
Sephanoides		
sephanoides	Green-backed Firecrown	Argentina and Chile
fernandensis	Juan Fernandez Firecrown	Juan Fernandez Island
Boissonneaua		
flavescens	Buff-tailed Coronet	Venezuela to Ecuador
matthewsii	Chestnut-breasted Coronet	Colombia to Peru
jardini	Velvet-purple Coronet	Colombia and Ecuador
Heliangelus		
mavors	Orange-throated Sunangel	Venezuela and Colombia
spencei	Merida Sunangel	Venezuela
amethysticollis	Amethyst-throated Sunangel¶¶	Venezuela to Bolivia
strophianus	Gorgeted Sunangel	Colombia and Ecuador
exortis	Tourmaline Sunangel	Colombia and Peru
viola	Purple-throated Sunangel	Ecuador to Peru
regalis (Fitzpatrick et al., 1979)	Royal Sunangel	Peru
micrastur	Little Sunangel	Ecuador to Peru
speciosa	Green-throated Sunangel†¶	Unknown
rothschildi	Rothschild Sunangel†¶	Unknown
luminosus	Glistening Sunangel†¶	Unknown
Eriocnemis		
nigrivestis	Black-breasted Puffleg	Ecuador
soderstromi	Söderström Puffleg§**	Ecuador
vestitus	Glowing Puffleg	Venezuela to Ecuador
godini	Turquoise-throated Puffleg	Ecuador, Colombia?
cupreoventris	Coppery-bellied Puffleg	Venezuela and Colombia
luciani	Sapphire-vented Puffleg	Colombia to Peru
isaacsonii	Isaacson Puffleg§¶	Unknown
mosquera	Golden-breasted Puffleg	Colombia and Ecuador
glaucopoides	Blue-capped Puffleg	Bolivia to Argentina

| Genus and Species | 2. Subfamily Trochilinae | |
	Common Name	Range
mirabilis (de Schauensee, 1967)	Colorful Puffleg	Colombia
alinae	Emerald-bellied Puffleg	Colombia to Peru
derbyi	Black-thighed Puffleg	Colombia and Ecuador
Haplophaedia (Eriocnemis)		
aureliae	Greenish Puffleg	Panama to Bolivia
lugens	Hoary Puffleg	Colombia and Ecuador
Ocreatus		
underwoodii	Booted Racket-tail	Venezuela to Bolivia
Lesbia		
victoriae	Black-tailed Trainbearer	Colombia to Peru
nuna	Green-tailed Trainbearer	Venezuela to Bolivia
Sappho (Lesbia)		
sparganura	Red-tailed Comet	Bolivia to Argentina
Polyonymus (Lesbia)		
caroli	Bronze-tailed Comet	Peru
Zodalia (Lesbia?)		
glyceria	Purple-tailed Comet†¶	Colombia and Ecuador
Metallura		
phoebe	Black Metaltail	Peru and Bolivia
iracunda (Wetmore, 1946)	Perija Metaltail	Colombia and Venezuela
williami	Veridian Metaltail	Colombia and Ecuador
baroni	Violet-throated Metaltail	Ecuador
odomae (Graves, 1980)	Neblina Metaltail	Peru
theresiae	Coppery Metaltail	Peru
eupogon	Fire-throated Metaltail	Peru and Bolivia
aeneocauda	Scaled Metaltail	Venezuela to Bolivia
tyrianthina	Tyrian Metaltail	Ecuador, Venezuela, Bolivia
Ramphomicron (Chalcostigma)		
purpureicauda	Purple-tailed Thornbill†¶	Ecuador
microrhynchum	Purple-backed Thornbill	Venezuela to Peru
dorsale	Black-backed Thornbill	Colombia
Chalcostigma		
ruficeps	Rufous-capped Thornbill	Ecuador and Bolivia
olivaceum	Olivaceous Thornbill	Peru and Bolivia
stanleyi	Blue-mantled Thornbill	Ecuador and Bolivia
heteropogon	Bronze-tailed Thornbill	Venezuela and Colombia
herrani	Rainbow-bearded Thornbill	Colombia and Ecuador
Oxypogon		
guerinii	Bearded Helmetcrest	Venezuela and Colombia
Opisthoprora		
euryptera	Mountain Avocetbill	Colombia and Ecuador

continued on next page

*Possibly conspecific with *prevostii*.
†Known from only a few specimens.
§Known from one specimen.
‡Possibly a variant of *poortmani*.
#Probably an artifact.
¶Probably a hybrid.
**Taxonomic status uncertain.
††Possibly should be considered as two species.

§§Probably conspecific with *exima*.
‡‡Includes *sybillae*, sometimes considered a separate species.
##Includes *cinaereicauda*, possibly should include *calolaema*.
¶¶Includes *H. clarisse clarisse* of Peters.
***Probably conspecific with *heloisa*.
†††Probably conspecific with *flammula*.
§§§Probably conspecific with *ardens*.

2. Subfamily Trochilinae

Genus and Species	Common Name	Range
Taphrolesbia		
griseiventris	Gray-bellied Comet	Peru
Aglaiocercus		
kingi	Long-tailed Sylph	Venezuela to Bolivia
coelestis	Violet-tailed Sylph	Colombia and Ecuador
Oreonympha		
nobilis	Bearded Mountaineer	Peru
Augastes		
scutatus	Hyacinth Visorbearer	Brazil (E.)
lumachellus	Hooded Visorbearer	Brazil (E.)
(Schistes)		
geoffroyi	Wedge-billed Hummingbird	Venezuela to Bolivia
Heliothryx		
barroti	Purple-crowned Fairy	Mexico to Ecuador
aurita	Black-eared Fairy	Guianas to Bolivia, Brazil
Heliactin		
cornuta	Horned Sungem	Surinam to Brazil
Loddigesia		
mirabilis	Marvellous Spatuletail	Peru
Heliomaster		
constantii	Plain-capped Starthroat	Mexico to Costa Rica
longirostris	Long-billed Starthroat	Mexico to Bolivia
squamosus	Stripe-breasted Starthroat	Brazil (E.)
furcifer	Blue-tufted Starthroat	Colombia to Argentina
Rhodopsis		
vesper	Oasis Hummingbird	Peru to Chile
Thaumastura		
cora	Peruvian Sheartail	Peru
Microstilbon		
burmeisteri	Slender-tailed Woodstar	Bolivia to Argentina
Myrtis		
fanny	Purple-collared Woodstar	Ecuador and Peru
Eulidia (Myrtis)		
yarrellii	Chilean Woodstar	Chile
Calliphlox (Calothorax)		
amethystina	Amethyst Woodstar	Bolivia to Argentina
Tilmatura (Calothorax)		
dupontii	Sparkling-tailed (Dupont) Hummingbird	Mexico to Nicaragua
Calothorax		
(Calothorax)		
lucifer	Lucifer Hummingbird	USA to Mexico
pulcher	Beautiful Hummingbird	Mexico
(Philodice)		
mitchellii	Purple-throated Woodstar	Colombia and Ecuador
evelynae	Bahama Woodstar	Bahamas
bryantae	Magenta-throated Woodstar	Costa Rica and Panama
(Doricha)		
enicura	Slender Sheartail	Mexico to Honduras
eliza	Mexican Sheartail	Mexico
Myrmia (Acestrura)		
micrura	Short-tailed Woodstar	Ecuador and Peru

2. Subfamily Trochilinae

Genus and Species	Common Name	Range
Acestrura		
mulsant	White-bellied Woodstar	Colombia to Bolivia
decorata	Decorated Woodstar§¶	Colombia
bombus	Little Woodstar	Ecuador and Peru
heliodor	Gorgeted Woodstar	Panama to Ecuador
berlepschi	Esmeralda Woodstar	Ecuador
harterti	Hartert Woodstar§¶	Colombia
Chaetocercus (Acestrura)		
jourdanii	Rufous-shafted Woodstar	Venezuela, Colombia, Trinidad
Archilochus		
(Calypte)		
anna	Anna Hummingbird	USA and Mexico
costae	Costa Hummingbird	USA and Mexico
helenae	Bee Hummingbird	Cuba
(Archilochus)		
colubris	Ruby-throated Hummingbird	USA and Canada to Panama (winter)
alexandri	Black-chinned Hummingbird	Canada to Mexico
(Stellula)		
calliope	Calliope Hummingbird	Canada to Mexico
(Mellisuga)		
minima	Vervain Hummingbird	West Indies
Selasphorus		
(Atthis)		
heloisa	Bumblebee Hummingbird	Mexico
ellioti	Wine-throated Hummingbird††***	Mexico to Honduras
(Selasphorus)		
flammula	Volcano (Rose-throated) Hummingbird	Costa Rica
torridus	Heliotrope-throated Hummingbird†††	Costa Rica and Panama
simoni	Cerise-throated Hummingbird§§§	Costa Rica
ardens	Glow-throated Hummingbird	Panama
rufus	Rufous Hummingbird	Alaska to Mexico
sasin	Allen Hummingbird	USA and Mexico
scintilla	Scintillant Hummingbird	Costa Rica and Panama
platycercus	Broad-tailed Hummingbird	USA to Guatemala

continued on next page

*Possibly conspecific with *prevostii*.
†Known from only a few specimens.
§Known from one specimen.
‡Possibly a variant of *poortmani*.
#Probably an artifact.
¶Probably a hybrid.
**Taxonomic status uncertain.
††Possibly should be considered as two species.

§§Probably conspecific with *exima*.
‡‡Includes *sybillae*, sometimes considered a separate species.
##Includes *cinaereicauda*, possibly should include *calolaema*.
¶¶Includes *H. clarisse clarisse* of Peters.
***Probably conspecific with *heloisa*.
†††Probably conspecific with *flammula*.
§§§Probably conspecific with *ardens*.

	2. Subfamily Trochilinae	
Genus and Species	Common Name	Range
Lophornis		
(Lophornis)		
ornata	Tufted Coquette	Guianas to Brazil, Trinidad
gouldii	Dot-eared Coquette	Brazil (N. & Central)
magnifica	Frilled Coquette	Brazil (E. & Central)
delattrei	Rufous-crested Coquette	Mexico to Bolivia
strictolopha	Spangled Coquette	Venezuela to Peru
melaniae	Dusky Coquette§**	Colombia
chalybea	Festive Coquette	Venezuela to Brazil
pavonina	Peacock Coquette	Guyana and Venezuela
insignibarbis	Bearded Coquette§¶	Unknown
helenae	Black-crested Coquette	Mexico to Costa Rica
adorabilis	White-crested Coquette	Costa Rica and Panama
(Discosura)		
longicauda	Racket-tailed Coquette	Guianas to Brazil, Venezuela
(Popelairia)		
popelairii	Wire-crested Thorntail	Colombia to Peru
langsdorffi	Black-bellied Thorntail	Venezuela to Brazil, Peru
letitiae	Coppery Thorntail†	Bolivia
conversii	Green Thorntail	Costa Rica to Ecuador

*Possibly conspecific with *prevostii*.
†Known from only a few specimens.
§Known from one specimen.
‡Possibly a variant of *poortmani*.
#Probably an artifact.
¶Probably a hybrid.
**Taxonomic status uncertain.
††Possibly should be considered
as two species.

§§Probably conspecific with *exima*.
‡‡Includes *sybillae*, sometimes considered a separate species.
##Includes *cinaereicauda*, possibly should include *calolaema*.
¶¶Includes *H. clarisse clarisse* of Peters.
***Probably conspecific with *heloisa*.
†††Probably conspecific with *flammula*.
§§§Probably conspecific with *ardens*.

Synoptic Identification Guide to Hummingbirds of the World

The enormous number of species, in addition to the great similarities among the females and young of some closely related species, make construction of a complete key to the hummingbirds of the world almost impossible; in any case, such a key would not be appropriate for a semi-technical book. However, the following key should provide a limited guide to hummingbird identification. It narrows down the possible identity of any unknown hummingbird to a relatively few species, based on fairly conspicuous features. In some cases the features are typical only of adults, and occasionally only of adult males. Nevertheless, it comprises some 325 species— essentially all of the well-verified species of hummingbirds—and contains sufficient redundancy so that users may "key out" several species in as many as five or six different places. The key is largely based on a similar one provided for the strictly South American species by de Schauensee (1966), but contains considerable modifications and additions. Numbers within the key correspond to the numbered sequence of vernacular hummingbird names listed in Appendix Five. The latter list contains an index to major references that provide colored plates for each species, which should assist further in identification efforts.

Although there are a few fairly comprehensive older keys to hummingbirds (e.g., Ridgway, 1911, and Elliott, 1878), no modern comprehensive key exists for all hummingbirds. A recent book by Poley (1976) provides a limited key (in German) to more than 300 species of hummingbirds, which should offer additional help to any reader who desires more information than is provided here. Another recent book by Behnke-Pederson (1972) provides descriptions (in Danish) of 228 species (through *Cyanophaia*), including range maps for many South American forms.

BODY PLUMAGE CHARACTERISTICS

I. Body plumage mostly shining green, usually without contrasting colors
    A. With contrasting crown
        1. Bill black
            South American: 93, 138, 182, 242
            Central American: 113
        2. Bill pink to reddish basally

    South American: 105, 111–113, 142
    West Indian: 90, 115
  B. Without contrasting crown
      1. Larger (more than 100 mm) species
          South American: 12, 47, 57–59, 205, 217
          Central American: 52, 57
          West Indian: 65, 79
      2. Smaller (less than 100 mm) species
          a. Lower mandible pink basally
              South American: 67, 75, 77, 82, 101, 119, 131, 132,
              145, 146, 151
              Central American: 78, 109, 140, 143, 145, 151, 152
              West Indian: 80
          b. Bill entirely black
              South American: 76, 83, 85–87, 118, 147, 163, 164,
              212, 236–238, 241, 245, 256–262
              West Indian: 81
II. Body plumage not mostly shining green; underparts often dif-
     ferent from upperparts
     A. Breast color different from that of belly
         1. Belly green or grayish (breast violet-blue or purple)
             South American: 48, 50–51, 99, 102–103, 133–134, 136,
             191, 228, 257
             Central American: 99, 106, 134, 164
         2. Belly not green or grayish
             a. Breast blue or purple
                 South American: 50, 74, 98, 100, 174, 176
                 Central American: 54
                 West Indian: 68
             b. Breast green
                 South American: 91, 153, 163, 190, 211, 213, 239, 243
                 Central American: 106, 137, 148
                 West Indian: 69
             c. Breast black, South American: 215
         3. Narrow throat patch, usually of more than one color,
             coming to a point on breast; all South American: 266–
             271, 282–283
         4. Small, isolated glittering patch on center of throat
             South American: 180–181, 183–188, 208, 211–216, 227,
             234, 236, 259, 260
             Central American: 56, 166, 183, 284
         5. White or pale buff patch or band on breast
             South American: 7, 10–11, 116, 157, 177, 191, 201–203,
             207, 209, 223–226, 244, 275, 277–279, 293, 297, 303–309
             Central American: 294, 299–301, 330, 337
             West Indian: 278
         6. All or mostly purple or black above
             South American: 55, 92, 208, 214, 254–255, 264–265, 268
             Central American: 46
         7. Upper back dull brown or black, lower back and rump

iridescent; all South American: 200–203
8. Rump crossed by white or buff band, size very small
   South American: 327–335, 338–342
   Central American: 330, 336–337, 342
B. Breast color not distinctly different from belly
   1. Underparts all or mostly white, gray, or black
      a. Underparts whitish
         aa. No metallic gorget
             South American: 116, 125–126, 128, 138–139, 219, 280–282
             Central American: 15, 21, 98–99, 127, 137, 140, 155, 156, 280
             West Indian: 316
         bb. Metallic gorget present
             South American: 288–292, 297, 302–303, 307
             Central American: 169, 172, 284–285, 295–296, 299, 310, 315, 317–326
             West Indian: 298, 312
      b. Underparts gray
         aa. Size small (less than 100 mm)
             South American: 39, 70, 72, 76–77, 82–83, 85–87, 95, 98–99, 103, 285
             Central American: 72, 151, 158
         bb. Size larger (more than 100 mm)
             aaa. Throat striped, bill curved
                  South American: 11, 13, 16, 18, 20–22, 26
                  Central American: 13
             bbb. Throat unstriped, bill straight
                  South American: 40, 42, 49–50, 53, 91–93, 122–123, 163–164, 195–197, 218, 287
                  Central American: 46
      c. Underparts black or blackish
         aa. Throat iridescent
             South American: 234, 254–255
             Central American: 73, 91, 168, 173, 198
             West Indian: 64, 66, 71
         bb. Throat not iridescent
             South American: 6, 39, 55, 194, 202, 204, 247, 339, 342
             Central American: 13, 40, 160, 165
   2. Underparts not all or mostly white, gray, or black
      a. Underparts all or mostly uniform buff to chestnut
         aa. Bill distinctly curved, tail variably pointed
             South American: 3–5, 14–15, 25, 27–29, 31, 33–36, 44
             Central American: 4, 5, 11, 15, 22, 35
         bb. Bill straight or nearly straight, tail rounded to forked
             aaa. Tail with rufous present
                  aaaa. Dusky band across chest

South American: 32, 290, 293, 297, 303, 305–306, 309

Central American: 330

    bbbb. No dusky band present

South American: 25, 44, 114, 179, 200, 221, 327–331

Central American: 43, 149, 295–296

  bbb. No rufous in tail

    aaaa. Size very large (wing more than 100 mm)

South American: 199, 205

    bbbb. Size smaller (wing less than 100 mm)

South American: 121, 174–175, 178, 206, 210–211, 274, 288, 291–292

Central American: 107, 169–171, 294, 300

b. Underparts spotted or streaked

  aa. Throat or underparts spotted, or white to buff with green disks

    aaa. Size larger (more than 100 mm)

South American: 52, 117–118, 120, 182–183, 188, 190–191, 197, 201, 210–211, 213, 217, 248, 251–252, 265, 272

Central American: 52, 54, 183

    bbb. Size smaller (less than 100 mm)

South American: 102, 111–114, 124, 128–129, 134, 136, 174, 176, 204, 245

Central American: 134, 336

  bb. Underparts streaked, or with a conspicuous streak down belly

    aaa. Underparts streaked, all South American: 1–2, 37–38

    bbb. A conspicuous streak down belly

South American: 60–61, 63, 70, 195, 283, 286

Central American: 61–63, 342

BILL CHARACTERISTICS

I. Upper mandible pink, red, or flesh-colored basally, with a black tip, normal shape

  A. South American: 75, 77, 102–103, 105, 111–112, 117, 121, 151, 154, 327–331

  B. Central American: 106–110, 130, 140, 141, 143–144, 149–52, 155–156, 162, 330, 336–337

  C. West Indian: 115

II. Bill mostly or entirely blackish, but of unusual configuration

  A. Bill longer than body: 217

  B. Bill very short (exposed culmen to 1 cm)

West Indian: 71, 316

Central American: 165

South American: 70, 72, 264, 265

C. Bill wedge-shaped in dorsal view: 279–281

D. Bill toothed or fringed on edges: 1–2

E. Bill slightly upturned toward tip: 67, 272

F. Bill sharply decurved and sickle-shaped: 37, 38

III. Nostril with rudimentary operculum, bill stout and shorter than head (exposed culmen to 15 mm)

A. South American: 327–334

B. Central American: 330, 335–337

HEAD CHARACTERISTICS

I. Throat with a pendant tuft, tail forked, South American

A. Head crested: 271

B. Head not crested: 266–269, 276

II. Cheek feathers variably lengthened, bill reddish basally: 327–334

III. Crested; throat not tufted nor cheek plumes present

A. South American: 74, 270, 282

B. West Indian: 71, 115

IV. Blue-violet to reddish ear-patch present

A. With dark band across tail: 56–59

B. Tail largely white, unbanded: 280–281

TAIL CHARACTERISTICS

I. Tail of fairly normal shape (not unusually long, forked or racquet-shaped)

A. Tail at least partially white other than on tip

1. Entire tail white: 210

2. Outer tail feathers entirely or mostly white

South American: 10–11, 47, 54–55, 117, 125, 195–196, 198, 204, 209–210, 219, 222, 271, 276, 280–282

Central American: 46, 157–159, 161–162, 165–167, 214

B. Outer tail feathers entirely buff or chestnut

South American: 5, 10, 38, 44–45, 48, 70, 114, 151, 153–154, 179–181, 192, 197, 200, 202, 220

Central American: 106–107, 143, 148–152, 155–156, 330, 337

II. Shape of tail unusual

A. Racquet-like tips present: 248, 283, 338

B. Tail forked

1. Size small (less than 100 mm)

South American: 91–92, 282, 289, 339–342

Central American: 78, 294–296, 300–301, 311, 313–314

West Indian: 81, 298, 316

2. Size larger (more than 100 mm)

South American: 51, 183, 188, 190–193, 228–229, 248–

252, 273
Central American: 91, 183, 189, 342
West Indian: 79, 80, 115
C. Tail with central feathers pointed, and tipped with white or buff: 12–36
D. Outer tail feathers distinctly narrowed, or all feathers ending in long points
   1. All tail feathers long and pointed: 339–342
   2. Outer feathers unusually narrow: 295, 303–307, 311, 324
E. Central tail feathers extremely short, often hidden by coverts
   1. Outermost pair of rectrices very narrow, Central American: 295–296
   2. Outer pair not narrower than rest, South American: 291–292, 302–309

WING CHARACTERISTICS

I. Wing very long (more than 100 mm, total length more than 200 mm) South American: 199, 205
II. Specialized primaries present
A. Entire shafts of primaries unusually broad and flattened: 41–52
B. Primary shafts somewhat thickened basally: 53
C. Outermost (tenth) primary specialized
   1. Outermost primary distinctly shorter than ninth: 113, 115
   2. Outermost primary unusually narrow over entire length: 200–204
   3. Outermost primary with attenuated (pointed) tip: 323–326
   4. Outermost primary with incised (notched) tip: 113, 317
D. Outer web of ninth primary abruptly incised for at least terminal third: 327–342
III. Wing color unusual
A. Wing greenish, West Indian: 68
B. Wing steel-blue, South American: 205
C. Wing reddish brown
Central American: 157–162, 173
South American: 200–203

APPENDIX FIVE

Identification Numbers

of Hummingbirds in Appendix Four,
and Index to Colored Plates from Books in the
General Reference List of Bibliography or Elsewhere

Illustration sources exclude North American species that are generally well illustrated and Gould's plates, unless these species are not illustrated elsewhere. In such cases, original Gould plate numbers are indicated in parentheses. Entire names in parentheses indicate uncertain taxonomic status, including possible hybrids, variants, and species known from unique or only a few specimens.

ID No.	Hummingbird	References
1.	Tooth-billed Hummingbird	3, 4
2.	Saw-billed Hermit	4, 17
3.	Hook-billed Hermit	17
4.	Bronzy Hermit	3, 14
5.	Rufous-breasted Hermit	3, 4, 8, 10, 14, 17
6.	Sooty Barbthroat	
7.	Bronze-tailed Barbthroat	Grantsau, 1969
8.	Christina Barbthroat	
9.	Black Barbthroat	
10.	Pale-tailed Barbthroat	4, 5, 17
11.	Band-tailed Barbthroat	3, 11, 14, 17
12.	White-whiskered Hermit	8, 9, 17
13.	Green Hermit	3, 14
14.	Tawny-bellied Hermit	4
15.	Long-tailed Hermit	1, 3, 14, 17, 19
16.	Great-billed Hermit	7 (pl. 17)
17.	Margaretta Hermit	
18.	Scale-throated Hermit	17
19.	Black-billed Hermit	Ruschi, 1973b
20.	White-bearded Hermit	8
21.	Pale-bellied Hermit	3, 14
22.	Straight-billed Hermit	10, 17
23.	Needle-billed Hermit	7 (pl. 21)
24.	Koepcke Hermit	Weske and Terborgh, 1977
25.	Dusky-throated Hermit	7 (pl. 30)
26.	Sooty-capped Hermit	8, 17
27.	Planalto Hermit	8, 17
28.	Buff-bellied Hermit	
29.	Cinnamon-throated Hermit	
30.	Maranhão Hermit	
31.	Broad-tipped Hermit	
32.	Reddish Hermit	8, 10
33.	White-browed Hermit	
34.	Gray-chinned Hermit	7 (pl. 36)

continued on next page

ID No.	Hummingbird	References
35.	Little Hermit	3, 10, 11, 13, 14
36.	Minute Hermit	7 (pl. 38)
37.	White-tipped Sicklebill	1, 3, 8, 17, 18, 19
38.	Buff-tailed Sicklebill	4
39.	Blue-fronted Lancebill	4, 5, 17
40.	Green-fronted Lancebill	3, 4, 14
41.	Wedge-tailed Sabrewing	3, 11, 13
42.	Gray-breasted Sabrewing	4, 5, 8, 17
43.	Rufous Sabrewing	3, 11, 13
44.	Rufous-breasted Sabrewing	5
45.	Buff-breasted Sabrewing	
46.	Violet Sabrewing	1, 3, 9, 11, 14
47.	White-tailed Sabrewing	5, 17
48.	Lazuline Sabrewing	5, 8, 17
49.	Santa Marta Sabrewing	
50.	Napo Sabrewing	17
51.	Swallow-tailed Hummingbird	4, 9, 10, 17, 19
52.	Scaly-breasted Hummingbird	3, 11, 14, 19
53.	Sombre Hummingbird	17
54.	White-necked Jacobin	3, 4, 10, 11, 13, 14, 18
55.	Black Jacobin	4, 8, 17
56.	Brown Violet-ear	3, 5, 11, 13, 14
57.	Green Violet-ear	3, 5, 11, 13, 14, 17
58.	Sparkling Violet-ear	1, 4, 5, 9, 17, 18
59.	White-vented Violet-ear	7 (pl. 223)
60.	Green-throated Mango	17
61.	Green-breasted Mango	3, 5, 11, 13, 17
62.	Veraguan Mango	3
63.	Black-throated Mango	3, 4, 5, 8, 10, 14, 18, 19
64.	Antillean Mango	2
65.	Green Mango	2
66.	Jamaican Mango	2
67.	Fiery-tailed Awlbill	4, 17
68.	Purple-throated Carib (Awlbill)	2, 17, 19
69.	Greent-throated Carib	2, 17
70.	Ruby-topaz Hummingbird	4, 8, 9, 10, 18
71.	Antillean Crested Hummingbird	2
72.	Violet-headed Hummingbird	3, 4, 14
73.	Emerald-chinned Hummingbird	3, 11, 13, 17
74.	Black-breasted Plovercrest	4, 8, 17, 19
75.	Blue-chinned Sapphire	5, 10
76.	Blue-tailed Emerald	3, 5, 10, 17, 18
77.	Glittering Emerald	8, 19
78.	Fork-tailed Emerald	3, 11, 13
79.	Cuban Emerald	2
80.	Hispaniolan Emerald	2
81.	Puerto Rican Emerald	2
82.	Red-billed Emerald	4

ID No.	Hummingbird	References
83.	Coppery Emerald	5
84.	(Berlepsch Emerald)	
85.	Narrow-tailed Emerald	5
86.	Green-tailed Emerald	7 (pl. 357)
87.	Short-tailed Emerald	5, 17
88.	(Cabanis Emerald)	
89.	(Natterer Emerald)	
90.	Blue-headed Hummingbird	2
91.	Crowned (Fork-tailed) Woodnymph	3, 4, 10, 13, 14, 17, 19
92.	Long-tailed Woodnymph	7 (pl. 100)
93.	Violet-capped Woodnymph	8, 17
94.	(Lerch Woodnymph)	
95.	(Berlioz Woodnymph)	
96.	(Emerald Woodnymph)	
97.	(Nerkhorn Hummingbird)	
98.	Violet-bellied Hummingbird	3, 14, 18
99.	Sapphire-throated Hummingbird	3, 14
100.	Sapphire-bellied Hummingbird	
101.	Shining-green Hummingbird	5
102.	Rufous-throated Sapphire	4, 5, 8, 13, 17
103.	White-chinned Sapphire	5, 10
104.	(Flame-rumped Sapphire)	
105.	Gilded Hummingbird	8, 19
106.	Blue-throated Goldentail	3, 11, 13, 14
107.	Black-fronted Hummingbird	3, 14
108.	White-eared Hummingbird	
109.	Dusky Hummingbird	3, 13
110.	Broad-billed Hummingbird	
111.	Blue-headed Sapphire	3
112.	Golden-tailed Sapphire	7 (pl. 325)
113.	Violet-capped Hummingbird	3, 14
114.	Pirre Hummingbird	3, 14
115.	Streamertail	1, 2, 8, 17, 19
116.	White-throated Hummingbird	17
117.	White-tailed Goldenthroat	1, 10
118.	Tepui Goldenthroat	7 (pl. 296)
119.	Green-tailed Goldenthroat	10
120.	Many-spotted Hummingbird	
121.	Buffy Hummingbird	7 (pl. 56)
122.	Tumbes Hummingbird	
123.	Spot-throated Hummingbird	
124.	Olive-spotted Hummingbird	
125.	White-bellied Hummingbird	17
126.	Green-and-White Hummingbird	
127.	White-bellied Emerald	3, 11, 13
128.	White-chested Emerald	5
129.	Versicolored Emerald	5, 8, 17

continued on next page

ID No.	Hummingbird	References
130.	Honduras Emerald	3
131.	Glittering-throated Emerald	5, 9, 10
132.	Tachira Emerald	5
133.	Sapphire-spangled Emerald	5, 17
134.	Blue-chested Hummingbird	3, 14
135.	(Blue-spotted Hummingbird)	
136.	Purple-chested Humming-bird	
137.	Mangrove Hummingbird	3
138.	Andean Emerald	4, 9, 18
139.	Plain-bellied Emerald	10
140.	Red-billed Azurecrown	3, 11
141.	(Small-billed Azurecrown)	
142.	Indigo-capped Humming-bird	7 (pl. 323)
143.	Berylline Hummingbird	3, 11, 13, 17
144.	Blue-tailed Hummingbird	3, 11, 13
145.	Steely-vented Hummingbird	3, 5
146.	Copper-rumped Humming-bird	5, 8
147.	Green-bellied Hummingbird	5
148.	Snowy-breasted Humming-bird	3, 14
149.	Cinnamon Hummingbird	3, 11, 13
150.	Buff-bellied Hummingbird	
151.	Rufous-tailed Hummingbird	
152.	Escudo Hummingbird	
153.	Chestnut-bellied Humming-bird	
154.	Amazilia Hummingbird	
155.	Green-fronted Hummingbird	13
156.	Violet-crowned Humming-bird	
157.	(White-tailed Hummingbird)	
158.	Stripe-tailed Hummingbird	3, 11, 13, 14
159.	Blue-capped (Oaxaca) Hum-mingbird	Rowley and Orr, 1964
160.	Black-bellied Hummingbird	3, 14
161.	White-tailed Emerald	3, 14
162.	Coppery-headed Emerald	
163.	White-vented Plumeleteer	3, 4, 14, 17
164.	Bronze-tailed Plumeleteer	3, 14, 17
165.	Snowcap	3, 8, 14
166.	Fiery-throated Hummingbird	3, 14
167.	Blue-throated Hummingbird	
168.	Amethyst-throated Hum-mingbird	3, 11
169.	Green-throated Mountain-gem	3, 11, 13
170.	White-bellied Mountain-gem	3
171.	White-throated (Variable) Mountain-gem	3, 9, 14

ID No.	Hummingbird	References
172.	Purple-throated Mountain-gem	3, 14
173.	Garnet-throated Hummingbird	3, 11, 13, 19
174.	Speckled Hummingbird	5
175.	Blossomcrown	4
176.	Whitetip	4, 9
177.	Ecuadorean Piedtail	17
178.	Peruvian Piedtail	
179.	Brazilian Ruby	4, 8, 17
180.	Gould Jewelfront	4
181.	Fawn-breasted Brilliant	7 (pl. 325)
182.	Violet-fronted Brilliant	5
183.	Green-crowned Brilliant	3, 14, 17
184.	Velvet-browed Brilliant	5
185.	Black-throated Brilliant	7 (pl. 93)
186.	Pink-throated Brilliant	
187.	Rufous-webbed Brilliant	
188.	Empress Brilliant	4, 17
189.	Rivoli (Magnificent) Hummingbird	
190.	Scissor-tailed Hummingbird	5
191.	Violet-chested Hummingbird	4, 5
192.	Crimson Topaz	1, 8, 9, 10, 19
193.	Fiery Topaz	4, 17
194.	Black-breasted Hillstar	4, 17
195.	Andean Hillstar	8, 9, 19
196.	White-sided Hillstar	17
197.	Wedge-tailed Hillstar	7 (pl. 73)
198.	White-tailed Hillstar	17
199.	Giant Hummingbird	1, 4, 8, 9, 19
200.	Shining Sunbeam	8, 9, 17
201.	Purple-backed Sunbeam	
202.	White-tufted Sunbeam	7 (pl. 180)
203.	Black-hooded Sunbeam	4, 17, 19
204.	Mountain Velvetbreast	5
205.	Great Sapphirewing	9, 17
206.	Bronzy Inca	5
207.	Brown Inca	8, 9, 18
208.	Black Inca	17
209.	Collared Inca	1, 4, 8, 9, 18
210.	White-tailed Starfrontlet	4
211.	Golden-bellied Starfrontlet	5, 19
212.	Dusky Starfrontlet	
213.	Blue-throated Starfrontlet	5, 19
214.	Buff-winged Starfrontlet	9
215.	Violet-throated Starfrontlet	7 (pl. 239)
216.	Rainbow Starfrontlet	4, 9, 17
217.	Sword-billed Hummingbird	1, 4, 8, 9, 17, 18
218.	Green-backed Firecrown	9, 19
219.	Fernandez Firecrown	17

continued on next page

ID No.	Hummingbird	References
220.	Buff-tailed Coronet	5, 18
221.	Chestnut-breasted Coronet	
222.	Velvet-purple Coronet	4, 8, 9, 18, 19
223.	Orange-throated Sunangel	5, 9
224.	Merida Sunangel	5
225.	Amethyst-throated Sunangel	4
226.	Gorgeted Sunangel	9, 17
227.	Tourmaline Sunangel	18
228.	Purple-throated Sunangel	7 (pl. 241)
229.	Royal Sunangel	Fitzpatrick et al., 1979
230.	Little Sunangel	
231.	(Green-throated Sunangel)	
232.	(Rothschild Sunangel)	
233.	(Glistening Sunangel)	
234.	Black-breasted Puffleg	7 (pl. 276)
235.	(Soderstrom Puffleg)	
236.	Glowing Puffleg	5, 9
237.	Turquoise-throated Puffleg	7 (pl. 277)
238.	Coppery-bellied Puffleg	5, 9, 17
239.	Sapphire-vented Puffleg	4, 8, 9, 18
240.	(Isaacson Puffleg)	
241.	Golden-breasted Puffleg	7 (pl. 274)
242.	Blue-capped Puffleg	
243.	Colorful Puffleg	4
244.	Emerald-bellied Puffleg	7 (pl. 280)
245.	Black-thighed Puffleg	7 (pl. 279)
246.	Greenish Puffleg	3, 14
247.	Hoary Puffleg	7 (pl. 282)
248.	Booted Racket-tail	4, 8, 17, 19
249.	Black-tailed Trainbearer	4, 8, 9, 18
250.	Green-tailed Trainbearer	17
251.	Red-tailed Comet	1, 4, 17, 19
252.	Bronze-tailed Comet	4
253.	(Purple-tailed Comet)	7 (pl. 176)
254.	Black Metaltail	
255.	Perija Metaltail	4
256.	Veridian Metaltail	Graves, 1980
257.	Violet-throated Metaltail	Graves, 1980
258.	Neblina Metaltail	Graves, 1980
259.	Coppery Metaltail	Graves, 1980
260.	Fire-throated	Graves, 1980
261.	Scaled Metaltail	Graves, 1980
262.	Tyrian Metaltail	5
263.	(Purple-tailed Thornbill)	
264.	Purple-backed Thornbill	4, 5, 8, 19
265.	Black-backed Thornbill	*Ibis*, 1880 (p. 172)
266.	Rufous-capped Thornbill	7 (pl. 188)
267.	Olivaceous Thornbill	
268.	Blue-mantled Thornbill	17
269.	Bronze-tailed Thornbill	5
270.	Rainbow-bearded Thornbill	1, 4, 19
271.	Bearded Helmetcrest	4, 8, 9, 17, 19
272.	Mountain Avocetbill	4, 19

ID No.	Hummingbird	References
273.	Gray-bellied Comet	4
274.	Long-tailed Sylph	1, 8, 18
275.	Violet-tailed Sylph	4, 19
276.	Bearded Mountaineer	4, 19
277.	Hyacinth Visorbearer	8
278.	Hooded Visorbearer	4, 19
279.	Wedge-billed Hummingbird	1, 4, 5, 8, 9
280.	Purple-crowned Fairy	3, 4, 11, 13, 18, 19
281.	Black-eared Fairy	8, 9, 10
282.	Horned Sungem	4, 8, 17, 19
283.	Marvellous Spatulletail	1, 4, 9, 17, 18, 19
284.	Plain-capped Starthroat	3, 11, 13
285.	Long-billed Starthroat	8, 11, 13, 14, 18, 19
286.	Stripe-breasted Starthroat	
287.	Blue-tufted Starthroat	4, 8, 17, 19
288.	Oasis Hummingbird	4, 17
289.	Peruvian Sheartail	4, 9
290.	Slender-tailed Woodstar	4
291.	Purple-collared Woodstar	17
292.	Chilean Woodstar	Johnson, 1967
293.	Amethyst Woodstar	4, 5, 8, 10
294.	Sparkling-tailed (Dupont) Hummingbird	3, 11, 13
295.	Lucifer Hummingbird	
296.	Beautiful Hummingbird	3, 13
297.	Purple-throated Woodstar	4
298.	Bahama Woodstar	2
299.	Magenta-throated Woodstar	3, 14
300.	Slender Sheartail	3, 11, 19
301.	Mexican Sheartail	3, 13
302.	Short-tailed Woodstar	4
303.	White-bellied Woodstar	4, 18
304.	(Decorated Woodstar)	
305.	· Little Woodstar	
306.	Gorgeted Woodstar	3, 5, 17
307.	Esmeralda Woodstar	
308.	(Hartert Woodstar)	
309.	Rufous-shafted Woodstar	5, 9
310.	Anna Hummingbird	
311.	Costa Hummingbird	
312.	Bee Hummingbird	1, 2, 19
313.	Ruby-throated Hummingbird	
314.	Black-throated Hummingbird	
315.	Calliope Hummingbird	
316.	Vervain Hummingbird	2, 9
317.	Bumblebee Hummingbird	13
318.	Wing-throated (Elliot) Hummingbird	3, 11, 19
319.	Volcano (Rose-throated) Hummingbird	3, 14

continued on next page

ID No.	Hummingbird	References
320.	Heliotrope-throated Hummingbird	3
321.	Cerise-throated Hummingbird	3
322.	Glow-throated Hummingbird	14
323.	Rufous Hummingbird	
324.	Allen Hummingbird	
325.	Scintillant Hummingbird	3, 14
326.	Broad-tailed Hummingbird	
327.	Tufted Coquette	4, 5, 9, 10, 17, 19
328.	Dot-eared Coquette	7 (pl. 118)
329.	Frilled Coquette	1, 8 17
330.	Rufous-crested Coquette	3, 13, 14
331.	Spangled Coquette	4, 5
332.	(Dusky Coquette)	
333.	Festive Coquette	5, 17
334.	Peacock Coquette	1, 5
335.	(Bearded Coquette)	
336.	Black-crested Coquette	3, 11, 13
337.	White-crested (Adorable) Coquette	1, 3, 14, 19
338.	Racket-tailed Coquette	4, 8, 17, 19
339.	Wire-crested Thorntail	1, 17, 18, 19
340.	Black-bellied Thorntail	5, 8, 17
341.	(Coppery Thorntail)	
342.	Green Thorntail	3, 4, 14, 18

APPENDIX SIX

Hummingbird- Adapted Plants in North America

DICOTYLEDONS

ACANTHACEAE
Anisacanthus thurberi. Chuparosa, Desert Honeysuckle. Arizona, southwestern New Mexico, and northern Mexico.
Beloperone californica. Chuparosa. Deserts of southern California, Arizona, and northern Mexico.
Jacobinia ovata. Southern Arizona and northern Mexico.

BALSAMACEAE
Impatiens capensis. Spotted Touch-me-not. Newfoundland and Quebec to Saskatchewan, south to South Carolina, Alabama, and Oklahoma.

BIGNONIACEAE
Campsis radicans. Trumpet Vine, Trumpet Creeper. New Jersey to Ohio, south to Florida and Texas.

BORAGINACEAE
Cordia sebestana. Florida Keys, Everglades, and West Indies.

BROMELIACEAE
Tillandsia balbisiana. Southern peninsular Florida, West Indies, Mexico, Central and South America.
T. fasciculata. Peninsular Florida, West Indies, Mexico, Central and South America.
T. flexuosa. Southern peninsular Florida, West Indies, and South America.

CACTACEAE
Echinocereus triglochidiatus. Hedgehog Cactus, Claret Cup Hedgehog. Southeastern California to New Mexico and Colorado, south to northern Mexico.

CAMPANULACEAE
Lobelia cardinalis. Cardinal-flower, Scarlet Lobelia. Widespread in the southwest, eastern United States, Mexico, and Central America.
L. laxiflora. Southern Arizona to Central America.

CAPRIFOLIACEAE
Lonicera arizonica. Honeysuckle. Arizona, New Mexico, Texas, and Utah.
L. canadensis. Fly-Honeysuckle. Nova Scotia and eastern Quebec to Saskatchewan, south to Pennsylvania, Ohio, Indiana, and Minnesota, and in the mountains of North Carolina.
L. ciliosa. Orange Honeysuckle. Northern California to British Columbia, east to Montana.
L. involucrata ledebourii. Twinberry. California coast.
L. sempervirens. Trumpet Honeysuckle. Connecticut to Florida and west to Oklahoma.

CARYOPHYLLACEAE
Silene californica. Indian Pink. Central California to southern Oregon.

S. laciniata. Catchfly. California to western Texas and Mexico.

S. regia. Royal Catchfly. Ohio to eastern Missouri, south to Alabama and Georgia.

S. rotundifolia. Roundleaf Catchfly. West Virginia and southern Ohio to Alabama and Georgia.

S. virginica. Fire Pink. New Jersey and western New York to southern Ontario, south to Georgia and Oklahoma.

CONVOLVULACEAE — *Ipomoea coccinea*. Star-glory, Small Red Morning-glory. Pennsylvania and Rhode Island south to Georgia, west to Illinois, Kansas, Oklahoma, western Texas and Arizona, and south to the tropics.

I. microdactyla. Morning-glory. Extreme southern Florida and the West Indies.

FOUQUIERIACEAE — *Fouquieria splendens*. Ocotillo. Deserts from southeastern California to western Texas, and northern Mexico.

HIPPOCASTANACEAE — *Aesculus pavia* (var. *pavia*). Buckeye. North Carolina to Florida and eastern Texas, and inland to southern Illinois and southern Missouri.

LABIATEAE — *Clinopodium coccineum*. Florida to Georgia and Alabama.

Monarda didyma. Bee-balm, Oswego-tea. Minnesota to Michigan, south to New Jersey, West Virginia, and Ohio, and along the mountains to northern Georgia.

M. fistulosa. Wild Bergamont. Quebec to Manitoba and British Columbia, south to Georgia, Louisiana, and Arizona, and west to the Rocky Mountains and California.

Monardella macrantha. Mountain-pennyroyal. Central California to northern Baja California.

Satureja mimyloides. Mint. Central and southern California.

Salvia henryi. Sage. Southern Arizona to western Texas and Mexico.

S. lemmoni. Sage. Southern Arizona and northern Mexico.

S. spathacea. Pitcher Sage. California Coast Range.

Stachys chamissonis. Hedge-nettle. Coastal California.

S. ciliata. Hedge-nettle. Oregon to British Columbia.

S. coccinea. Hedge-nettle. Southern Arizona to western Texas and Mexico.

Trichostema lanatum. Woolly Blue-curls, Romero. Coast Ranges of central and southern California.

NYCTAGINACEAE — *Allionia coccinea*. Southern California, Arizona, New Mexico, and northern Mexico.

ONAGRACEAE — *Zauchneria californica*. California-fuschia. California to southern Oregon, east to New Mexico, south to northern Mexico.

Z. cana. California-fuschia. Central and southern California.

Z. garrettii. California-fuschia. Eastern California to Utah and western Wyoming.

Z. septentrionalis. California-fuschia. Northern California.

LEGUMINACEAE — *Astragalus coccineus*. Locoweed, Rattleweed, Milkvetch. Desert mountains of eastern California, southwestern Arizona, and northern Baja California.

Erythrina flabelliformis. Coral-bean, Chilicote. Southern Arizona, southwestern New Mexico, and northern Mexico.

E. herbacea. Coral-tree. Florida to Texas and North Carolina, and northeastern Mexico.

LOGANIACEAE   *Spigelia marilandica*. Pinkroot, Wormgrass. North Carolina to southern Indiana, southern Missouri, and Oklahoma, south to Florida and Texas.

MALVACEAE   *Hibiscus coccineus*. Alabama, Georgia, and Florida.

Malvaviscus arboreus (var. *drummondii*). Turks-head. Southern Florida to Texas, West Indies, and Mexico.

POLEMONIACEAE   *Collomia rawsoniana*. South-central Sierra Nevada, California.

Gilia splendens (var. *grantii*). Gilia. San Bernardino and San Gabriel Mountains, southern California.

G. subnuda. Gilia. Northern Arizona to Nevada, east to New Mexico and Colorado.

Ipomopsis (Gilia) aggregata. Gilia. Widespread in western North America.

I. arizonica. Gilia. Eastern California to Arizona and Utah.

I. rubra. Gilia. Florida to Texas, Oklahoma, and North Carolina.

I. tenuifolia. Gilia. Extreme southern California and northern Baja California.

Polemonium pauciflorum. Polemonium. Southeastern Arizona and northern Mexico, and Davis Mountains in Texas.

P. brandegei. Honey Polemonium. Rocky Mountains in Colorado.

RANUNCULACEAE   *Aquilegia canadensis*. Columbine. Nova Scotia to Saskatchewan south to Florida and Texas.

A. desertorum. Columbine. Northern Arizona.

A. elegantula. Rocky Mountain Red Columbine. Arizona and New Mexico, north to southern Utah and Colorado, and south to northern Mexico.

A. eximia. Columbine. Coast Range in California.

A. formosa. Columbine. California to Alaska, east to Utah and Montana.

A. shockeyi. Columbine. Desert mountains of eastern California and Nevada.

A. triternata. Columbine. Eastern Arizona to western New Mexico and western Colorado.

Delphinium barbeyi. Subalpine Larkspur. Wyoming to Colorado and Utah.

D. cardinale. Scarlet Larkspur. Central California to Baja California.

D. nelsoni. Low Larkspur, Nelson Lonspur. Idaho to Utah and South Dakota.

D. nudicaule. Larkspur. Central California to southern Oregon.

RUBIACEAE   *Bouvardia glaberrima*. Bouvardia. Southern Arizona and New Mexico to northern Mexico.

B. ternifolia. Texas and adjacent New Mexico south to Mexico.

Hamelia patens. Southern peninsular Florida and West Indies

SAXIFRAGACEAE   *Ribes sanguineum*. Red Flowering Currant. California to British Columbia.
Ribes speciosum. Currant, Fuschia-flowered Gooseberry. Coast from central California to northern Baja California.

SCROPHULARIACEAE   *Castilleja affinis*. Paintbrush. California.
C. angustifolia. Paintbrush. Eastern Oregon to southern British Columbia and northwestern Wyoming.
C. applegatei. Paintbrush. Central California to eastern Oregon, east to western Wyoming.
C. austromontana. Paintbrush. Southern Arizona, southern New Mexico, and northern Mexico.
C. brevilobata. Paintbrush. Northern California and southern Oregon.
C. breweri. Paintbrush. Sierra Nevada in California.
C. coccinea. Painted-cup, Indian Paintbrush. Massachusetts to Ontario and Manitoba, south to South Carolina, Mississippi, and Oklahoma.
C. chromosa. Early Paintbrush. Southern California to eastern Oregon, east to New Mexico, Colorado, and Wyoming.
C. covilleana. Paintbrush. Central Idaho and western Montana.
C. crista-galli. Paintbrush. Idaho to western Wyoming.
C. cruenta. Paintbrush. Southeastern Arizona.
C. culbertsonii. Paintbrush. Sierra Nevada in California.
C. elmeri. Paintbrush. Cascade Mountains in Washington.
C. exilis. Paintbrush. Widespread in western North America.
C. foliolosa. Paintbrush. California.
C. franciscana. Paintbrush. Central Coast Range in California.
C. fraterna. Paintbrush. Wallowa Mountains in Oregon.
C. haydeni. Paintbrush. Northern New Mexico to Colorado.
C. hispida. Indian Paintbrush. Oregon to British Columbia, east to Montana.
C. hololeuca. Paintbrush. Chennel Islands, California.
C. inconstans. Paintbrush. Northern New Mexico.
C. indivisa. Paintbrush. Southeastern Oklahoma and Texas.
C. integra. Orange Paintbrush. Arizona to western Texas, south to northern Mexico, and north to Colorado.
C. lanata. Paintbrush. Arizona and northern Mexico to western Texas.
C. latifolia. Seaside Painted Cup. Montery coast in California.
C. laxa. Paintbrush. Southern Arizona and northern Mexico.
C. lemmonii. Paintbrush. Sierra Nevada in California.
C. leschkeana. Paintbrush. Point Reyes in California.
C. linariaefolia. Wyoming Paintbrush, Narrow-leaved Paintbrush. California to Oregon, east to New Mexico, Colorado, and Wyoming.
C. martinii. Paintbrush. Southern California to Baja California.
C. miniata. Scarlet Paintbrush. Widespread in western North America.
C. minor. Paintbrush. Arizona, New Mexico, and northern Mexico.

C. nana. Paintbrush. Sierra Nevada in California.

C. neglecta. Paintbrush. Tiburon peninsula in California.

C. organorum. Paintbrush. Organ Mountains in New Mexico.

C. parviflora. Rosy Paintbrush. California to Alaska and northern Rocky Mountains.

C. patriotica. Paintbrush. Southeastern Arizona and northern Mexico.

C. payneae. Paintbrush. Cascade Mountains from northern California to central Oregon.

C. peirsonii. Paintbrush. Sierra Nevada in California.

C. plagiotoma. Paintbrush. San Gabriel Mountains in California.

C. pruinosa. Paintbrush. Central California to Oregon.

C. rhexifolia. Splitleaf Painted Cup, Rosy Paintbrush. Northern Oregon to British Columbia, east to Colorado and Alberta.

C. roseana. Paintbrush. Coast Range in California.

C. rupicola. Paintbrush. Oregon to British Columbia.

C. sessiliflora. Downy Paintbrush, Plains Paintbrush. Wisconsin and northern Illinois to Saskatchewan, and south to Missouri, Texas, and Arizona.

C. septentrionalis. Northern Paintbrush, Yellow Paintbrush. Labrador and Newfoundland to Vermont, Michigan, South Dakota, and Alberta, south to Colorado and Utah.

C. stenantha. Paintbrush. California.

C. suksdorfii. Paintbrush. Oregon to British Columbia.

C. subincluosa. Paintbrush. Sierra Nevada in California.

C. uliginosa. Paintbrush. Pitkin Marsh in Sonoma County (California).

C. wightii. Paintbrush. Coastline from central California to Washington.

C. wootoni. Paintbrush. White and Sacramento Mountains in New Mexico.

Displacus (Mimulus) aurantiacus. Bush Monkey-flower. California and Oregon.

D. flemingii. Monkey-flower. Channel Islands in California.

D. puniceus. Monkey-flower. Coastal southern California and northern Baja California.

Galvezia speciosa. Islands of southern California and Baja California.

Keckia (Penstemon) cordifolia. Beard Tongue. Central California to northern Baja California.

K. corymbosa. Bear Tongue. Northern California.

K. ternata. Southern California and northern Baja California.

Macranthera flammea. Northern Florida to eastern Louisiana and Georgia.

Mimulus cardinalis. Crimson Monkey-flower, Scarlet Monkey-flower. California to Oregon, east to Arizona and Nevada.

M. eastwoodiae. Monkey-flower. Northeastern Arizona and southeastern Utah.

Pedicularis densiflora. Indian Warrier, Lousewort. California to southern Oregon and northern Baja California.

Penstemon barbatus. Penstemon. Arizona to Utah and southern

Colorado, and south into Mexico.

P. bridgesii. Scarlet Penstemon. California and Baja California to Colorado and New Mexico.

P. cardinalis. Penstemon. South-central New Mexico, Guadaloupe Mountains in Texas.

P. centranthifolius. Scarlet Bugler. Coast Range in central California to Baja California.

P. clevelandii. Penstemon. Southern California and Baja California.

P. crassulus. Penstemon. Central New Mexico.

P. eatonii. Penstemon. Southern California to Arizona and Utah.

P. labrosus. Scarlet Penstemon. Southern California and northern Baja California.

P. lanceolatus. Penstemon. Southeastern Arizona and southwestern New Mexico, to northern Mexico.

P. newberryi. Mountain Pride. Central California to northern Oregon.

P. parryi. Penstemon. Southern Arizona and northern Mexico.

P. pinifolius. Penstemon. Southeastern Arizona and southwestern New Mexico, to northern Mexico.

P. rupicola. Rock Penstemon. Northern California to Washington.

P. subulatus. Penstemon. Arizona.

P. utahensis. Penstemon. Eastern California to northern Arizona and Utah.

Scrophularia coccinea (= macrantha). Figwort. Southwestern New Mexico.

MONOCOTYLEDONS

AGAVACEAE   *Agave schottii* (?). Century Plant, Maguey. Southern Arizona to southwestern New Mexico and northern Mexico.

A. utahensis (?). Century Plant, Maguey. Southeastern California to northern Arizona and southern Utah.

LILIACEAE   *Brodiaea ida-maia*. Fire-cracker Plant. Northern California to southern Oregon.

B. venusta. Brodiaea. Northwestern California.

Fritillaria recurva. Scarlet Fritillary. Central California to southern Oregon.

Lilum maritimum. Coast Lily. Northern coastal California.

L. parvum. Alpine Lily. Sierra Nevada, California, to southern Oregon.

ORCHIDACEAE   *Spiranthes orchoides*. Ladies Tresses. Florida, Mexico, Central America, South America, and the West Indies.

Glossary

Adaptive peak	A genetic combination that approximates the maximum fitness for a specific population in a particular place and time.
Advertisement behavior	Communication, especially by various displays, evolved to increase the conspicuousness of an individual; frequently associated with territoriality.
Aggregation	A grouping of individuals attracted to some commonly exploited environmental resource.
Agonistic	Referring to aggressive interactions between individuals, ranging from attack to escape behavior.
Altricial	Referring to the condition of being hatched or born in a relatively undeveloped state, usually blind and without locomotory abilities.
Altruism	Behavior that increases the fitness of another individual at the expense of the individual performing it, including both nurturing behavior (usually between parent and offspring) and succoring behavior (nonparental assistance given to other, sometimes unrelated, individuals).
Angulated	Forming a distinct angle.
Anthesis	The period or time of blossoming in plants.
Apical	At the apex or tip.
Apodiformes	The avian order that includes swifts (suborder Apodi) and hummingbirds (family Trochilidae).
Arroyo	A gulley, creek, or dry creek bed (Spanish).
Attenuated	Tapering to a narrow tip.
Allopatric	Having geographically separated distributions, at least during the breeding season.
Auriculars	Feathers surrounding the ear opening of birds.
Axillars	Feathers located at the base of the underside of the wing.
Barbicels	Hooklet-like outgrowths toward the tip or pennulum of a barbule; also called hamuli.
Barbs	The individual subunits of a feather, which extend diagonally outward in pairs from the central shaft and which contain the feather pigments responsible for its colors.
Barbules	The individual subunits of a barb, which extend diagonally out-

273

ward in pairs from the main axis of each barb.

Barranca A cliff or gorge (Spanish).

Boreal Northern or northerly.

Calorie A physiological unit used to express the heat output of an organism and the energy value of its food, equal to 1000 gram calories of heat equivalent; also called kilocalorie, the equivalent of 1000 "small" calories.

Chapparal A vegetation type dominated by evergreen shrubs, usually growing in dense thickets.

Choripetalous A blossom condition in which the corolla is made up of separate petals.

Cinnamomeous Yellowish or reddish brown, the color of cinnamon.

Cloud forest Tropical montane forest at elevation where clouds or mist are frequent, usually rich in epiphytic plants and tree ferns.

Coevolution The development of genetic traits in two species that help to facilitate interactions, usually to their mutual advantage.

Coleopteran Referring to the insect order of beetles.

Communication Behavior patterns of a individual that alter the probability of behavior in another individual in an adaptive manner.

Community The organisms that occupy a particular habitat.

Congregation A grouping of individuals attracted to one another on the basis of social interactions among them.

Conspecific Belonging to the same species; likewise applied to genera (congeneric).

Contour feathers The body feathers in general, exclusive of more specialized types.

Convergent evolution The evolution of structural similarities in organisms that are not closely related, often because of similar ecological adaptations.

Corolla Collectively, the petals of a flower.

Courtship Communication between individuals of opposite sexes that facilitates pair-bonding or fertilization; see also *display*.

Culmen The distance from the tip of a bird's beak to its base, or to the limit of feathering on its forehead (exposed culmen).

Cuneate Wedge-shaped.

Dendrogram A diagram of phyletic relationships, drawn in the form of a branching tree.

Dicotyledons Plants having two seed leaves, usually broad-leaved and net-veined.

Dipteran Referring to the insect order of flies, mosquitoes, and gnats, all having two functional wings.

Display Behavior patterns ("signals") that have been evolved ("ritualized'') to provide communication functions for an organism, usually through stereotypic performance and exaggeration.

Diurnal Referring to the hours of daylight; diurnal segregation is a special type of habitat segregation (*q.v.*).

Distal Away from the main body axis, as opposed to proximal.

Double-rounded A tail condition in which the central and outermost pairs of tail feathers are shorter than the intermediate ones, producing a double-convex profile.

Dusky Blackish, or dark brownish black.

Ecotone A transitional area between two community types.

Egocentric Behavioral adaptations that are directed toward the survival and health of the individual.

Endemic Referring to species or groups that are native to and restricted to a particular area; see also relict.

Entomophilous Referring to plants adapted for pollination by insects.

Epigamic Referring to social interactions that lead toward or facilitate mating; see also *courtship*.

Epiphyte A plant that depends on other plants for its support but not its nutrition, usually located above ground level.

Femoral Referring to the region of the upper leg.

Fitness The relative genetic contribution of an individual toward future generations of its species.

Fledging period The period between hatching and initial flight in birds; in hummingbirds essentially synonymous with nestling period (*q.v.*).

Form A taxonomically neutral term for a species or some subdivision of a species.

Fusiform Spindle-shaped, tapering at both ends.

Generalist A species with broad foraging or habitat requirements, a "jack-of-all-trades" not dependent on a single environmental resource.

Genus (plural, *genera*). A taxonomic category within a family representing a grouping of related species.

Gleaning Foraging for insects or similar food from leafy or bark surfaces.

Gorget A patch of irridescent color in the throat region of some hummingbirds.

Graduated Referring to tail shape in which the rectrices shorten progressively from the central pair outwardly.

Guild A group of species that exploits the same class of environmental characteristics in a similar way, whether or not they are closely related.

Guttate Shaped like a teardrop.

Habitat The physical, chemical, and biotic characteristics of a specific environment.

Habitat segregation A physical division of environmental resources by two or more of the resource users, such as the two sexes of a species, by age classes or by different species having similar niche adaptations; the resources may be subdivided horizontally, vertically, by microhabitats, or by usage time periods (diurnal, seasonal).

Hawking Capturing insects while in flight.

Herbaceous Referring to a nonwoody plant (herb), including both grasslike and nongrasslike plants (forbs).

Homeothermal Warm-blooded, capable of maintaining a constant body temperature; also called endothermal.

Hybridization The production of progeny of unlike genetic lines, such as between subspecies (intraspecific hybridization), separate species (interspecific), and more rarely between genera (intergeneric).

Hymenopteran Referring to the insect order of bees, wasps, and ants.

Hyoid apparatus The paired cartilaginous elements that support the tongue and that in hummingbirds are greatly elongated, allowing for unusual extension.

Hypothermia A condition of lower-than-normal body temperature and a sleep-like state (torpidity, *q.v.*).

Inflorescence A flower cluster.

Innate Inherited, such as instinctive patterns of behavior.

Instinctive behavior Innate responses that typically are more complex than simple reflexes or taxes, and that are dependent upon specific external stimuli ("releasers") as well as variable and specific internal states ("drives" or "tendencies") for their expression.

Interference The optical process responsible for iridescent color in feathers, brought about by the reciprocal action of waves of reflected light, which may either reinforce or cancel each other.

Intergeneric Between separate genera; likewise applied to species (interspecific).

Iridescence A spectral color formed by selective interference and reflection of specific wavelengths of light, rather than by differential pigment absorption and reflection, as is the case with simple feather coloration; see also *interference*.

Isabella Brown, tinged with reddish yellow.

Isolating mechanism An innate property of an individual that prevents successful mating and subsequent offspring with individuals of genetically unlike populations; mechanisms that prevent successful mating, rather than control the subsequent development of offspring, are called premating mechanisms, and include heritable ecological, morphological, behavioral, and temporal differences between populations.

Isotherm	A line on a map connecting points having the same average temperature.
Jugulum	The lower portion of the throat.
Juvenal	Referring to the plumage stage of juvenile birds during which fledging normally occurs, and immediately following any downy stage.
Lek	An area occupied by males of species that display in groups in relatively small, contiguous territories; in hummingbirds usually called a singing assembly. Often also used as an adjective (lek behavior, synonymous with arena behavior) and sometimes as a verb (lekking).
Loral	Referring to the area (lore) between the eye and the base of the bill in birds.
Lumbar	Referring to the lower back region.
Malar	Referring to the area extending from the base of the mandible backward below the eye, sometimes forming a moustache-like streak.
Mandible	The lower component of the beak or bill in birds.
Mating system	Patterns of mating within a population, including length and strength of pair bond, the number of mates, degree of inbreeding, and the like.
Maxilla	The upper component of the beak or bill in birds.
Melanin	A pigment of hair and feathers that is insoluble in water and organic solvents and is responsible for blackish, brown, brownish yellow, and reddish brown coloration.
Mesial	Toward the middle, medial.
Micron	A micromillimeter (0.001 mm).
Monocotyledons	Plants having a single seed leaf, typically narrow-leaved and parallel-veined.
Monotypic	Referring to a taxonomic category that has only one unit in the category immediately subordinate to it, such as a genus with only one species.
Nectarivorous	Adapted for foraging on nectar.
Neotropical region	The zoogeographic region that includes all of South America, Middle America, and Mexico north to the central highlands, as well as the West Indies.
Nestling period	The period between hatching and leaving the nest; in hummingbirds essentially synonymous with the fledging period.
Niche	Structural, physiological, and behavioral adaptations of a species to its environment.
Nidicolous	The condition in which the young are raised in the nest until fledging or nearly so.

Nocturnal	Referring to the hours of darkness.
Nuptial plumage	Plumage associated with the breeding season.
Obsolete	Rudimentary, nearly lacking.
Occiput	The region of the head formed by the back of the skull.
Oligocene	An early geological epoch in the Cenozoic Period, extending from about 25 to 40 million years before the present.
Operculum	A shelf-like structure partially covering the nasal opening.
Orbital	The head region associated with the eyes; suborbital and postorbital areas are those below and behind the eyes, respectively.
Ornithophilous	Referring to plants adapted for pollination by birds.
Pair-bonding	Individualized association between members of the opposite sex lasting for variable periods, but longer than that necessary only to attain fertilization.
Páramo	The moist vegetational zone above timberline in the Andes.
Phyletic	Referring to an evolutionary lineage; synonymous with phylogenetic.
Pileum	The crown of the head, from the forehead to the occiput.
Pollination	The transfer of pollen from the anther to the stigma of the same flower (self-pollination) or of another flower (cross-pollination).
Polygamy	A mating system in which individuals of one sex maintain simultaneous or serial individualized contacts (pair-bonds) with two or more members of the opposite sex, to attain multiple fertilization; includes both polyandry (pairing with multiple males) and polygyny (pairing with multiple females); see also *promiscuity*.
Promiscuity	A mating system in which no pair-bonds exist, and individual contacts between the sexes occur only at the time of fertilization, typically involving multiple matings by one sex or the other; see also *polygamy*.
Proximal	Toward the main body axis, as opposed to distal.
Protandry	The asynchronous development of sexual parts in a flower, with male structures developing earlier than female structures; in animals refers to the change of sex from male to female during development.
Psilopaedic	Hatched naked or nearly so.
Quasi-social	Referring to behavioral adaptations that facilitate aggregation behavior.
Racquet-like	Formed in the shape of a racket.
Rectrix	(plural, *rectrices*) The individual tail feathers of birds.
Reflectance	A measure of the relative amount of light reflected back from a surface, rather than absorbed by it or transmitted through it; when two light rays are reflected from the outer and inner sur-

face of a transparent substance they may either reinforce or cancel specific wavelengths of light; see also *interference* and *iridescence*.

Refractive index The ratio of the speed of light in air to its speed in any other transparent substance, resulting in differential bending of the light rays (refraction) in that substance.

Relict An organism belonging to an earlier time than the other members of the contemporary population in the region where the organism now occurs.

Remix (plural, *remiges*) The individual flight feathers (primaries and secondaries) of birds.

Reproductive isolation The prevention of successful interbreeding between individuals of different populations, attained through various genetically determined isolating mechanisms (*q.v.*).

Resaca A surfline or coastal edge (Spanish).

Resource A feature of the environment, the control of which contributes to an organism's fitness; resource partitioning is a division of such a feature, within or between two species, to reduce the intensity of competition over its control; see also *fitness* and *habitat segregation*.

Rictal Referring to the point where the mandible and maxilla join at the base of the bill.

Riparian Associated with riverbanks or lake shorelines.

Ritualization The evolutionary process by which behaviors gradually acquire communication function (become "signals"); the development of signaling behavior and associated signaling devices.

Rufous Brownish red to reddish.

Rufescent Somewhat tinged with reddish.

Serrate Toothed, saw-like.

Sexual dimorphism Here used to refer to species in which the sexes differ markedly as adults, and including both dichromatism (the sexes differ in color) and diethism (they differ in behavior).

Sexual selection Selection favoring divergence between the sexes of a species (sexual dimorphism), resulting from differential mating success produced by individual differences in heterosexual attraction or intrasexual dominance.

Singing assembly A group of two or more territorial males localized in a traditional area (lek or arena) for courtship and singing; see *lek*.

Social behavior Behavioral adaptations that result in congregating behavior and facilitate social interactions.

Solferino Bluish-red in color.

Specialist A species with narrow foraging or habitat adaptations, or both; a "master-of-one-trade" specialized for exploiting a single resource.

Speciation	The multiplication of species through the development of reproductive isolation in a population or group of populations.
Species	A "kind" of organism or, more technically, a group or groups of actually or potentially interbreeding populations that are reproductively isolated from all other populatoins; the term remains unchanged in the plural, and also refers to the taxonomic category below that of the genus and above that of the subspecies (abbreviated sp., plural spp).
Species group	A group of closely related species, usually with partially overlapping ranges.
Squamate	Scale-like.
Stamen	The part of the flower that produces pollen, including the anthers and their supporting filaments.
Standard metabolic rate	The heat production of an organism per unit of time, under controlled conditions; also called basal metabolic rate.
Stigma	The tip of the pistil in flowers, which receives the pollen.
Strategy	The evolved niche adaptations of a population that are associated with fitness in a particular environment, including mating strategies, foraging strategies, life history strategies, etc.; optimal strategies are those that maximize fitness while minimizing wastage of time, energy, gametes, or other limited attributes.
Style	The portion of the pistil that lies above the ovary and supports the stigma in flowers.
Subbasal	Toward or near the base.
Subspatulate	Slightly spoon-shaped in outline.
Subgenus	One or more species of a genus that differ from the rest of the genus as to be recognized taxonomically, but are not sufficiently distinctive to be considered a full genus.
Subspecies	A group of local populations of a species that occupies part of the species' range and differs taxonomically from other local populations; a geographic race (abbreviated spp., plural sspp.).
Superspecies	Two or more species with largely or entirely non-overlapping ranges, which are clearly derived from a common ancestor, but are too distinct to be considered a single species.
Subterminal	Toward or near the tip.
Sympatric	Having geographically overlapping distributions, at least during the breeding season.
Sympetalous	A blossom condition in which the corolla is partly to entirely fused, often forming a tube.
Syrinx	The structure in birds responsible for producing vocalizations, analogous to the larynx in mammals.
Taxon	A group of organisms belonging to a formally recognized taxon-

omic unit, such as a species or genus; taxonomy is the procedure by which taxa are identified, described, and classified.

Territory	An area having resources that are controlled or defended by an animal against others of its species (intraspeciic territories), or less often against individuals of other species (interspecific territories). Hummingbird territories usually control food supplies (feeding territories) and/or facilitate fertilization (mating station territories), but in other groups often include nesting or roosting sites as well.
Territoriality	The advertisement and agonistic behavior associated with territorial establishment and defense.
Torpidity	A sleep-like state of reduced body temperature (hypothermia) and metabolism, entered into during the night (noctivation) or during colder periods of the year (hibernation).
Transition Zone	A "life zone" that occurs between the relatively cooler Canadian Zone and the relatively hotter Austral Zone, and generally conforming to the lower coniferous forest belt in western mountains.
Traplining	Behavior of hummingbirds that do not defend a definite feeding territory, but instead visit a variety of flowers over a regularly traveled route.
Trochilidae	The family of birds that includes all the hummingbirds.
Vinaceous	Referring to the color of wine or grapes; reddish.
Wing disc loading	A statistic obtained by dividing the body weight by the area covered by the outstretched wings, as an estimate of work performed during flight in hummingbirds.
Xeric	Referring to a dry, desert-like environment.
Xerophilous	Referring to desert- or drought-adapted plants.
Zygomorphic	Blossoms in which the corolla exhibits bilateral or other nonradial symmetry, such as bilabiate blossoms.

Bibliography

I. *General References and Regional Identification Guides**

1. Austin, O. L., Jr. 1961. *Birds of the World*. Golden Press, New York.
2. Bond, J. 1971. *Birds of the West Indies*, 2nd ed. Houghton Mifflin, Boston.
3. Davis, L. I. 1972. *A Field Guide to the Birds of Mexico and Central America*. University of Texas Press, Austin.
4. de Schauensee, R. M. 1966. *The Species of Birds of South America*. Livingston Publishing Co., Narberth, Pa.
5. de Schauensee, R. M., and W. H. Phelps. 1978. *A Guide to the Birds of Venezuela*. Princeton University Press, Princeton.
6. Elliot, D. B. 1878. A classification and synopsis of the Trochilidae. *Smithsonian Institution, Contributions to Knowledge* 317:1–277.
7. Gould, J. 1849–61. *A Monograph of the Trochilidae, or Family of Hummingbirds*. Taylor and Francis, London. (Second ed. and supplements 1880–85)
8. Greenewalt, C. H. 1960a. *Hummingbirds*. Doubleday and the American Museum of Natural History, Garden City.
9. Grzimek, B., ed. 1972. *Grzimek's Animal Life Encyclopedia*, vol. 8. Van Nostrand Reinhold, New York.
10. Haverschmidt, F. 1968. *Birds of Surinam*. Oliver & Boyd, Edinburgh.
11. Land, H. 1970. *Birds of Guatemala*. Livingston Publishing Co., Narberth, Pa.
12. Peters, J. L. 1945. *Check-List of Birds of the World*, vol. 5. Harvard University Press, Cambridge.
13. Peterson, R. T., and E. L. Chalif. 1973. *A Field Guide to Mexican Birds*. Houghton. Mifflin, Boston.
14. Ridgeley, R. S. 1976. *A Guide to the Birds of Panama*. Princeton University Press, Princeton.
15. Ridgway, R. 1890. The hummingbirds. *Report of the U.S. National Museum for 1890*, pp. 253–383.
16. Ridgway, R. 1911. The birds of North and Middle America. Part V. *U.S. Natl. Mus. Bull.* 50:1–859.
17. Rutgers, A. 1972. *Birds of South America. Illustrations from the Lithographs of John Gould*. St. Martin's Press, New York. (Includes reproductions of 80 hummingbird plates)
18. Scheithauer, W. 1967. *Hummingbirds*. Thomas Y. Crowell, New York.
19. Skutch, A. F. 1973. *The Life of the Hummingbird*. Crown, New York.

II. *Other Literature Cited*

Aldrich, E. C. 1945. Nesting of the Allen hummingbird. *Condor* 47:137–148.
———. 1956. Pterylography and molt of the Allen hummingbird. *Condor* 58:121–133.
American Ornithologists' Union (AOU). 1957. *Check-List of North American Birds*, 5th ed.

*A listing of species illustrated by color plates in these references is keyed by number in Appendix Five of this book)

Lord Baltimore Press, Baltimore, Md.

Anderson, J. O., and G. Monson. 1981. Berylline hummingbirds nest in Arizona. *Continental Birdlife* 2:56–61.

Armitage, K. B. 1955. Territorial behavior in fall migrant rufous hummingbirds. *Condor* 57:239–240.

Austin, D. V. 1975. Bird flowers in the eastern United States. *Florida Sci.* 38:1–12.

Austin, G. T. 1970. Interspecific territoriality of migrant calliope and resident broad-tailed hummingbirds. *Condor* 72:234.

Baepler, D. H. 1962. The avifauna of the Soloma region in Huehuetenango, Guatemala. *Condor* 64:140–153.

Bendire, C. E. 1895. Life histories of North American birds. *U.S. Natl. Mus. Spec. Bull. 3.*

Bailey, A. M. 1927. Notes on the birds of southeastern Alaska. *Auk* 44:351–367.

———. 1974. Second nesting of broad-tailed hummingbirds. *Condor* 76:350.

Bailey, A. M., and R. J. Niedrach. 1965. *Birds of Colorado*, 2 vol. Denver Museum of Natural History, Denver.

Bailey, F. M. 1928. *Birds of New Mexico.* New Mexico Department of Fish and Game, Santa Fe.

Bakus, G. J. 1962. Early nesting of the Costa hummingbird in southern California. *Condor* 64:438–439.

Banks, R. C., and N. K. Johnson. 1961. A review of North American hybrid hummingbirds. *Condor* 63:3–28.

Baptista, L. F., and M. Matsui. 1979. The source of the dive-noise of the Anna's hummingbird. *Condor* 81:87–89.

Barash, D. P. 1972. Lek behavior in the broad-tailed hummingbird. *Wilson Bull.* 82:202–3.

Barbour, R. 1943. Cuban ornithology. *Mem. Nuttall Ornithol. Club* 9:1–129.

Baumgartner, M. 1981. To hold a hummingbird. *Bird Watcher's Digest* 3(3):18–21.

Behnke-Pederson, M. 1972. *Kolibrien*, vol. 1. Aage Poulsen, Skibby, Denmark.

Bené, F. 1947. The feeding and related behavior of hummingbirds with special reference to the black-chin, *Archilochus alexandri* (Bourcier and Mulsant). *Mem. Boston Soc. Nat. Hist.* 9:395–478.

Bent, A. C. 1940. Life histories of North American cuckoos, goatsuckers, hummingbirds and their allies. *U.S. Natl. Mus. Bull.* 176:1–506.

Berlioz, J. 1932. Notes critiques sur quelques Trochilidés du British Museum. *Oiseau* (N.S.) 2:530–534.

———. 1944. *La Vie des Colibris*. Histoires Naturelles, Paris.

———. 1965. Note critique sur les Trochilidés des genres *Timolia* et *Augasma*. *Oiseau* 35:1–8.

Blair, F., A. Blair, P. Brodkorp, F. Cagle, and G. Moore. 1968. *Vertebrates of the United States*, 2nd ed. McGraw-Hill, New York.

Borrero, J. I. 1965. Notas sobre el comportamiento del colibri coli-rojo (*Amazilia tzacatl*) y el mielero (*Coereba flaveola*), en Colombia. *El Hornero* 10:247–250.

———. 1975. Notas sobre el comportamiento reproductivo de *Amazilia tzacatl*. *Ardeola* 21:933–943.

Brandt, H. 1951. *Arizona and Its Bird Life.* Bird Research Foundation, Cleveland, Ohio.

Brown, J. H., and A. Kodric-Brown. 1979. Convergence, competition and mimicry in a temperate community of hummingbird-pollinated flowers. *Ecology* 60:1022–1035.

Brown, J. H., W. A. Calder, and A. Kodric-Brown. 1978. Correlates and consequences of body size in nectar-feeding birds. *Am. Zool.* 18:687–700.

Brudenell-Bruce, P. G. C. 1975. *The Birds of New Providence and the Bahama Islands.* Taplinger Publishing Co., New York.

Brunton, D. F., S. Andrews, and D. G. Paton. 1979. Nesting of the calliope hummingbird in Kananskis Provincial Park, Alberta. *Can. Field-Nat.* 93:449–451.

Butler, A. G. 1932. (Exhibition of a hybrid hummingbird, *Damophila amabilis* × *Amazilia tzacatl*). *Bull. Br. Ornithol. Club* 47:134.

Calder, W. A. 1971. Temperature relationships and mating of the calliope hummingbird. *Condor* 73:314–321.

———. 1973. Microhabitat selection during nesting of hummingbirds in the Rocky Mountains. *Ecology* 54:127–134.

———. 1976. Energy crisis of the hummingbird. *Nat. Hist.* 85(3): 24–29.

Carpenter, F. L. 1976. Ecology and evolution of an Andean hummingbird (*Oreotrochilus estella*). *Univ. Calif. Pub. Zool.* 106:1–74.

Carriker, M. A., Jr. 1910. An annotated list of the birds of Costa Rica, including Cocos Island. *Ann. Carnegie Mus.* 6:314–915.

Chapman, F. M. 1902. Notes on birds and mammals observed near Trinidad, Cuba, with remarks on the origin of West Indian bird life. *Am. Mus. Nat. Hist. Bull.* 4:279–330.

Chase, V. C., and P. H. Raven. 1975. Evolutionary and ecological relationships between *Aquilegia formosa* and *A. pubescens* (Ranunculaceae), two perennial plants. *Evolution* 29:474–486.

Clench, M. H., and R. C. Leberman. 1978. Weights of 151 species of Pennsylvania birds analyzed by month, age, and sex. *Bull. Carnegie Mus. Nat. Hist.* (5):1–87.

Clyde, D. P. 1972. Anna's hummingbird in adult male plumage feeds nestling. *Condor* 74:102.

Cogswell, H. L. 1949. Alternate care of two nests in the black-chinned hummingbird. *Condor* 51:176–178.

Cohn, J. M. W. 1968. The convergent flight mechanisms of swifts (Apodi) and hummingbirds (Trochili)(Aves). Ph.D. dissertation, University of Michigan, Ann Arbor.

Colwell, R. K., B. J. Betts, P. Bunnell, F. L. Carpenter, and P. Feinsinger. 1974. Competition for the nectar of *Centropogon valerii* by the hummingbird *Colibri thalassinus* and the flower-pecker *Diglossa plumbea*, and its evolutionary implications. *Condor* 76:447–452.

Conway, A. E., and S. R. Drennan. 1979. Rufous hummingbirds in eastern North America. *Am. Birds* 33:130–132.

Cook, R. E. 1969. Variation in species density of North American birds. *Syst. Zool.* 18:63–84.

Cottam, C., and P. Knappen. 1939. Food of some uncommon North American birds. *Auk* 49:479–481.

de Schauensee, R. M. 1964. *The Birds of Colombia and Adjacent Areas of South and Central America.* Livingston Publishing Co., Narberth, Pa.

———. 1967. *Eriocnemis mirabilis*, a new species of hummingbird from Colombia. *Not. Nat.* 402:1–2.

Demaree, S. R. 1970. Nest-building, incubation period and fledging in the black-chinned hummingbird. *Wilson Bull.* 82:225.

Des Granges, J. L. 1979. Organization of a tropical nectar feeding bird guild in a variable environment. *Living Bird* 17:199–236.

Diamond, A. W. 1973. Habitats and feeding stations of St. Lucia forest birds. *Ibis* 115:313–329.

Dickey, D. R., and A. J. van Rossem. 1938. The birds of El Salvador. *Field Mus. Nat. Hist. Zool. Ser.* 23:1–609.

Dubois, A. D. 1938. Observations at a rufous hummingbird's nest. *Auk* 55:629–641.

Dorst, R. 1962. Nouvelle recherches biologiques sur les Trochilidés des haut Andes péruviennes (*Oreotrochilus estella*). *Oiseau* 32:95–126.

Edgarton, H. E., R. J. Niedrach, and W. van Riper. 1951. Freezing the flight of humming-birds. *Nat. Geogr.* 100:245–261.

Edwards, E. P. 1973. *A Field Guide to the Birds of Mexico.* E. P. Edwards, Sweet Briar, Va.

Edwards, E. P., and R. E. Tassian. 1959. Avifauna of the Catemaco Basin of southern Veracruz, Mexico. *Condor* 61:325–337.

Elgar, R. J. 1980. Observations on the display of the blue-tailed emerald. *Avic. Mag.* 86:147–150.

English, T. S. 1928. A diary of the nesting of *Microlyssa exilis,* the crested hummingbird of Montserrat, West Indies. *Ibis* (12th series) 4:13–16.

———. 1934. Notes on a nest of *Microlyssa exilis. Ibis* (13th series) 4:838.

Feinsinger, P., and R. W. Colwell. 1978. Community organization among neo-tropical nectar-feeding birds. *Am. Zool.* 18:779–795.

Fitzpatrick, A. 1966. My friend rufous. *Fla. Nat.* 39:35–38, 54.

Fitzpatrick, J. W., D. E. Willard, and J. W., Terborgh. 1979. A new species of humming-bird from Peru. *Wilson Bull.* 91:177–186.

Foster, W. L., and J. Tate, Jr. 1966. The activities and coactions of animals at sapsucker trees. *Living Bird* 5:87–114.

Fox, R. P. 1954. Plumages and territorial behavior of the lucifer hummingbird in the Chi-sos Mountains, Texas. *Auk* 71:465–466.

Friedmann, H., L. Griscom, and R. T. Moore. 1950. Distributional check-list of the birds of Mexico. Part 2. *Pacific Coast Avifauna* (29):1–436.

Gass, C. L. 1979. Territory regulation, tenure and migration in rufous hummingbirds. *Can. J. Zool.* 57:914–923.

Gass, C. L., G. Angehr, and J. Centra. 1976. Regulation of food supply by feeding territo-riality in the rufous hummingbird. *Can. J. Zool.* 54:2046–2054.

Godfrey, W. E. 1966. The birds of Canada. *Nat. Mus. Can. Bull.* 203 (Biol. Ser. 73):1–428.

Grant, K. A., and V. Grant. 1968. *Hummingbirds and Their Flowers.* Columbia University Press, New York.

Grant, V. 1952. Isolation and hybridization between *Aquilegia formosa* and *A. pubescens. Aliso* 2:341–360.

Grantsau, R. 1968. Uma nova espécie de Phaethornis (Aves, Trochilidae). *Papeis Avulsos de Zoologia* 22 (article 7):57–59.

———. 1969. Uma nova espécie Threnetes (Aves, Trochilidae). *Papeis Avulsos de Zoologia* 22 (article 23):246–249.

Graves, G. R. 1980. A new species of metaltail hummingbird from northern Peru. *Wilson Bull.* 92:1–7.

Greenewalt, C. 1960b. The hummingbirds. *Nat. Geogr.* 118:658–679.

———. 1962. Dimensional relationships for flying animals. *Smithsonian Misc. Coll.* 144:1–46.

Grinnell, J., and A. H. Miller. 1944. The distribution of birds of California. *Pacific Coast Avifauna.* (21):1–608.

Gruson, E. S. 1972. *Words for Birds.* Quadrangle Press, New York.

Hartman, F. A. 1954. Cardiac and pectoral muscles of Trochilidae. *Auk* 71:467–469.

Hauser, D. C., and N. Currie, Jr. 1966. Hummingbird survives through December in North Carolina. *Auk* 83:138–139.

Hering, L. 1947. Courtship and mating of broad-tailed hummingbird in Colorado. *Condor* 49:126.

Hinman, D. A. 1928. Habits of the ruby-throated hummingbird. *Auk* 45:504–505.

Horvath, O. H. 1964. Seasonal differences in rufous hummingbird nest height and their relation to nest climate. *Ecology* 45:235–241.

Howell, T. R., and W. R. Dawson. 1954. Nest temperatures and attentiveness in the Anna hummingbird. *Condor* 56:93–96.

Hubbard, J. P. 1978. Revised Check-List of the Birds of New Mexico.*New Mexico Ornithological Society Publication No. 6*, Albuquerque.

Ingels, J. 1976. Observations on some hummingbirds of Martinique. *Avic. Mag.* 82:98–100.

James, R. L. 1948. Some hummingbird flowers east of the Mississippi. *Castenea* 13:97–109.

Johnson, A. W. 1967. *The Birds of Chile and Adjacent Regions of Argentina, Bolivia, and Peru*, vol. 2. Platt Establecimientos Graficos, Buenos Aires.

Kelly, J. W. 1955. History of the nesting of an Anna hummingbird. *Condor* 57:347–353.

Kobbe, W. H. 1900. The rufous hummingbirds of Cape Disappointment. *Auk* 17:8–15.

Kodric-Brown, A., and J. H. Brown. 1978. Influence of economics, interspecific competition, and sexual dimorphism on territoriality of migrant rufous hummingbirds. *Ecology* 59:285–296.

Kuban, J. F., and R. L. Neill. 1980. Feeding ecology of hummingbirds in the highlands of the Chiso Mountains, Texas. *Condor* 82:180–185.

Lack, D. 1973. The number of species of hummingbirds in the West Indies. *Evolution* 27:326–327.

———. 1976. *Island Biology, Illustrated by the Land Birds of Jamaica*. Blackwell, Oxford.

Lasiewski, R. C. 1962. Energetics of migrating hummingbirds. *Condor* 64:324.

———. 1964. Body temperature, heart and breathing rate, and evaporative water loss in hummingbirds. *Physiol. Zool.* 37:212–223.

Lasiewski, R. C., W. W. Weathers, and M. H. Bernstein. 1967. Physiological responses of the giant hummingbird, *Patagonia gigas*. *Comp. Biochem. Physiol.* 23:797–813.

Leberman, R. C. 1972. Identify, sex, and age it. Key to age and sex determination of ruby-throated hummingbirds in autumn. *Inl. Bird-Banding News* 44:197–202.

Leck, C. F. 1973. Dominance relationships in nectar-feeding birds at St. Croix. *Auk* 90:431–432.

Legg, K., and F. A. Pitelka. 1956. Ecological overlap of Anna and Allen hummingbirds nesting at Santa Cruz, California. *Condor* 58:393–405.

Lesson, R. P. 1829. *Histoire Naturelle des Oiseau-Mouches*. Arthus Bertrand, Paris.

———. 1830–31. *Histoire Naturelle de Colibris*. Arthus Bertrand, Paris.

———. 1832. *Les Trochilidées on les Colibris et les Oiseaux-Mouches*. Arthus Bertrand, Paris.

Levy, S. H. 1958. A possible United States breeding area for the violet-crowned hummingbird. *Auk* 75:350.

Ligon, J. S. 1961. *New Mexico Birds and Where to Find Them*. University of New Mexico Press, Albuquerque.

Linneaus, C. 1758. *Systema Naturae. Regnum Animale*. (10th ed. tomus I) L. Salvii, Holminae.

Lodge, G. E. 1896. Notes on some West-Indian humming-birds. *Ibis* 2(7th ser.):495–519.

Lowery, G. H., Jr. 1974. *Louisiana Birds*, 3rd ed. Louisiana State University Press, Baton Rouge.

Lyerly, S. B., B. F. Riess, and S. Ross. 1950. Color preference in the Mexican violet-eared hummingbird. *Colibri t. thalassinus* (Swainson). *Behaviour* 2:237–248.

Lynch, J., and P. L. Ames. 1970. A new hybrid hummingbird, *Archilochus alexandri* × *Selasphorus sasin. Condor* 72:209–212.

Lyon, D. L. 1973. Territorial and feeding activity of broad-tailed hummingbirds (*Selasphorus platycercus*) in *Iris missouriensis*. *Condor* 75:346–349.

———. 1976. A montane hummingbird territorial system in Oaxaca, Mexico. *Wilson Bull.* 88:280–299.

Lyon, D. L., J. Crandall, and M. McKone. 1977. A test of the adaptiveness of interspecific territoriality in the blue-throated hummingbird. *Auk* 94:448–454.

MacMillen, R. E., and F. L. Carpenter. 1977. Daily energy costs and body weight in nectarivorous birds. *Comp. Biochem. Physiol. A Comp. Physiol.* 56:439–441.

Marshall, J. T. 1957. Birds of pine-oak woodland in southern Arizona and adjacent Mexico. *Pacific Coast Avifauna* 32:1–125.

Martin, A., and A. Musy. 1959. *La Vie des Colibris*. Editions Delachaux et Niestlé, Neuchâtel, Switzerland.

Mayr, E., and L. L. Short, Jr. 1970. Species taxa of North American birds: a contribution to comparative systematics. *Publ. Nuttall Ornithol. Club* 9:1–127.

Miller, A. H., and R. C. Stebbins. 1964. *The Lives of Desert Animals in Joshua Tree National Monument*. University of California Press, Berkeley.

Miller, J. R. 1978. Notes on birds of San Salvador Island (Watlings), the Bahamas. *Auk* 95:281–288.

Miller, R. S., and R. E. Miller. 1971. Feeding activity and color preference of ruby-throated hummingbirds. *Condor* 73:309–313.

Mirsky, E. N. 1976. Song divergence in hummingbird and junco populations on Guadalupe Island. *Condor* 78:230–235.

Mobbs, A. J. 1971. Stretching attitudes in hummingbirds. *Avic. Mag.* 77:231.

———. 1973. Scratching and preening postures in hummingbirds. *Avic. Mag.* 79:200–204.

———. 1979. Methods used by the Trochilidae when capturing insects. *Avic. Mag.* 85:26–30.

Monroe, B. L., Jr. 1968. A distributional study of the birds of British Honduras. *Am. Ornithol. Union Monogr.* 7.

Moore, R. T. 1939a. Habits of the white-eared hummingbird in northern Mexico. *Auk* 56:442–445.

———. 1939b. The Arizona broad-billed hummingbird. *Auk* 56:313–319.

———. 1947. Habits of male hummingbirds near their nests. *Wilson Bull.* 59:21–25.

Morony, J. J., Jr., W. J. Bock, and J. Ferrand, Jr. 1975. *Reference List of the Birds of the World*. American Museum of Natural History, New York.

Morrison, P. 1962. Modification of body temperature by activity in Brazilian hummingbirds. *Condor* 64:315–323.

Nelson, R. C. 1970. An additional nesting record for the lucifer hummingbird in the United States. *Southwest. Nat.* 1:513–515.

Nickell, W. P. 1948. Alternate care of two nests by a ruby-throated hummingbird. *Wilson Bull.* 60:242–243.

Norris, E. A., C. E. Connell, and D. W. Johnston. 1957. Notes on fall plumages, weights and fat condition in the ruby-throated hummingbird. *Wilson Bull.* 69:155–163.

Northrop, J. I. 1891. The birds of Andros Island, Bahamas. *Auk* 8:64–80.

Oberholser, H. C. 1974. *The Bird Life of Texas*. (Ed. E. B. Kincaid.) 2 vols. University of Texas Press, Austin.

Olrog, C. C. 1963. *Lista y Distribución de las Aves Argentinas*. Instituto Miguel Lillo, Tucumán.

———. 1968. *Las Aves Sudamericanas*, vol. 1. Instituto Miguel Lillo, Tucumán.

Orr, R. T. 1939. Observations on the nesting of the Allen hummingbird. *Condor* 41:17–24.

Ortiz-Crespo, F. I. 1974. The giant hummingbird *Patagonia gigas* in Ecuador. *Ibis* 116:347–359.

Owre, O. T. 1976. Bahama woodstar in Florida: first specimen for continental North America. *Auk* 93:837–838.

Paynter, R. J., Jr. 1955. The ornithogeography of the Yucatán Peninsula. *Bull. Peabody Mus.* (9):1–347.

Pearson, O. P. 1954. The daily energy requirements of a wild Anna hummingbird. *Condor* 56:317–322.

————. 1960. Speed of the Allen hummingbird while diving. *Condor* 62:403.

Phillips, A. R. 1965. Notas sistematicas sobre aves Mexicanas. III. *Rev. Soc. Mex. Hist. Nat.* 1965:217–242.

————. 1975. The migration of Allen's and other hummingbirds. *Condor* 77:196–205.

Phillips, A. R., J. Marshall, and G. Monson. 1964. *Birds of Arizona.* University of Arizona Press, Tucson.

Primack, R. B., and H. F. Howe. 1975. Interference competition between a hummingbird *Amazilia tzacatl* and skipper butterflies (Hesperiidae). *Biotropica* 7:55–58.

Pickens, A. L. 1927. Unique method of pollination by the ruby-throat. *Auk* 44:14–17.

————. 1930. Favorite colors of hummingbirds. *Auk* 47:346–352.

————. 1944. Seasonal territory studies of ruby-throats. *Auk* 61:88–92.

Pickens, A. L., and L. P. Garrison. Two-year record of the ruby-throat's visits to a garden. *Auk* 48:532–537.

Pitelka, F. A. 1942. Territoriality and related problems in North American hummingbirds. *Condor* 44:189–204.

————. 1951a. Breeding seasons of hummingbirds near Santa Barbara, California. *Condor* 53:198–201.

————. 1951b. Ecologic overlap and interspecific strife in breeding populations of Anna and Allen hummingbirds. *Ecology* 32:641–661.

Poley, D. 1976. *Kolibris.* Neue Brehm-Bücherei 484. A. Ziemsen Verlag, Wittenberg Lutherstadt.

Pulich, W. M., and W. M. Pulich, Jr. 1963. The nesting of the lucifer hummingbird in the United States. *Auk* 80:370–371.

Pyke, G. H. 1980. The foraging behaviour of Australian honeyeaters: a review and some comparisons with hummingbirds. *Aust. J. Ecol.* 5:343–369.

Rising, J. D. 1965. Notes on behavioral responses of the blue-throated hummingbird. *Condor* 67:352–354.

Robertson, W. B., Jr. 1962. Observations on the birds of St. John, Virgin Islands. *Auk* 79:44–76.

Rowley, J. S. 1966. Breeding records of birds of the Sierra Madre del Sur, Oaxaca, Mexico. *Proc. West. Found. Vertebr. Zool.* 1:107–203.

Rowley, J. S., and R. Orr. 1964. A new hummingbird from southern Mexico. *Condor* 66:81–83.

Ruschi, O. 1965. [Position assumed by the female during incubation and the warming of the young in Trochilidae.] *Bol. Mus. Biol. Prof. Mello Leitão* (48):1–3.

————. 1972. Uma nova espécie de beija-flor do E. E. Santo. *Bol. Mus. Biol. Prof. Mello Leitão* (35):1–5.

————. 1973a. Uma nova especie de beija-flor do E. E. Santo. *Bol. Mus. Biol. Prof. Mello Leitão* (36):103.

————. 1973b. Uma nova especie de *Threnetes* (Aves, Trochilidae). *Bol. Mus. Biol. Prof. Mello Leitão* (37):1–6.

————. 1975. *Threnetes cristinae*, n. sp. *Bol. Mus. Biol. Prof. Mello Leitão* (83):1–3.

————. 1979. *Les Aves do Brasil.* Kosmos, Sao Paolo.

Russell, S. M. 1964. A distributional study of the birds of British Honduras. *Am. Ornithol. Union Monogr.* 1:1–195.

Russell, S. M., and D. W. Lamm. 1978. Notes on the distribution of the birds in Sonora, Mexico. *Wilson Bull.* 90:123–130.

Schäfer, E. 1952. Sobre la biologie de *Colibri coruscans*. *Bol. Soc. Venez. Cienc. Nat.* 15:153–162.

Schaldach, W. J. 1963. The avifauna of Colima and adjacent Jalisco, Mexico. *Proc. West. Found. Vertebr. Zool.* 1:1–100.

Schmidt-Marloh, D., and K.-L. Schuchmann. 1980. Zur Biologie des Blauen Veilchenohr-

Kolibris. *Bonn. Zool. Beitr.* 31:61–77.

Schuchmann, F.-L. 1979. Okologie und Ethologie des Anna-Kolibris (*Calypte anna*). *Natur Mus.* 109:149–155.

Schuchmann, K. L., D. Schmidt-Marloh, and H. Bell. 1979. Energetische Untersuchengen bei einer tropischen Kolibriart (*Amazilia tzacatl*). *J. Ornithol.* 120:78–85.

Selander, R. K. 1966. Sexual dimorphism and differential niche utilization in birds. *Condor* 68:113–151.

Short, L. L., Jr., and A. R. Phillips. 1966. More hybrid hummingbirds from the United States. *Auk* 83:253–265.

Simon, E. 1921. *Histoire Naturalle des Trochilidae* (*Synopsis et Catalogue*). Mulo, Paris.

Skutch, A. F. 1931. The life history of Reiffer's hummingbird (*Amazilia tzacatl tzacatl*) in Panama and Honduras. *Auk* 48:481–500.

———. 1952. Scarlet passion flower. *Nat. Mag.* 45:523–525, 550.

———. 1967. Life histories of Central American highland birds. *Nuttall Ornithol. Soc. Publ.* 7:1–213.

———. 1972. Studies of tropical American birds. *Nuttall Ornithol. Soc. Publ.* 10:1–228.

Slud, P. 1964. The birds of Costa Rica: distribution and ecology. *Am. Mus. Nat. Hist. Bull.* 128:1–430.

Smith, G. T. C. 1949. A high altitude hummingbird on the Volcano Cotapaxi. *Ibis* 111:17–22.

Smith, W. K., S. W. Roberts, and P. C. Miller. 1974. Calculating the nocturnal energy expenditure of a incubating Anna's hummingbird. *Condor* 76:176–183.

Snow, B. K. 1974. Lek behavior and breeding of Guy's hermit hummingbird, *Phaethornis guy*. *Ibis* 116:278–297.

Snow, B. K., and D. W. Snow. 1972. Feeding niches of hummingbirds in a Trinidad valley. *J. Anim. Ecol.* 41:471–485.

Snow, D. W. 1968. The singing assemblies of little hermits. *Living Bird* 7:47–55.

Snow, D. W., and B. K. Snow. 1980. Relationships between hummingbirds and flowers in the Andes of Colombia. *Bull. Br. Mus. (Nat. Hist.), Zool. Ser.* 38:105–139.

Snyder, D. E. 1966. *The Birds of Guyana*. Peabody Museum, Salem, Mass.

Sprunt, A., Jr. 1954. *Florida Bird Life*. Coward-McCann, New York.

Stewart, R. E. 1975. *Breeding Birds of North Dakota*. Tri-College Center for Environmental Studies, Fargo.

Stiles, F. G. 1971. On the field identification of California hummingbirds. *Calif. Birds* 2:41–54.

———. 1972a. Age and sex determination in rufous and Allen hummingbirds. *Condor* 74:25–32.

———. 1972b. Food supply and the annual cycle of the Anna hummingbird. *Univ. Calif. Publ. Zool.* 97:1–109.

———. 1975. Ecology, flowering phenology, and hummingbird pollination of some Costa Rica *Heliconia* species. *Ecology* 56:285–301.

———. 1976. Taste preferences, color preferences, and flower choice in hummingbirds. *Condor* 78:10–26.

———. 1978. Ecological and evolutionary implications of bird pollination. *American Zool.* 18:715–727.

———. 1980. The annual cycle in a tropical wet forest community. *Ibis* 122:322–343.

———. 1982. Aggressive and courtship displays of the male Anna's hummingbird. *Condor* 84:208–225.

Stiles, F. G., and L. L. Wolf. 1979. Ecology and evolution of lek mating behavior in the long-tailed hermit hummingbird. *Amer. Ornithol. Union Monogr.* 27:1–78.

Straw, R. M. 1956. Floral isolation in *Penstemon*. *Am. Nat*. 90:47–53.

Sutton, G. M., and T. D. Berleigh. 1940. Birds of Tamazunchale, San Luis Potosi. *Wilson Bull*. 52:221–233.

Sutton, G. M., and O. S. Pettingill. 1942. Birds of the Gomez Farias region, southeastern Tamaulipas. *Auk* 59:1–34.

Thompson, A. L., ed. 1974. *A New Dictionary of Birds*. McGraw-Hill, New York.

Todd, W. E. C. 1942. List of hummingbirds in the collection of the Carnegie Museum. *Ann. Carnegie Mus*. 29:271–370.

Toledo, V. M. 1974. Observations on the relationship between hummingbirds and *Erythrina* spp. *Lloydia*. 37:482–487.

Trousdale, B. 1954. Copulation of Anna hummingbird. *Condor* 56:110.

van der Pijl, L., and C. H. Dodson, 1966. *Orchid Flowers: Their Pollination and Evolution*. University of Miami Press, Coral Gables.

van Rossem, A. J. 1945. A distribution survey of the birds of Sonora, Mexico. *Occas. Pap. Mus. of Zool. La. State Univ*. (21):1–379.

Wagner, H. O. 1945. Notes on the life history of the Mexican violet-ear. *Wilson Bull*. 57:165–187.

———. 1946a. Food and feeding habitats of Mexican hummingbirds. *Wilson Bull*. 58:69–93.

———. 1946b. Observaciones sobre la vida de *Calothorax lucifer*. *An. Inst. Biol. Univ. Nac. Auton. Mex*. 17:289–299.

———. 1948. Die Balz des Kolibris *Selasphorus platycercus*. *Zool. Jahrb. Abt. Syst. Oekol. Geogr. Tiere* 77:267–278.

———. 1952. Bietrage zur Biologie des Blaukehlkolibris *Lampornis clemenciae* (Lesson). *Veroeff. Mus. Bremen, Reihe A Band* 2:5–44.

———. 1954. Versuch einer Analyse der Kolibribalz. *Z. Tierpsychol*. 11:182–212.

———. 1959. Bietrag zum Verhalten des Weissohrkolibris (*Hylocharis leucotis* Vieill.). *Zoologische Jahrbücher, Abteilung für Systematik Oekologie und Geographie der Tiere* 86:253–302.

Waser, N. M. 1976. Food supply and nest timing of broad-tailed hummingbirds in the Rocky Mountains. *Condor* 78:133–135.

———. 1978. Competition for hummingbird pollination and sequential flowering in two Colorado wildflowers. *Ecology* 59:934–944.

Waser, N. M., and D. W. Inouye. 1977. Implications of recaptures of broad-tailed hummingbirds banded in Colorado. *Auk* 94:393–395.

Wauer, R. H. 1973. *Birds of Big Bend National Park and Vicinity*. University of Texas Press, Austin.

Wells, S., and L. F. Baptista. 1979. Displays and morphology of an Anna × Allen hummingbird hybrid. *Wilson Bull*. 91:524–532.

Wells, S., R. A. Bradley, and L. F. Baptista. 1978. Hybridization in *Calypte* hummingbirds. *Auk* 95:537–549.

Welter, W. A. 1935. Nesting habits of ruby-throated hummingbird. *Auk* 52:88–89.

Welty, C. 1975. *The Life of Birds*, 2nd ed. W. B. Saunders, Philadelphia.

Weske, J. S., and J. W. Terborgh. 1977. *Phaethornis koepkeae*, a new species of hummingbird from Peru. *Condor* 79:143–147.

Wetmore, A. 1946. New birds from Colombia. *Smithson. Misc. Collect*. 106(16):1–14.

———. 1953. Further additions to the birds of Panama and Colombia. *Smithson. Misc. Collect*. 122(8):1–12.

———. 1963. Additions to records of birds known from the Republic of Panama. *Smithson. Misc. Collect*. 145(6):1–11.

———. 1968. The birds of the Republic of Panamá. *Smithson. Misc. Collect*. 150, pt. 2.

Wetmore, A., and W. H. Phelps, Jr. 1956. Further additions to the list of birds of Venezuela.

Proc. Biol. Soc. Wash. 69:1–10.

Weydemeyer, W. 1927. Notes on the location and construction of the nest of the calliope hummingbird. *Condor* 29:19–24.

———. 1971. Injured calliope hummingbird lifted by another. *Auk* 88:431.

Weymouth, R. D., R. C. Lasiewski, and A. J. Berger. 1964. The tongue apparatus in hummingbirds. *Acta Anat.* 58:252–270.

Whittle, C. L. 1937. A study of hummingbird behavior during a nesting season. *Bird-Banding* 8:170–173.

Wiley, R. H. 1971. Song groups in a singing assembly of little hermits. *Condor* 73:28–35.

Williamson, F. 1957. Hybrids of the Anna and Allen hummingbirds. *Condor* 59:118–123.

Witzeman, J. 1979. Plain-capped starthroats in the United States. *Continental Birdlife* 1:1–3.

Wolf, L. 1964. Nesting of the fork-tailed emerald in Oaxaca, Mexico. *Condor* 66:51–55.

Wolf, L., and F. R. Hainsworth. 1971. Environmental influence on regulated body temperatures in torpid hummingbirds. *Comp. Biochem. Physiol.* 41:167–173.

Wolf, L., and F. G. Stiles. 1970. Evolution of pair cooperation in a tropical hummingbird. *Evolution* 24:759–773.

Wolf, L., F. G. Stiles, and F. R. Hainsworth. 1976. Ecological organization of a tropical, highland hummingbird community. *J. Anim. Ecol.* 45:349–379.

Woods, R. S. 1927. The hummingbirds of California. *Auk* 44:297–318.

Wyman, L. E. 1920. Notes on the calliope hummingbird. *Condor* 22:206–207.

Zimmer, J. T. 1950–53. Studies on Peruvian birds, nos. 55–63. *Am. Mus. Novit.* 1449, 1450, 1463, 1475, 1513, 1540, 1595, 1604.

Zimmerman, D. A. 1973. Range expansion of Anna's hummingbird. *Am. Birds* 27:827–835.

Zimmerman, D. A., and S. H. Levy. 1960. Violet-crowned hummingbird nesting in Arizona and New Mexico. *Auk* 77:470.

Zusi, R. L. 1980. On the subfamilies of hummingbirds. Abstract of paper presented at 98th meeting, American Ornithologists' Union, Fort Collins, Colorado, 11–15 August 1980.

Index

The following index to vernacular names includes (in parentheses) the numbers assigned to each species in the synopsis of the family and used in the identification key. Numbers for the color plates are given in **bold**. Complete indexing is limited to the entries for the vernacular names used in this book. Indexing of the scientific names is limited to the principal account of each species and to the family synopsis.

SCIENTIFIC NAMES